INTRODUCTION

Title: "Royal LIONS: Lionhearted: Capturing Noble Power in Charcoal"
Welcome to "Royal Lions," where the noble essence of these magnificent creatures is brought to life in stunning detail across two volumes.

Welcome back to the world of "Royal Lions," where each design is meticulously crafted to capture the regal essence of these majestic creatures. In this third volume, we're excited to introduce a groundbreaking addition to our series: ready-to-tattoo stencils accompanying each photorealistic design. Our other 2 books in the series have the designs without stencils

With over 77 unique designs, this volume offers tattoo artists an unparalleled resource for creating stunning lion tattoos with ease. Each design is carefully adorned with ornate filigree and baroque ornamentation, symbolizing the royal heritage and indomitable spirit of these majestic animals and presented with it's corresponding tattoo stencil carefully numbered for easy access and identification, ensuring a seamless tattooing process from start to finish.

From serene lion portraits to fierce expressions of power, each design embodies the spirit and quality that "Royal Lions" is known for. Now, with the added feature of ready-to-tattoo stencils, artists can bring these captivating designs to life on skin with precision and accuracy.

In addition to the physical book, we're thrilled to offer a downloadable printable PDF, providing even more convenience for artists in need of quick access to the stencils. Elevate your tattooing game with "Royal Lions Vol. 3," the ultimate resource for bringing the regal beauty of lions to life

Explore the Lion as a symbol of regal pride and majestic grace.
It reigns as the eternal ruler in the material realm, teaching that true authority transcends the tangible.

Yet, deeper still, the Lion becomes a reflection of the Higher Self, conveying wisdom and nobility beyond words.

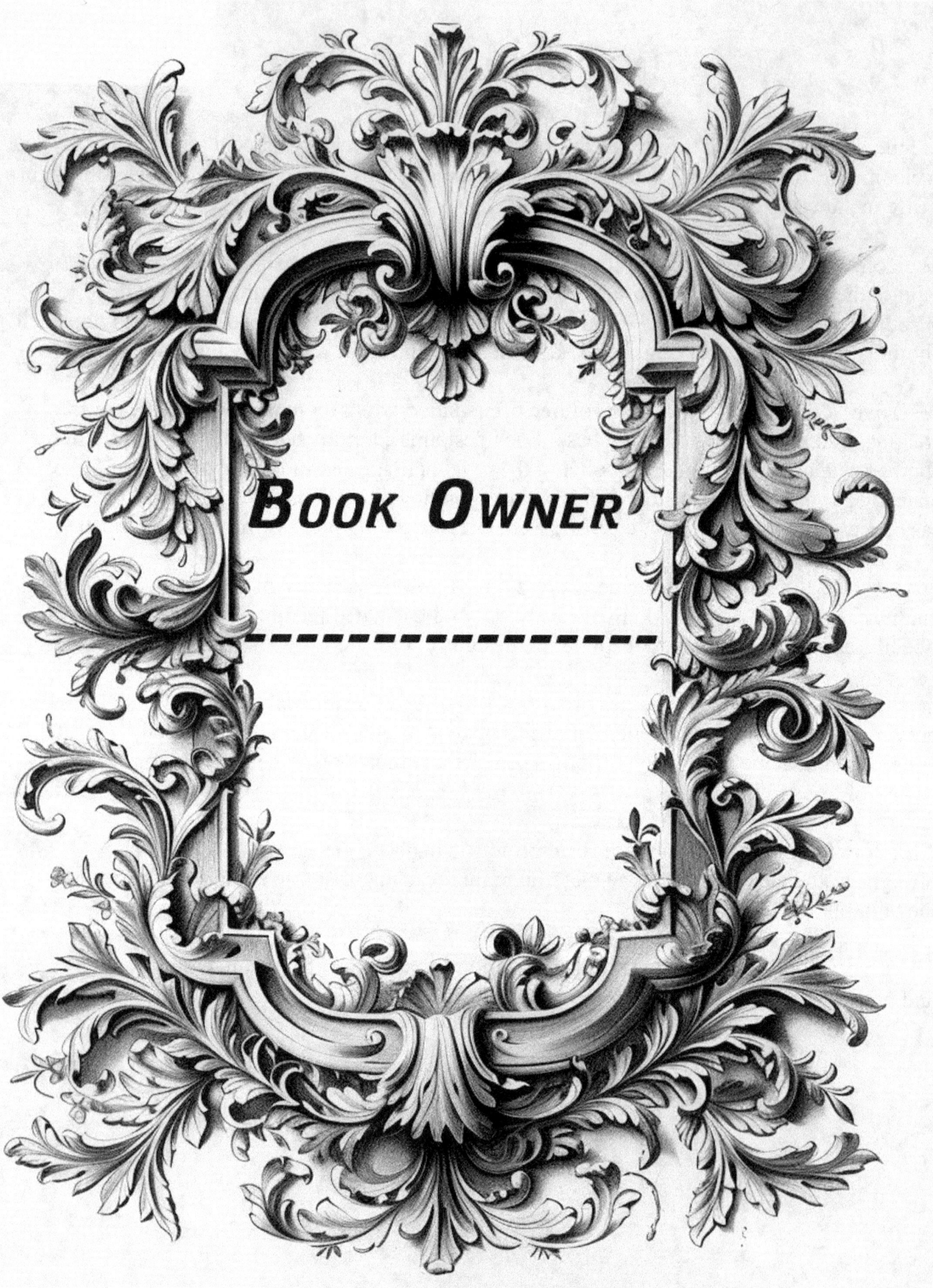

COPYRIGHT

All rights reserved. No part of this book may be reproduced in any form or by any electronic or mechanical means. Including information storage and retrieval systems, or making brushes for any graphics program , without written permission from the author, except for brief quotations linking to the author and buying page.

The buyer-owner of this book has the right to photocopy samples for personal use only. i.e. making a tattoo his own or for a client as a tattoo artist.

Thank you for respecting my works as an author and wish you enjoy your tattooing with best results.

Copyright © 2024 Alex Metsovas DivineTattoo Designs
ISBN: 9798320631462

See more of my books here :

amazon.com/author/alexartbooks

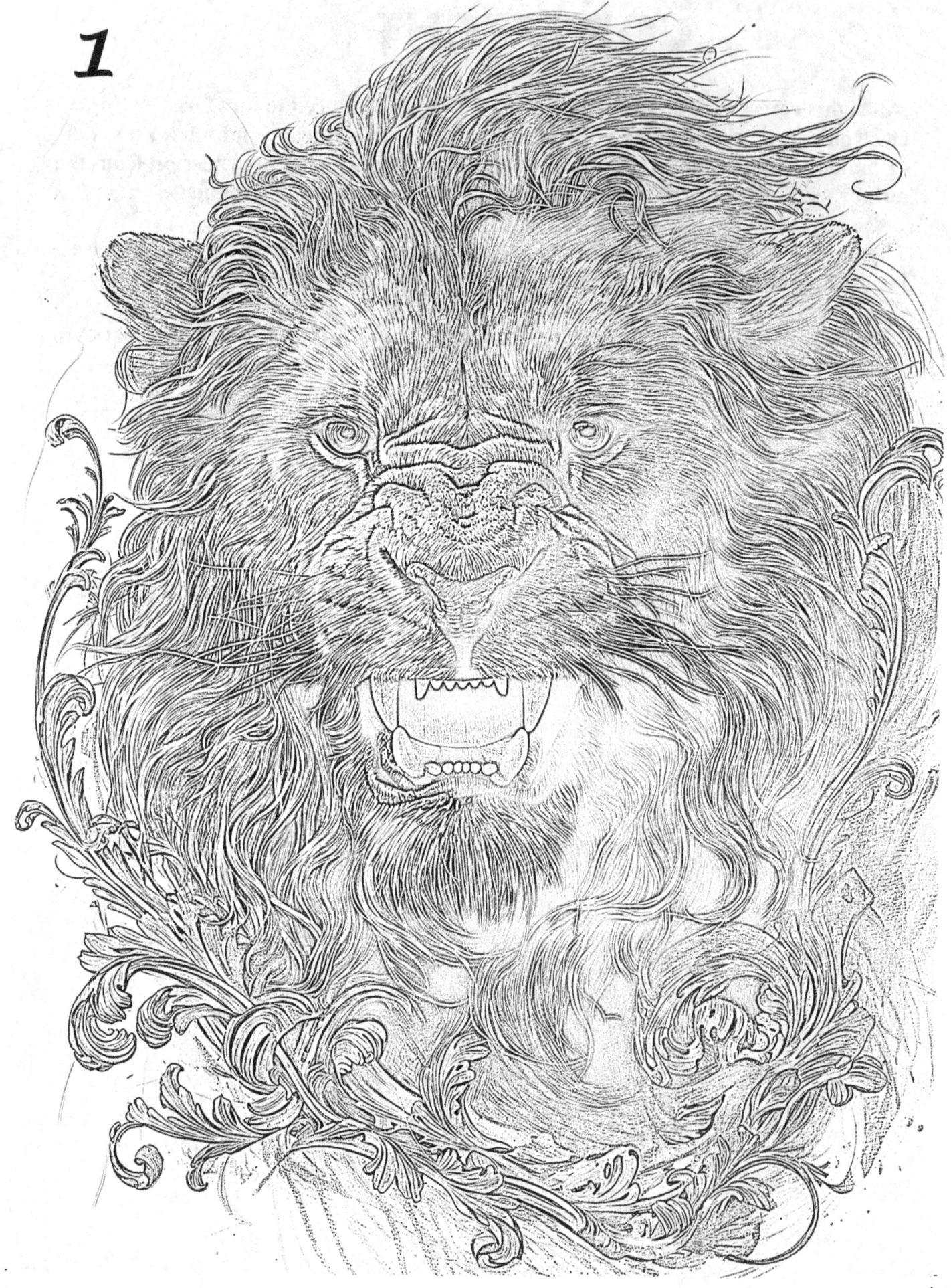

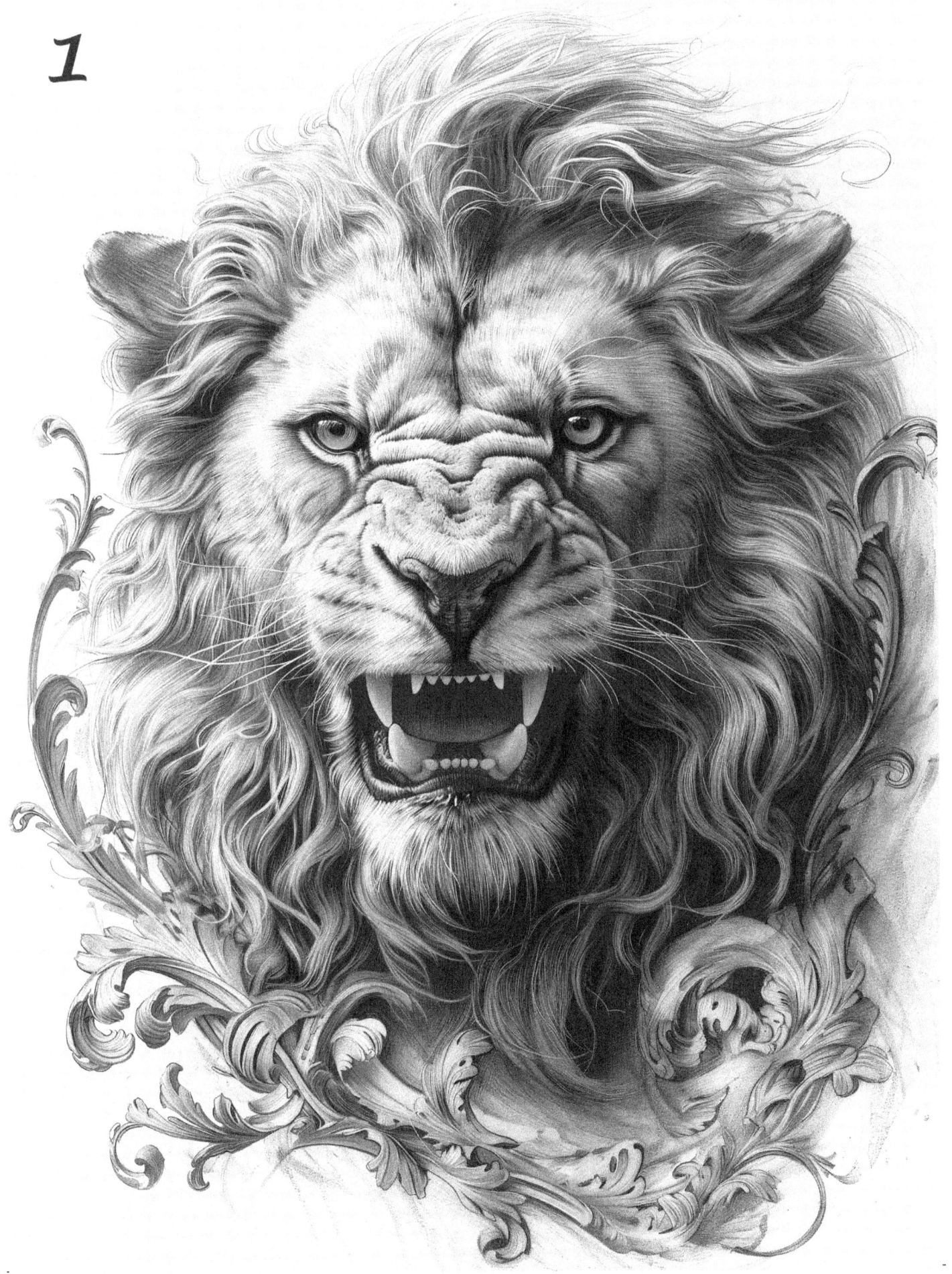

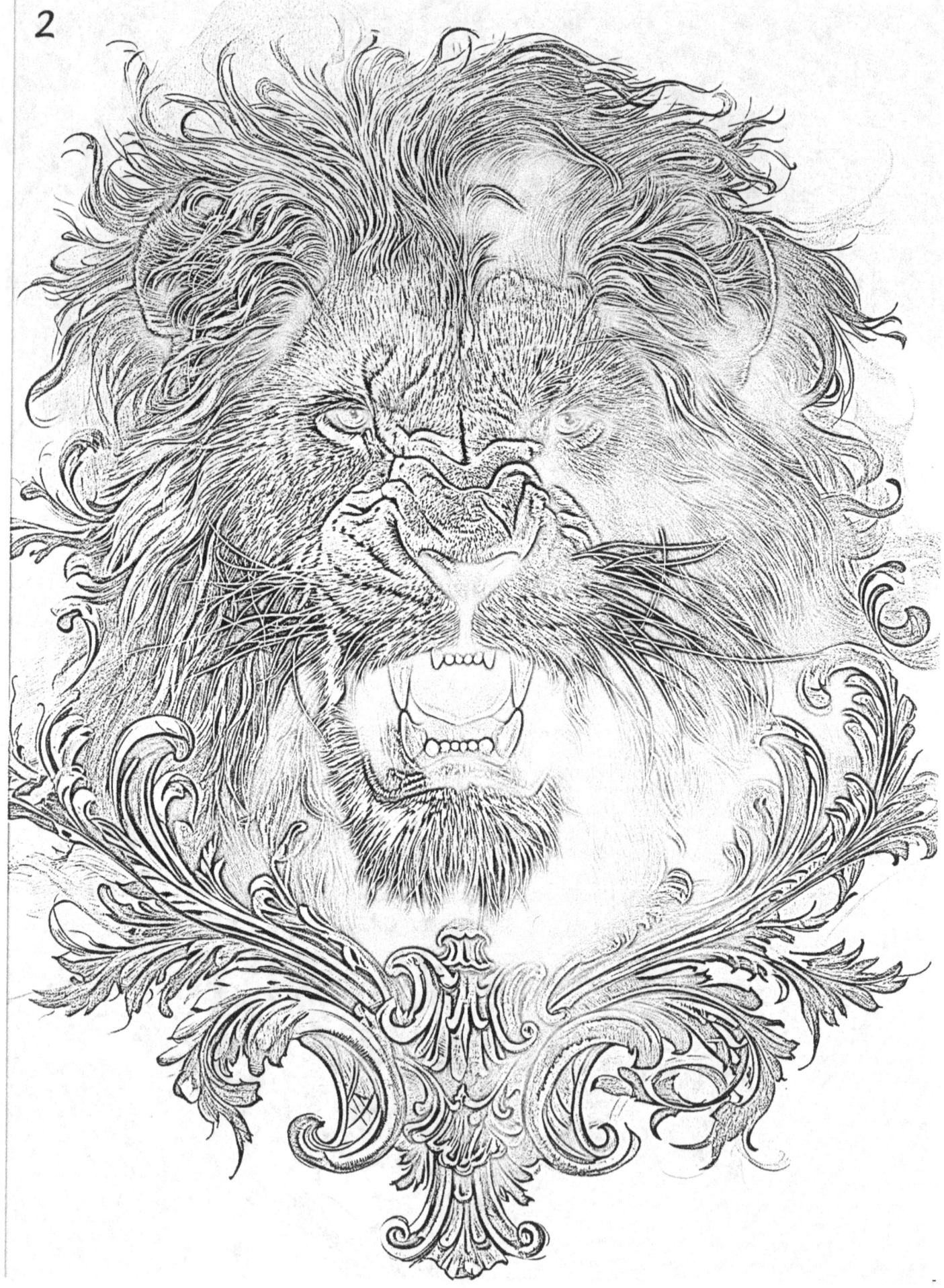

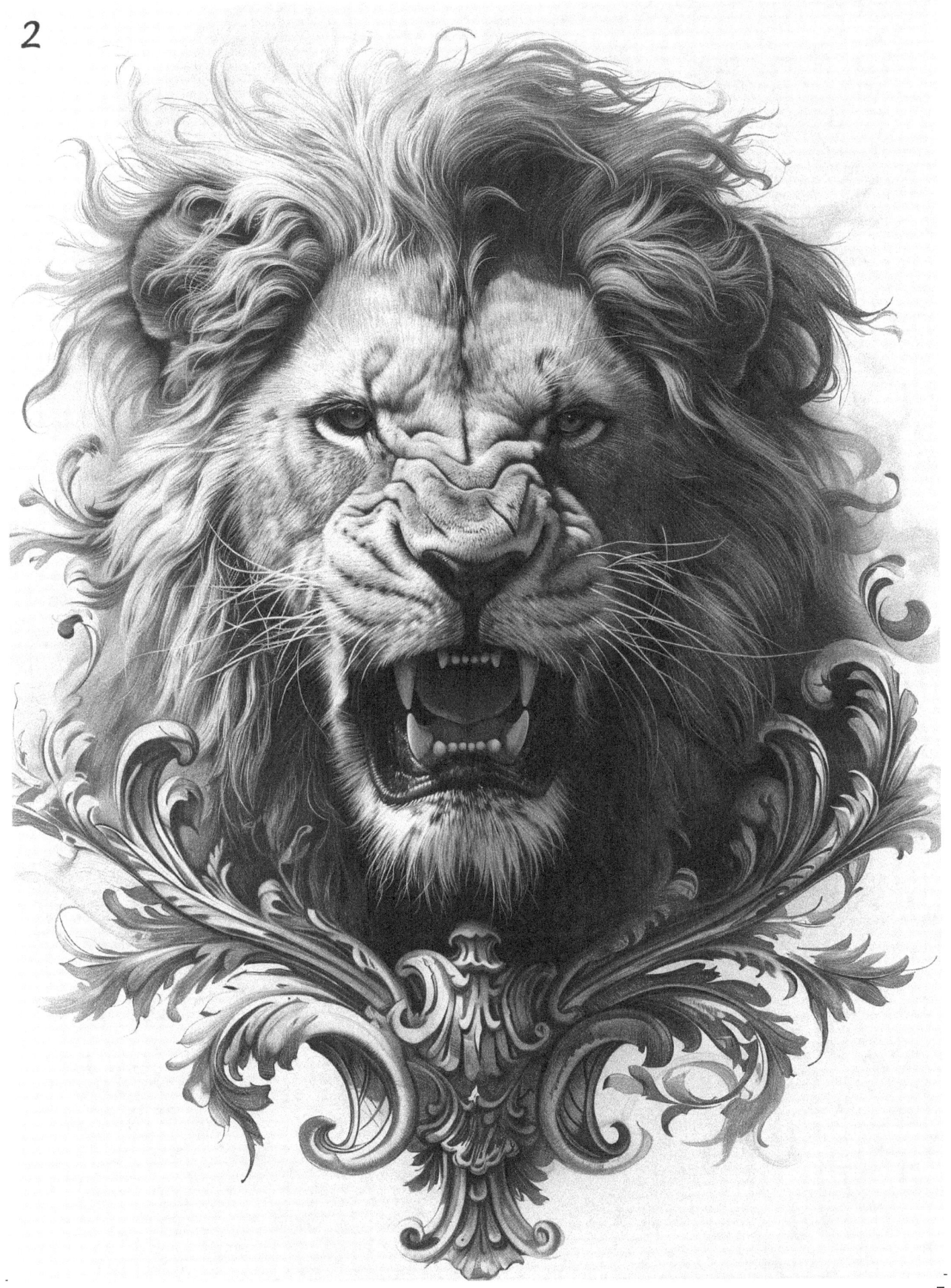

3

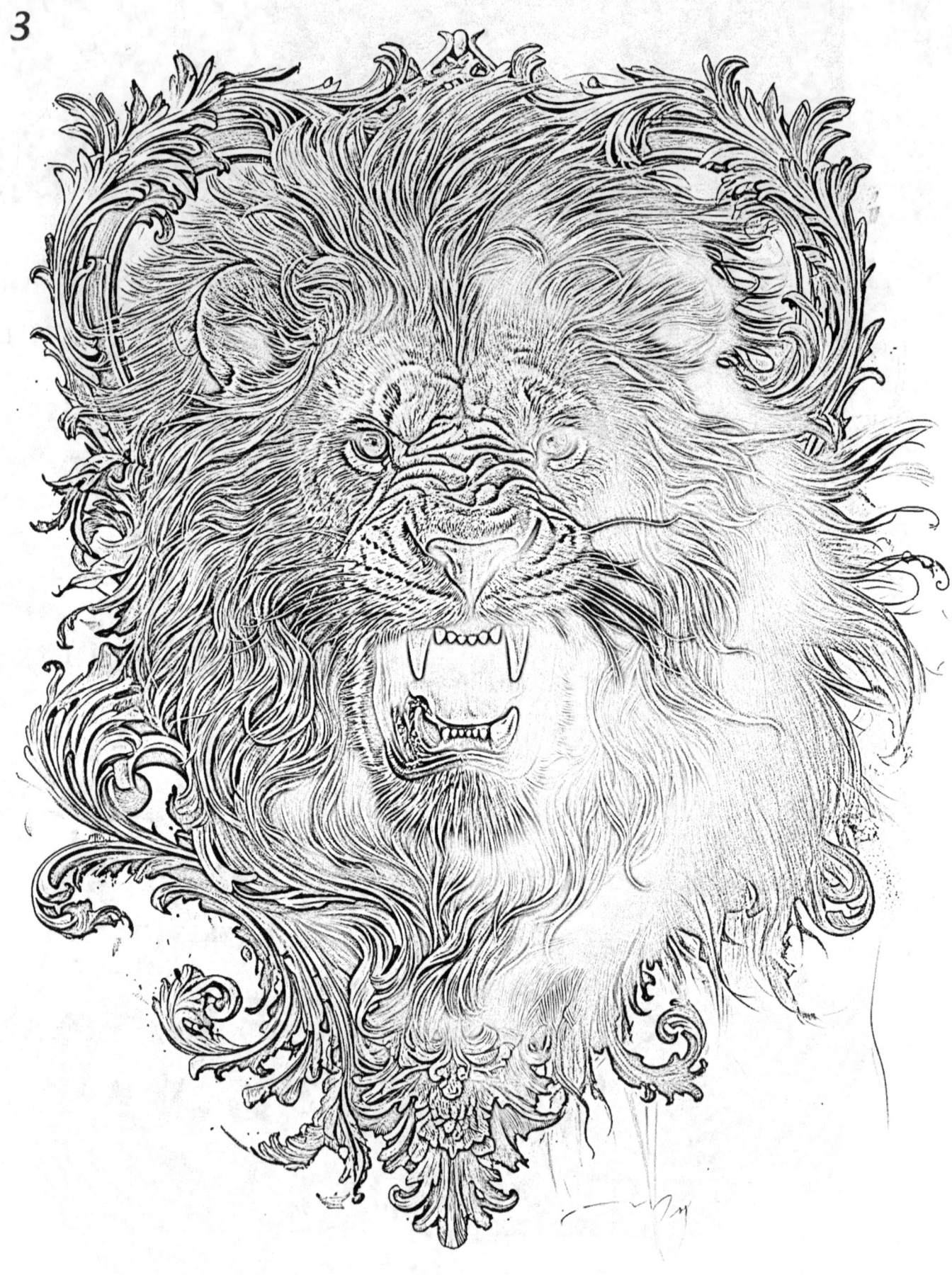

3

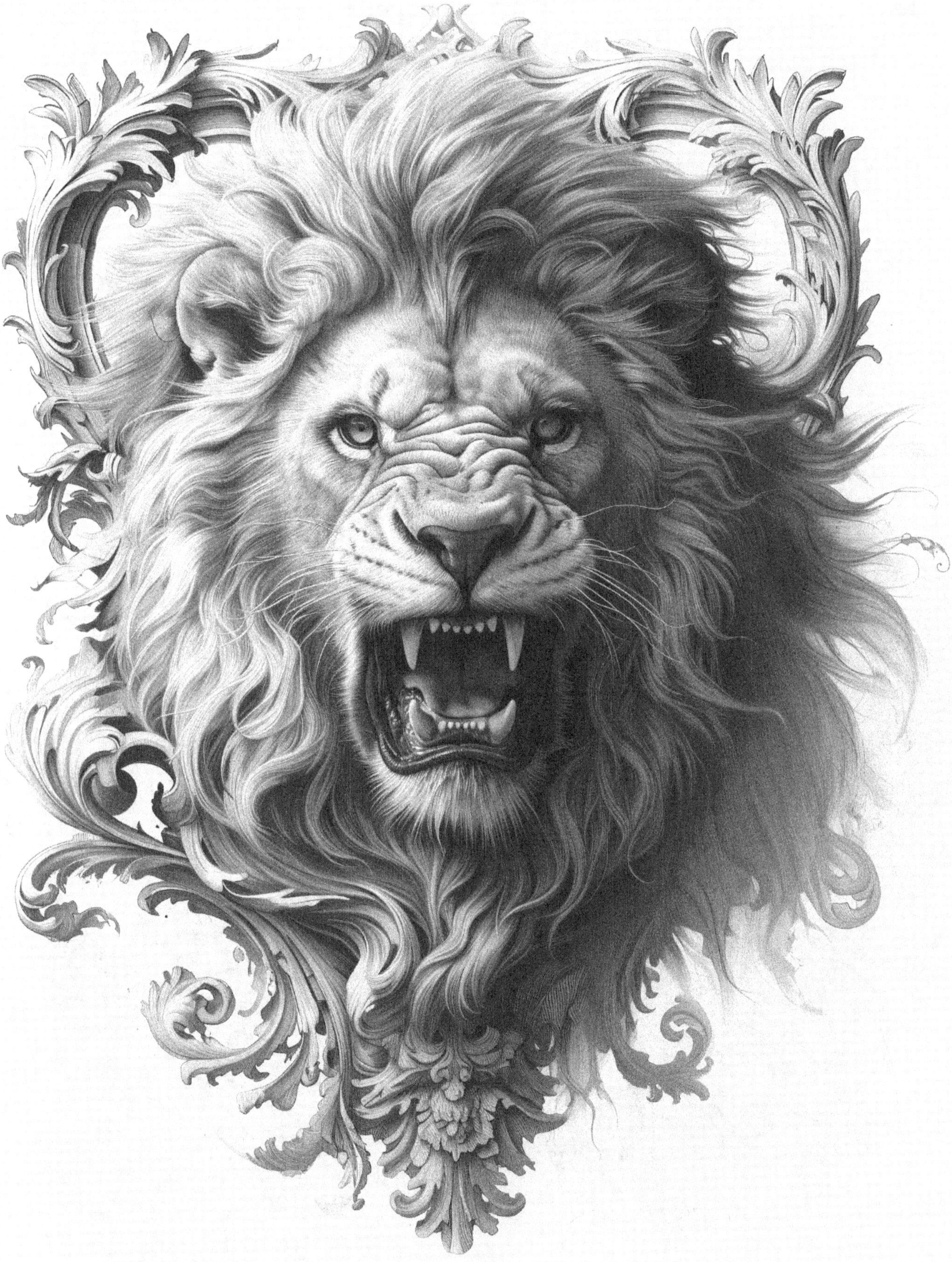

4

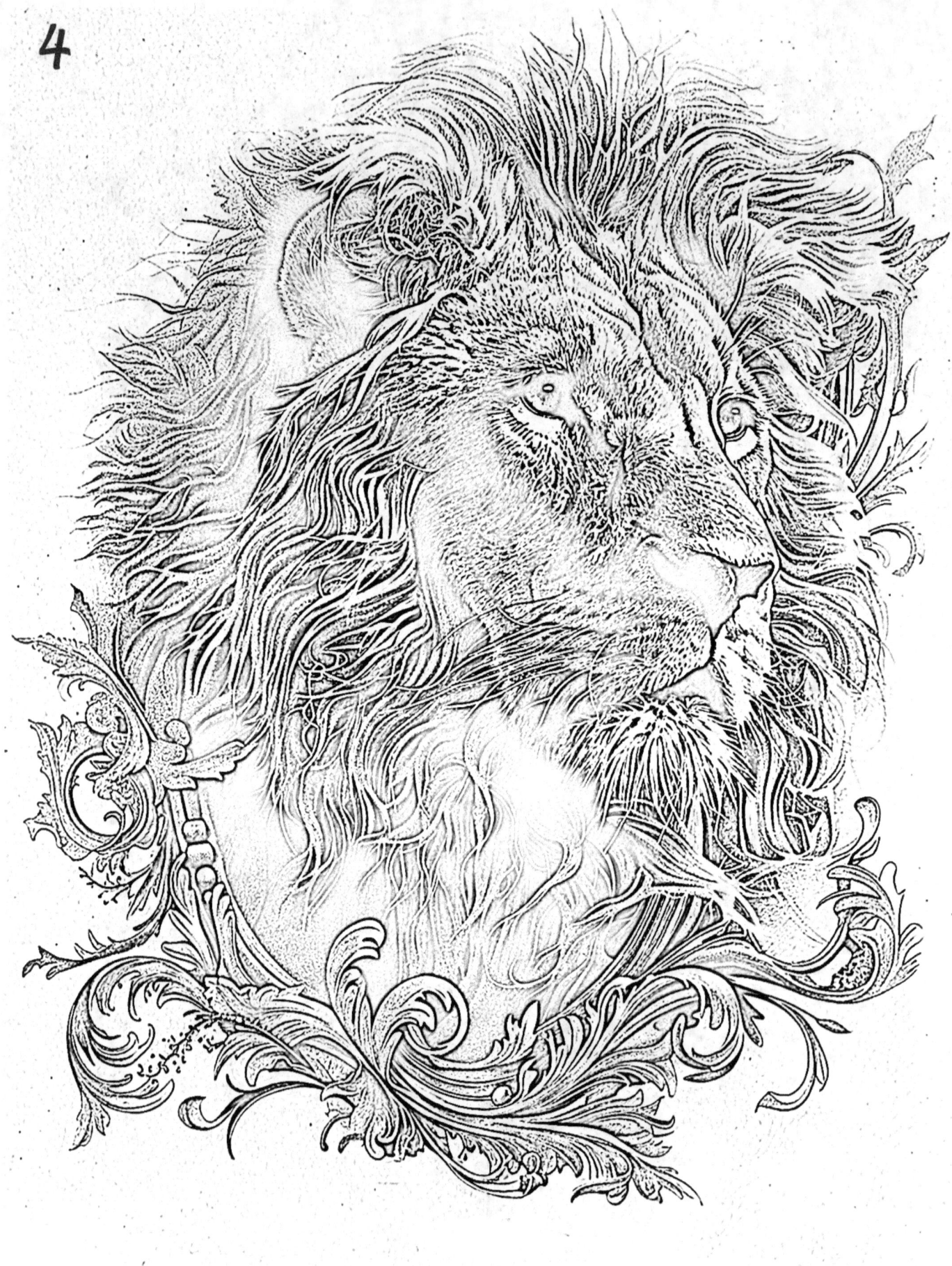

4

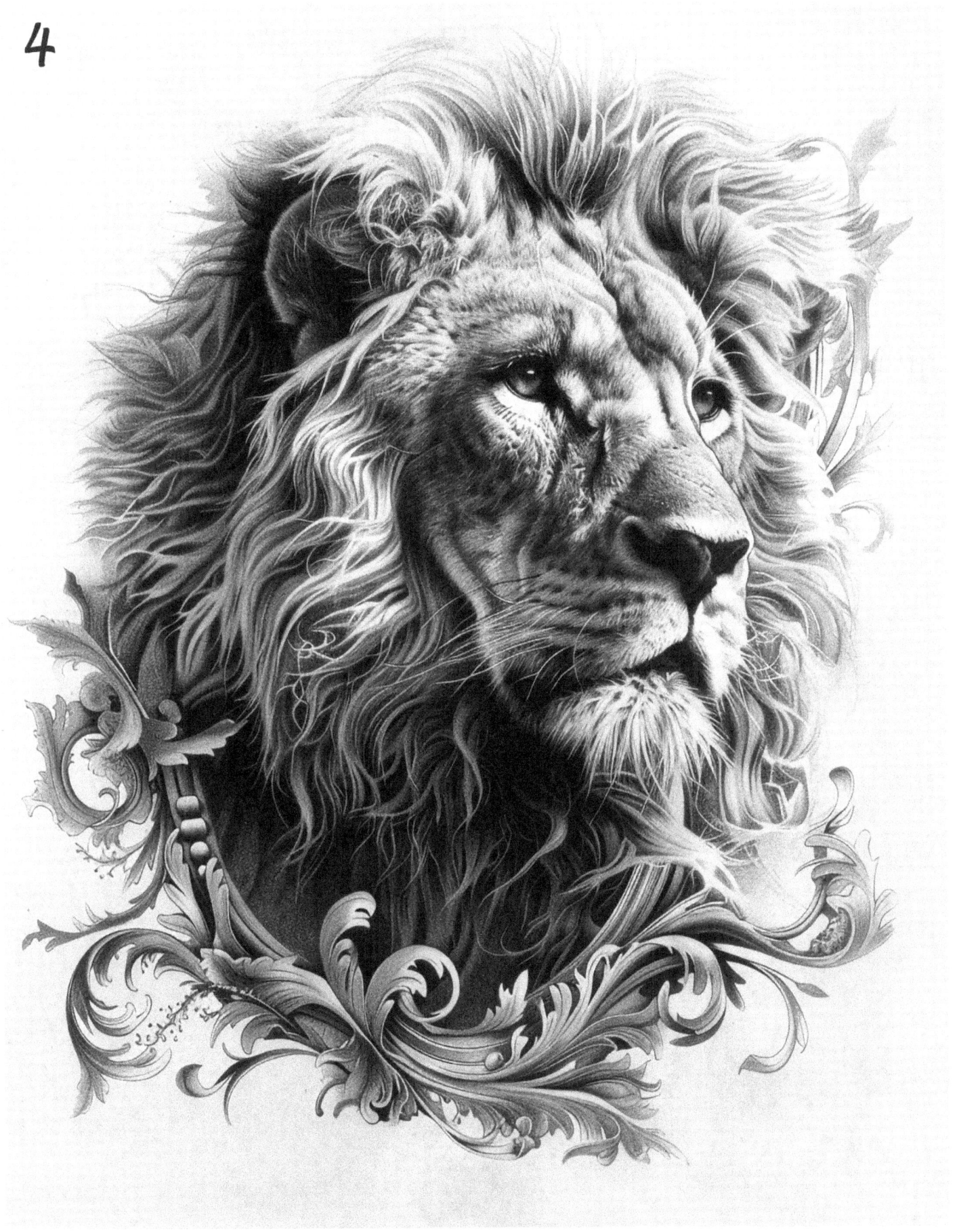

5

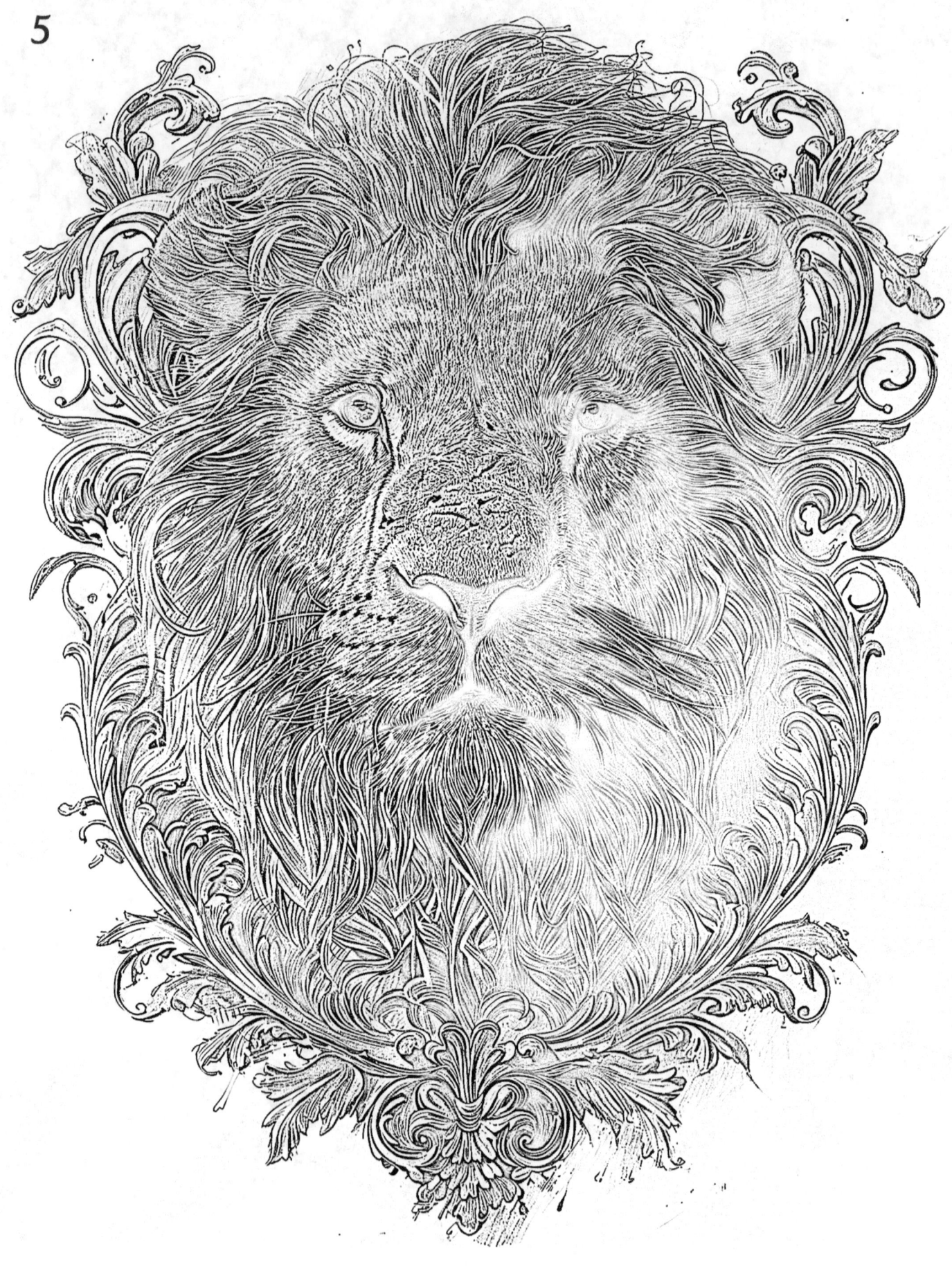

5

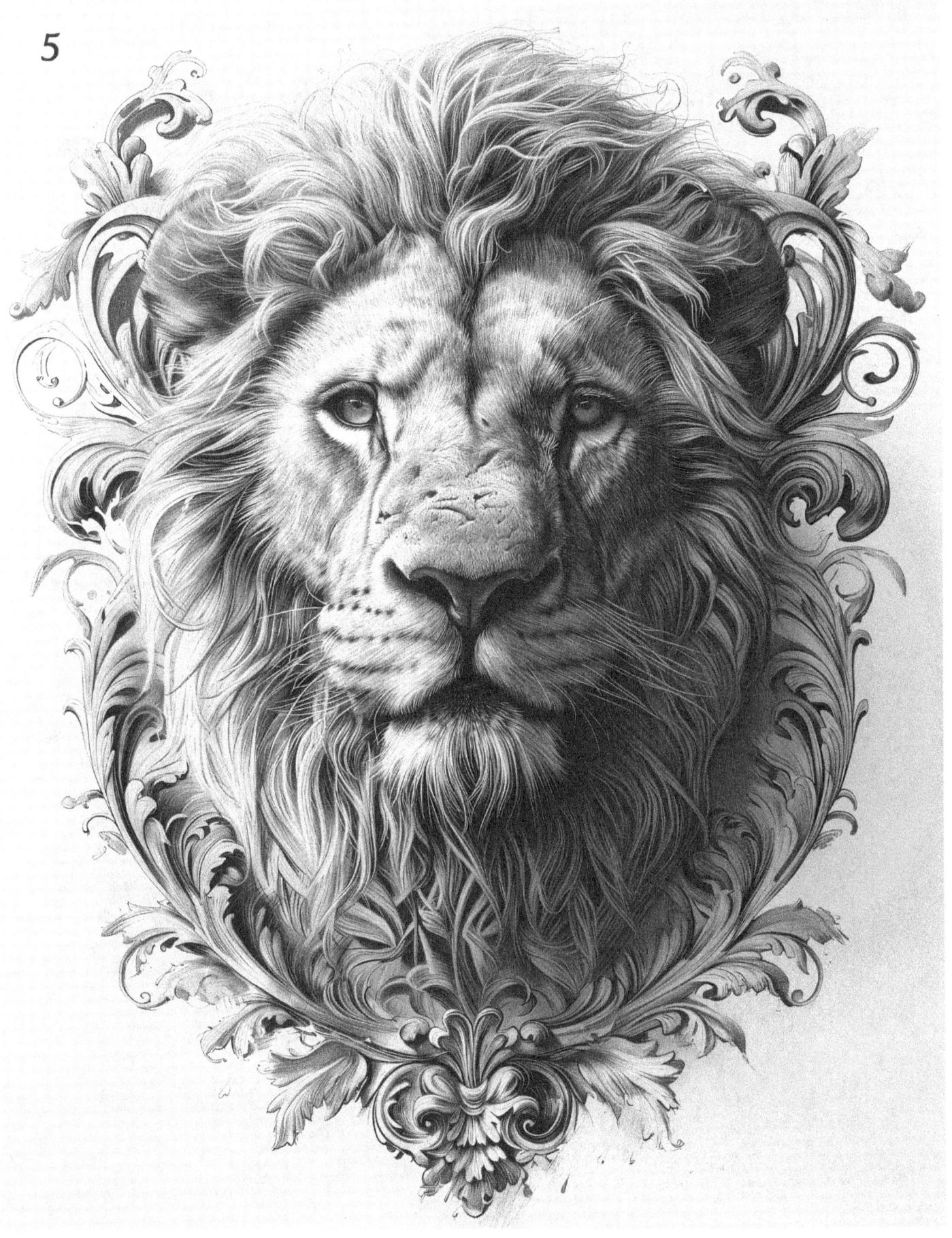

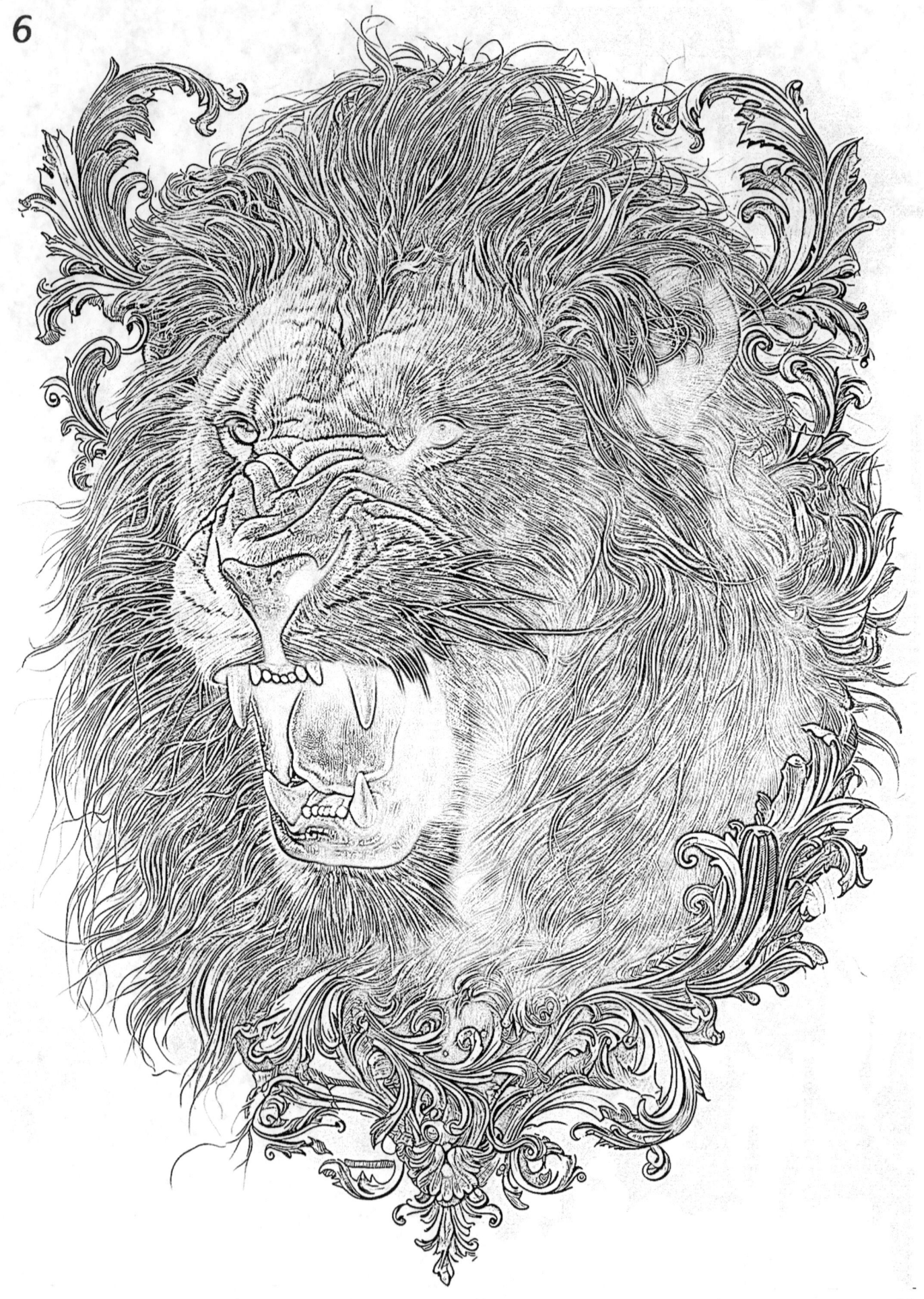

6

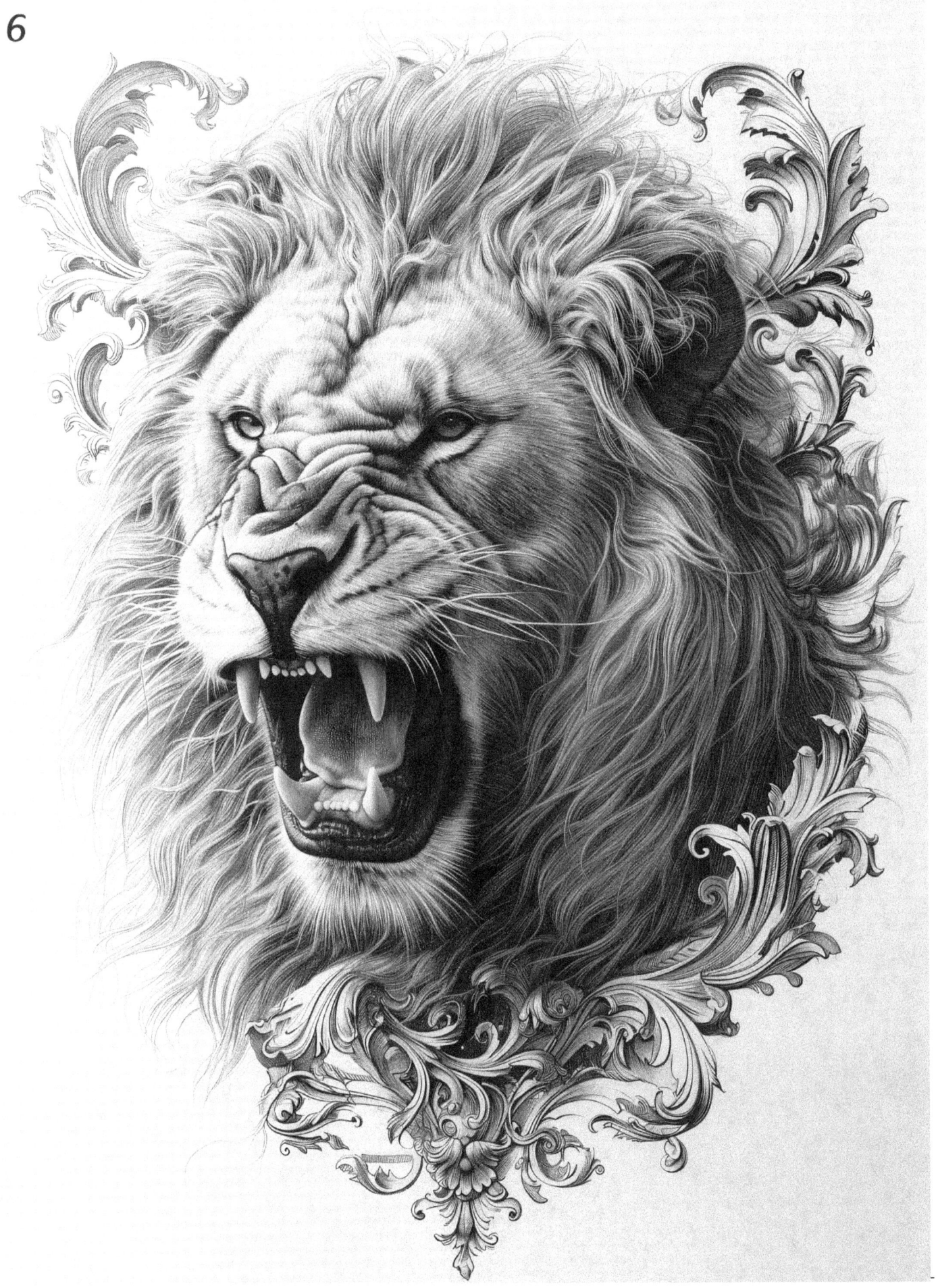

7

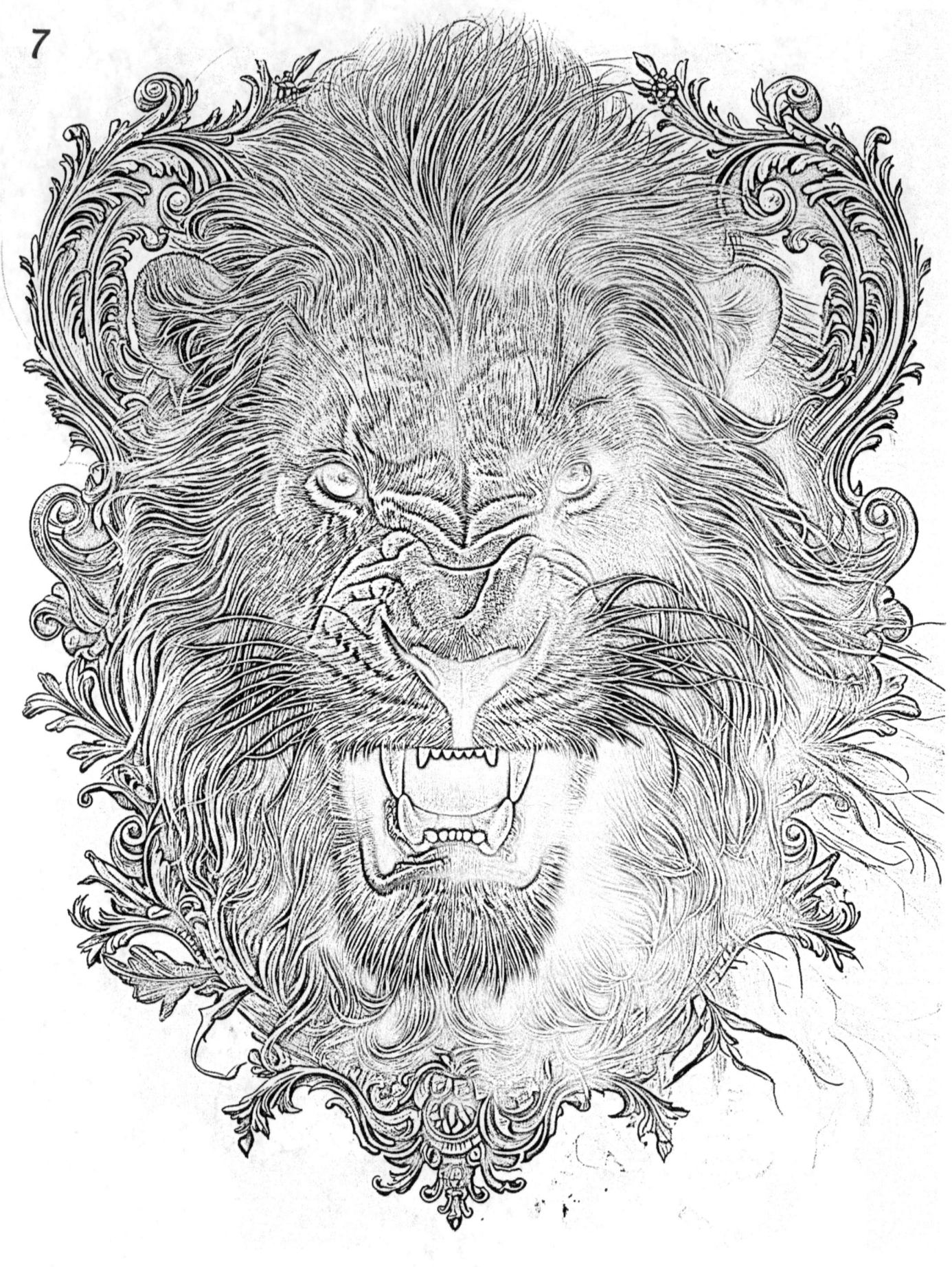

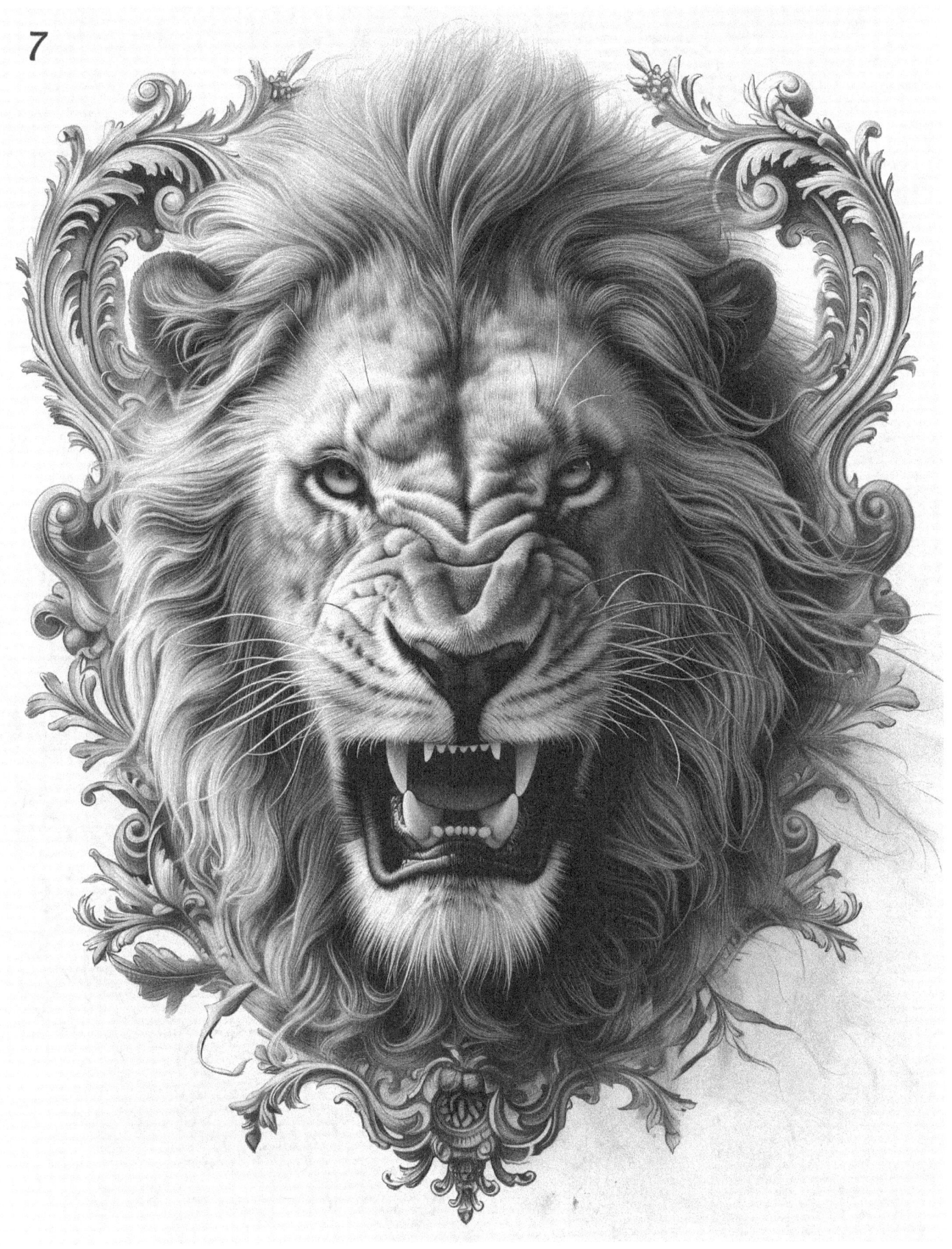

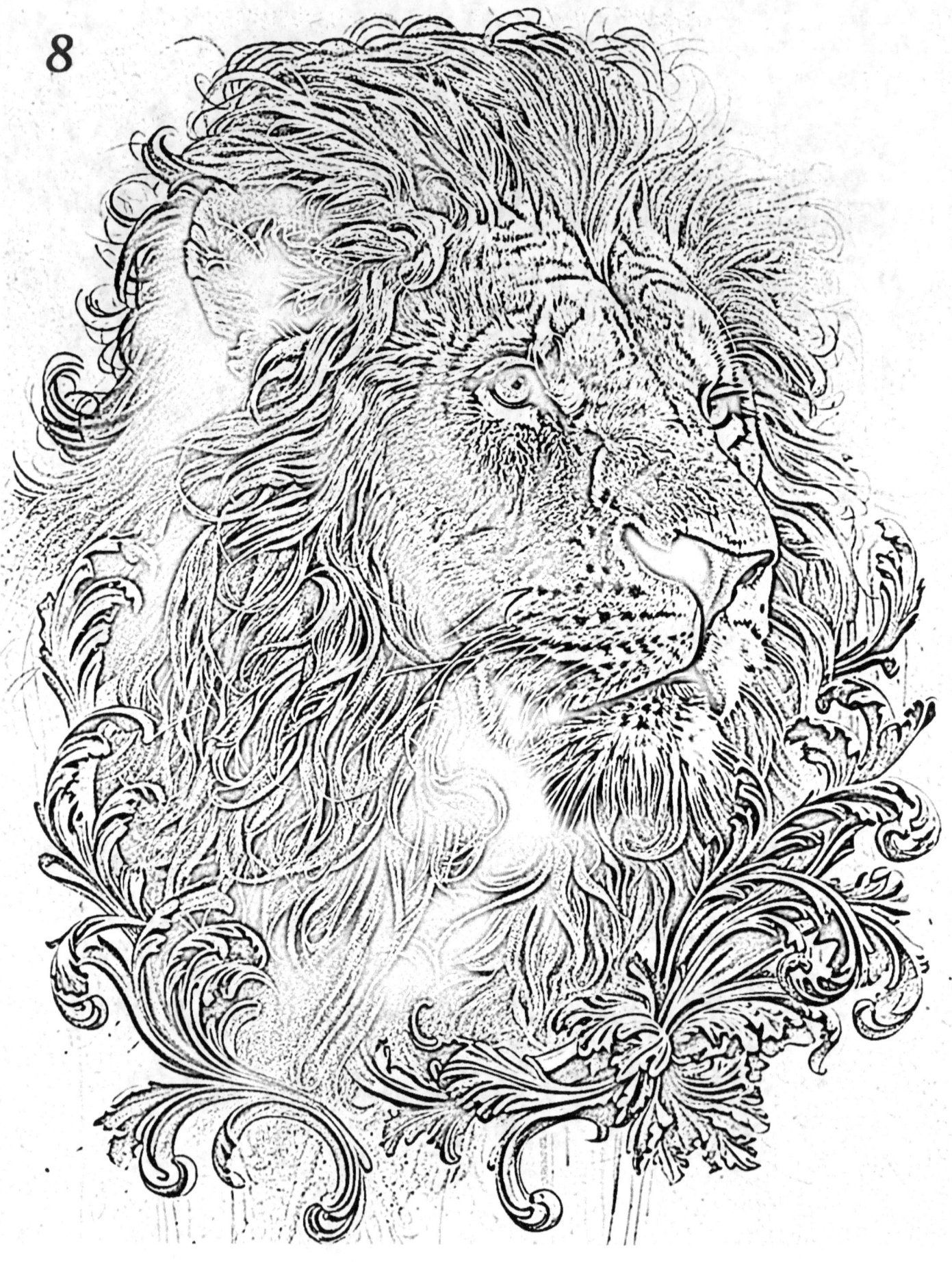

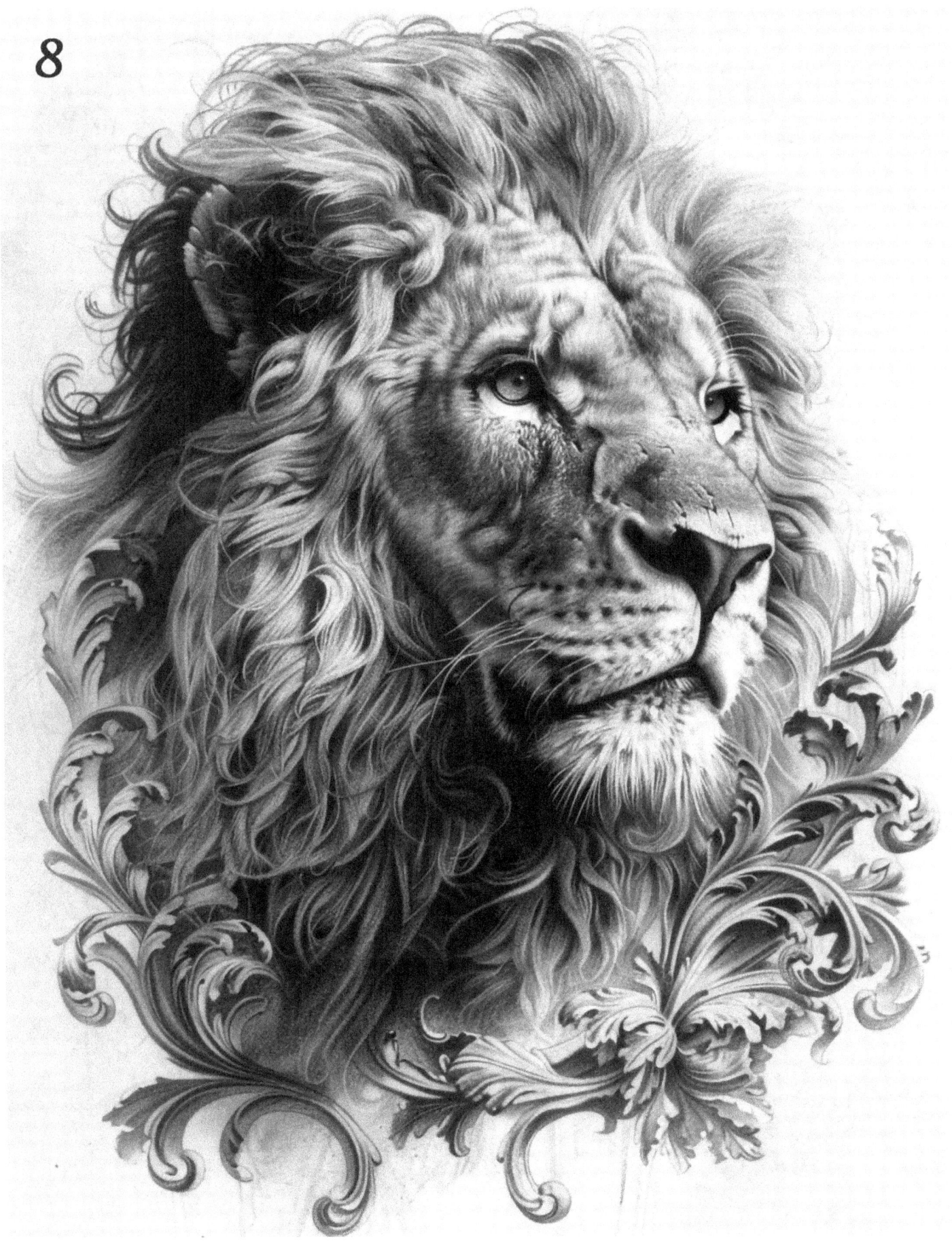

9

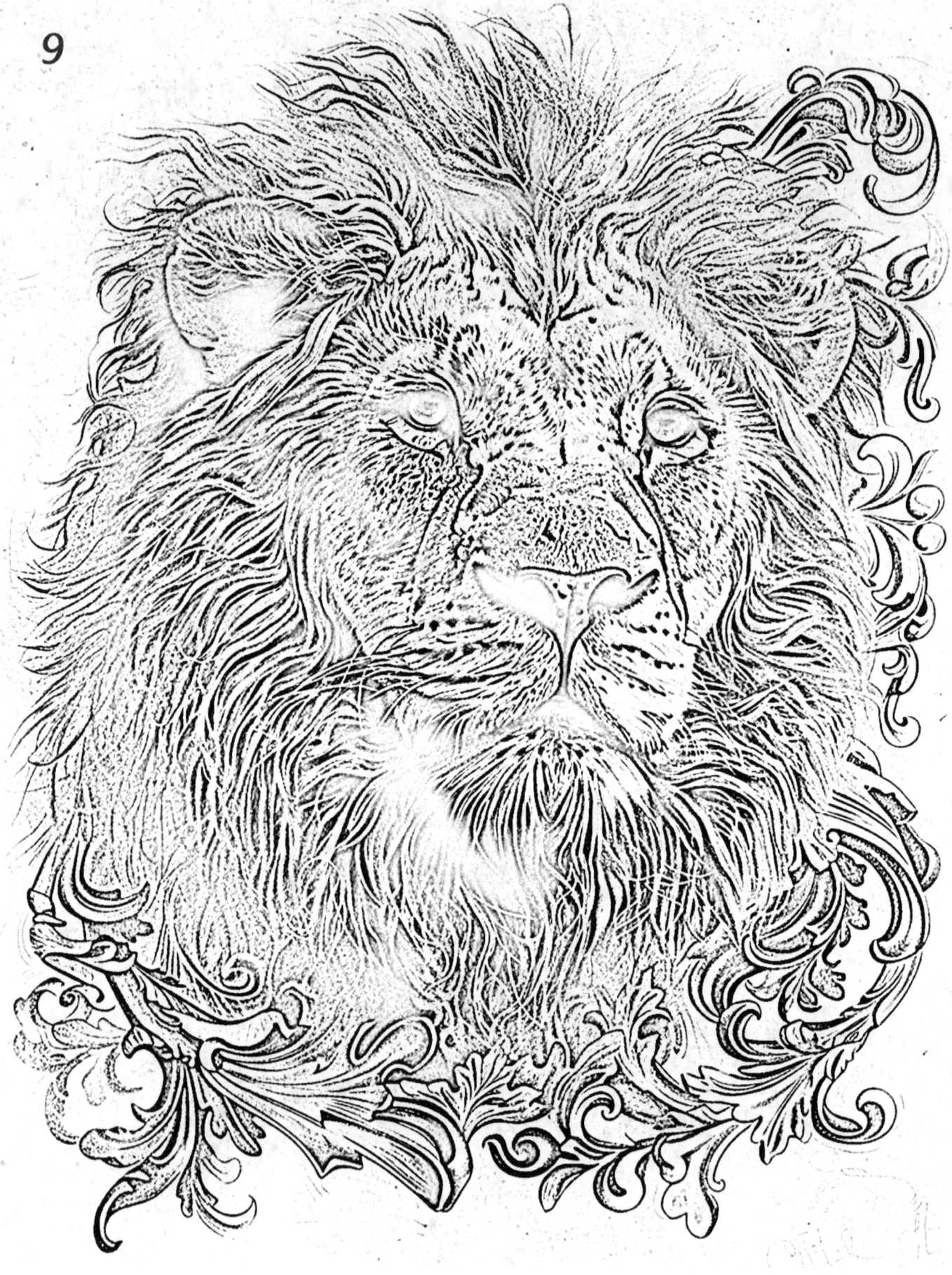

9

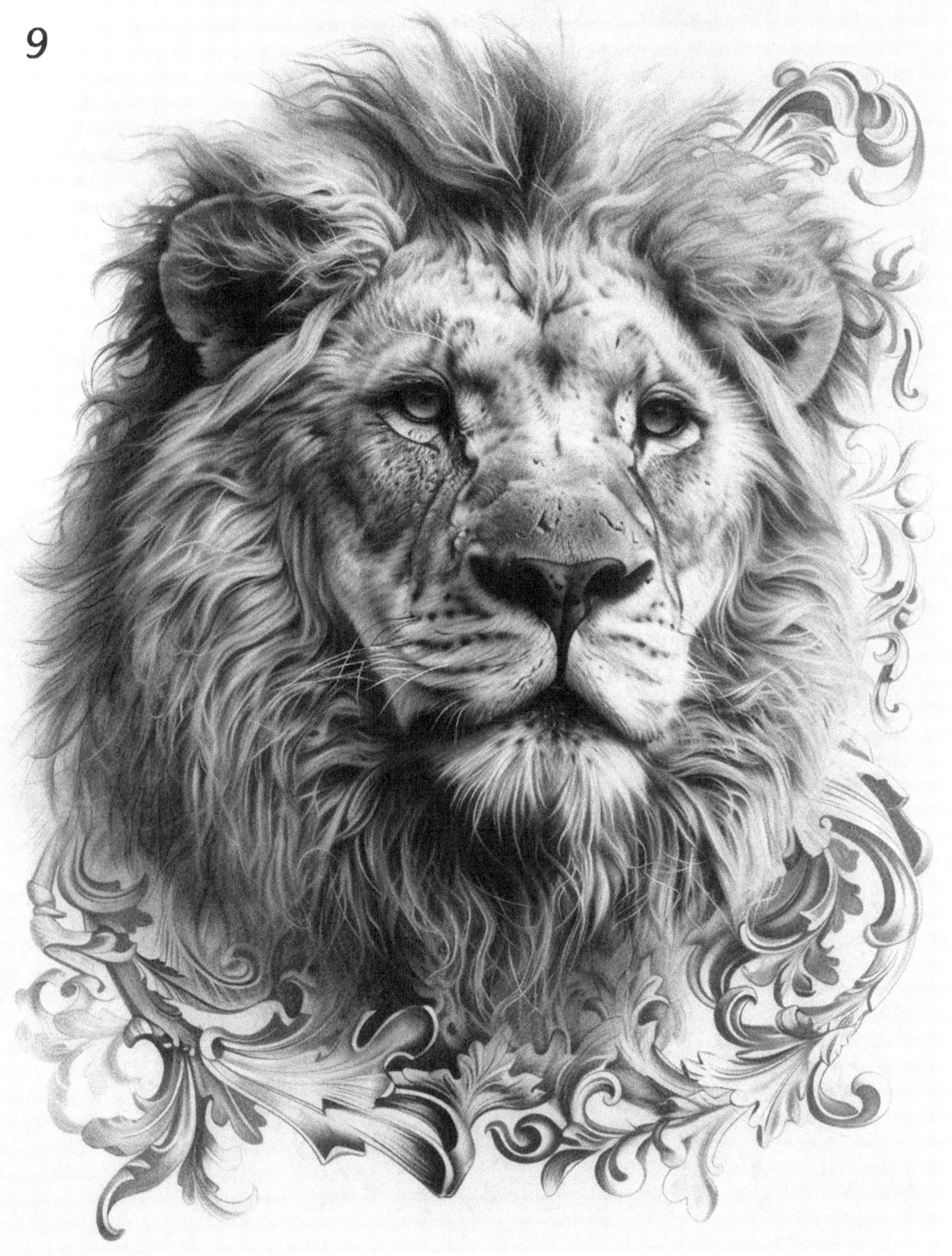

10

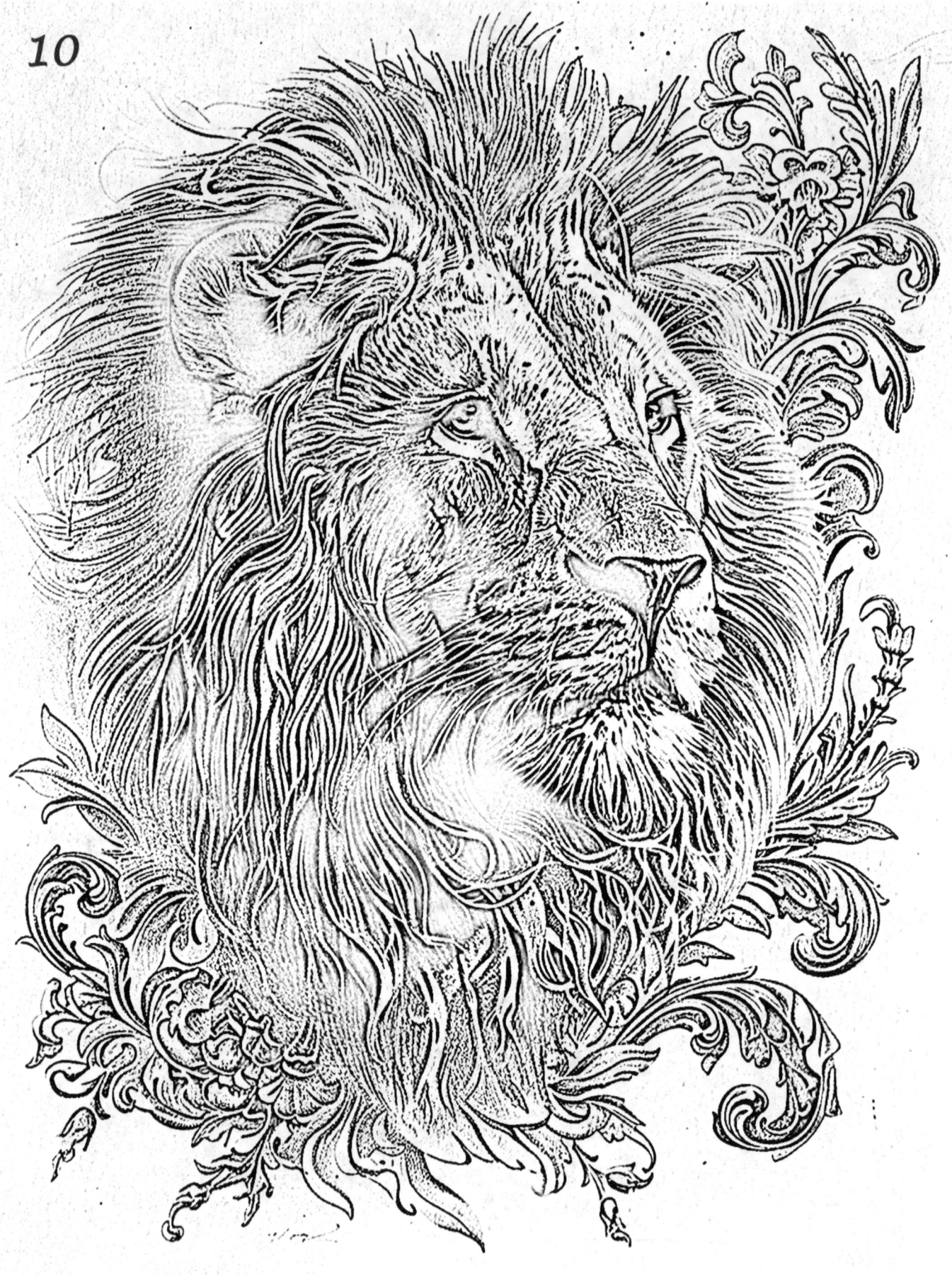

10

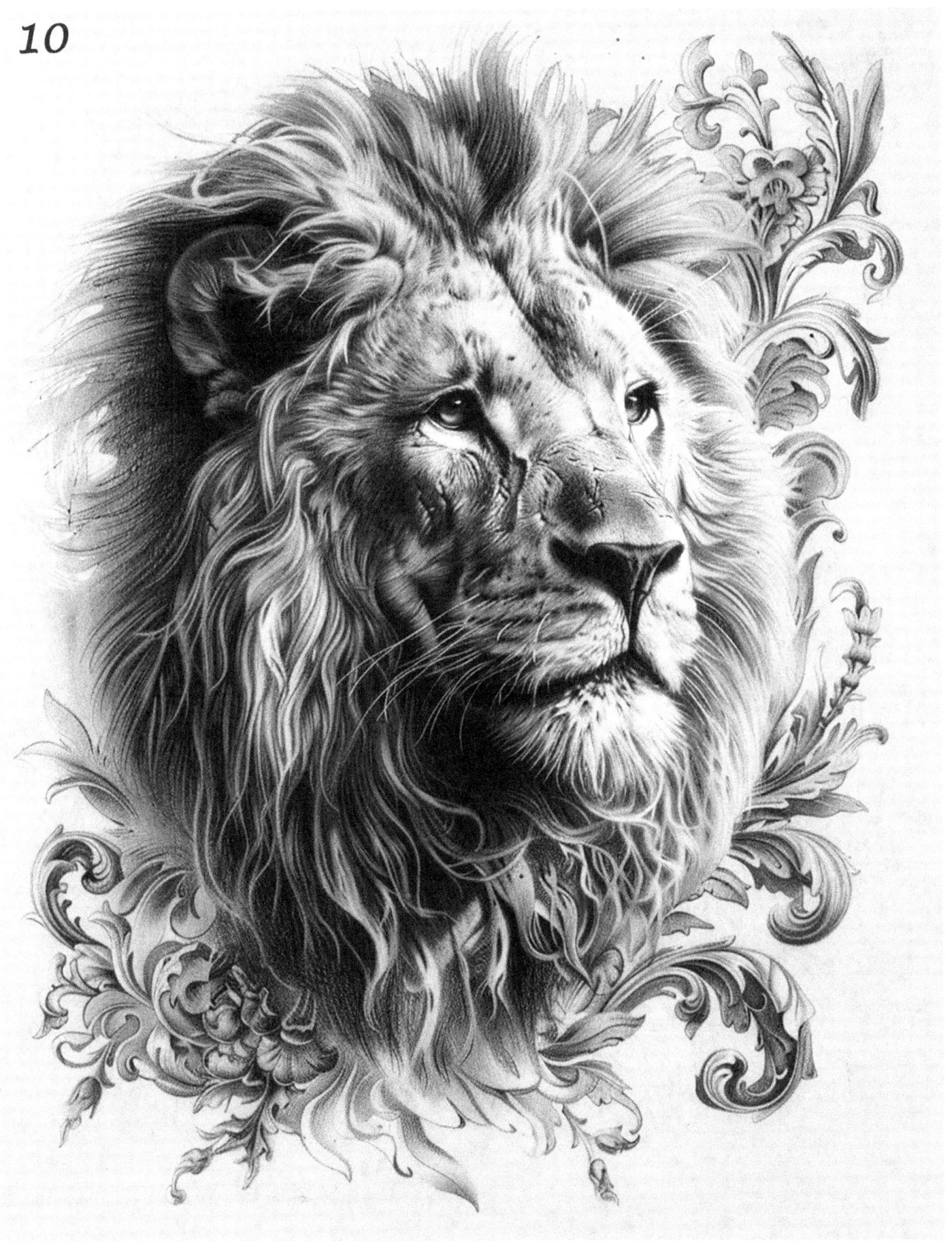

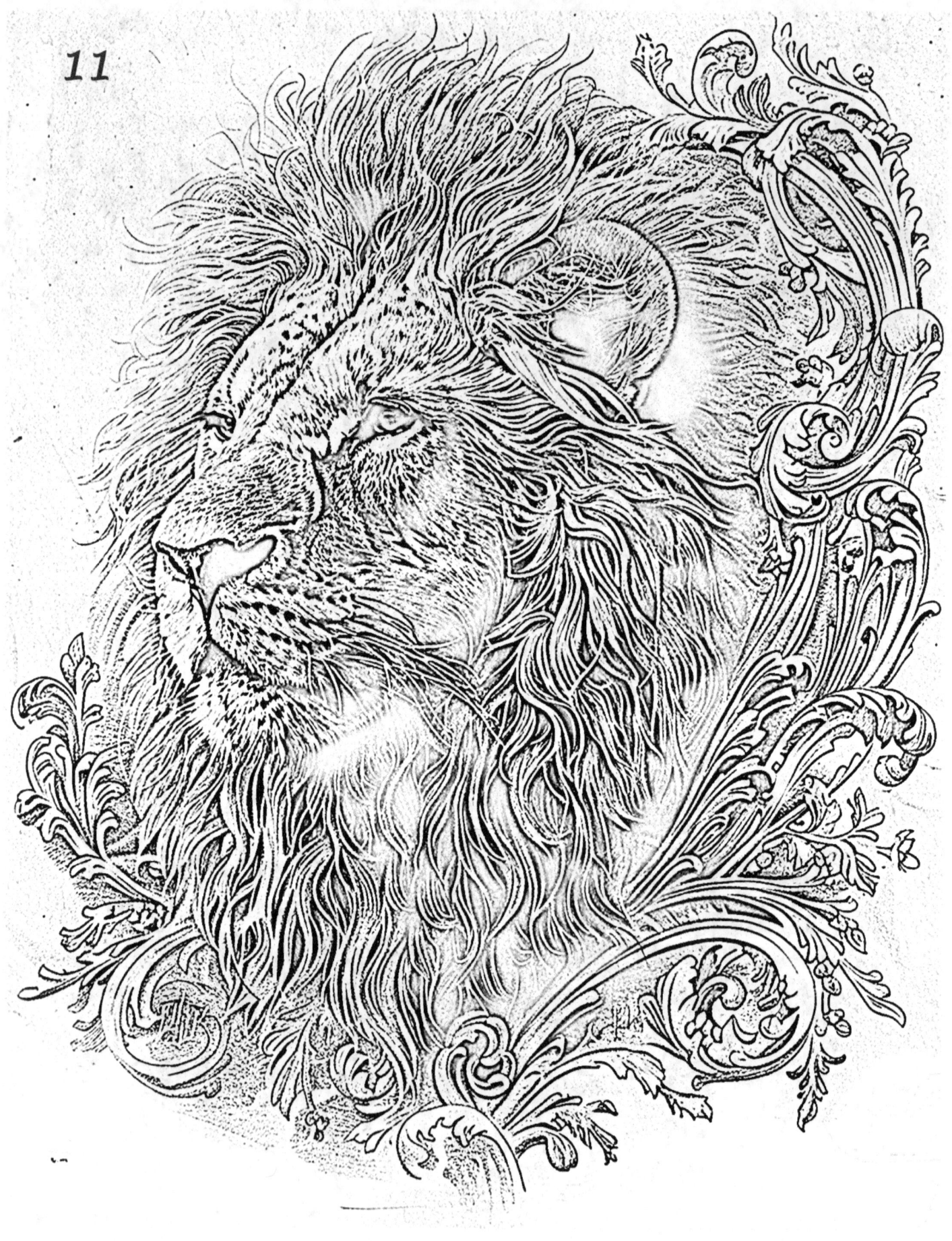

11

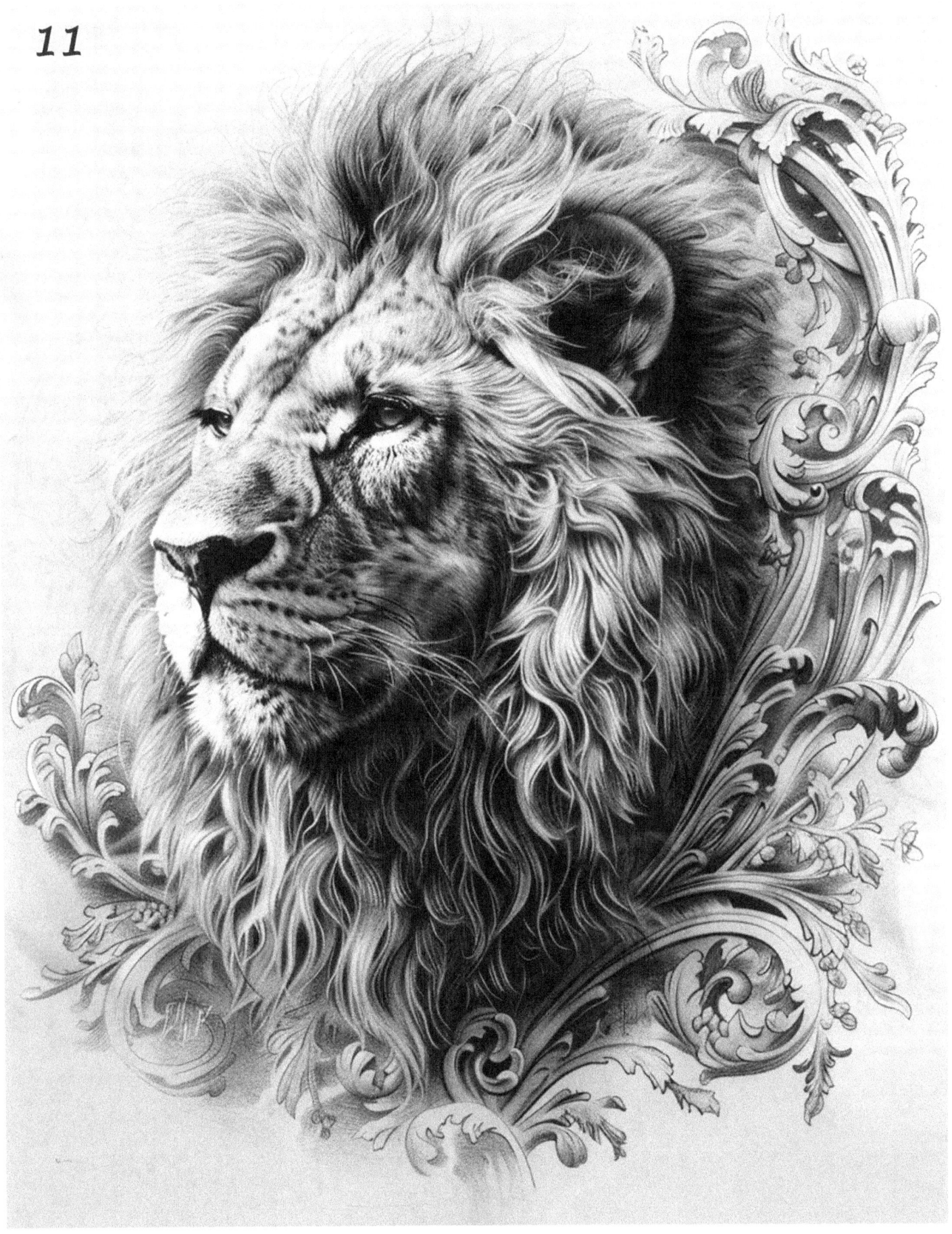

12

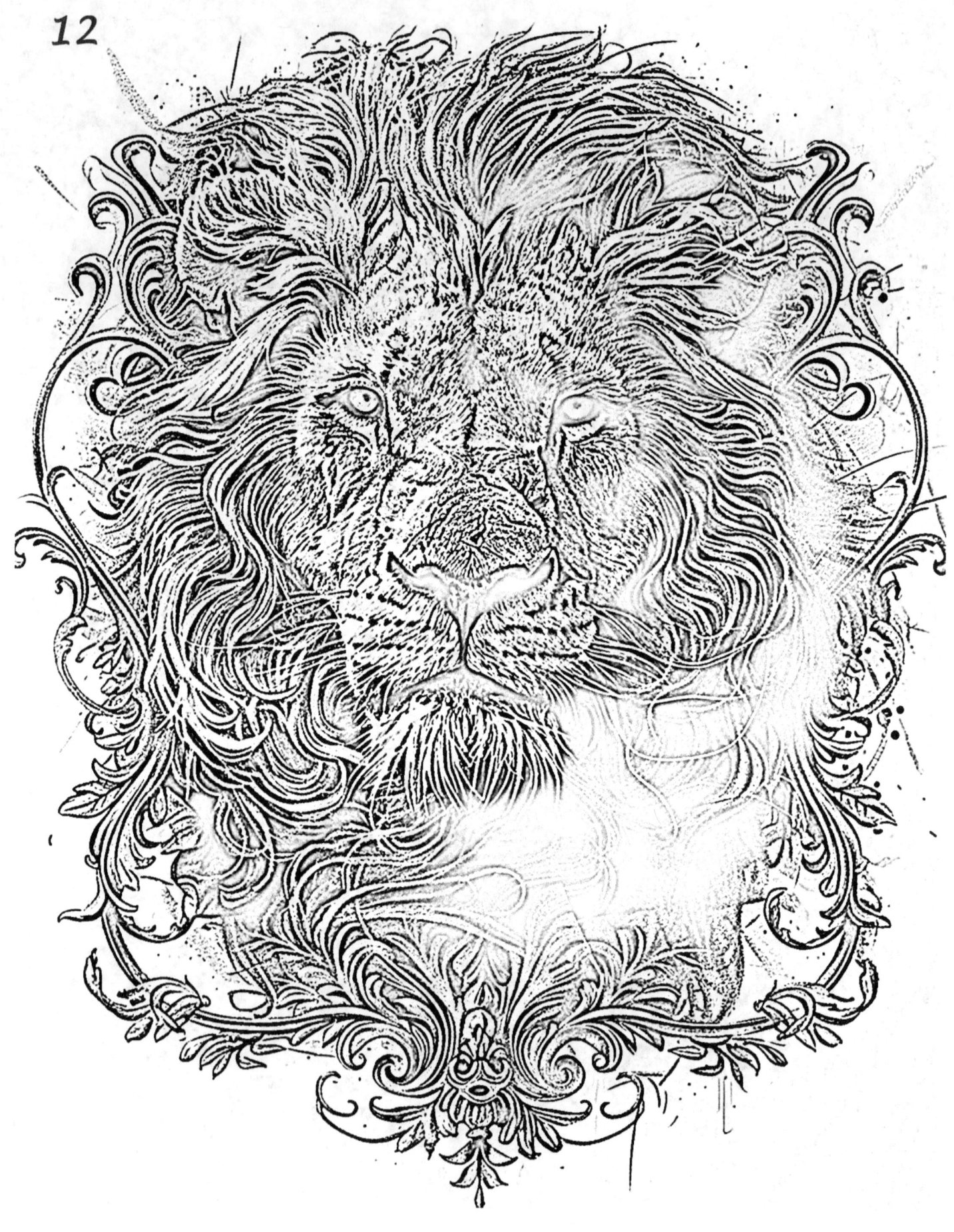

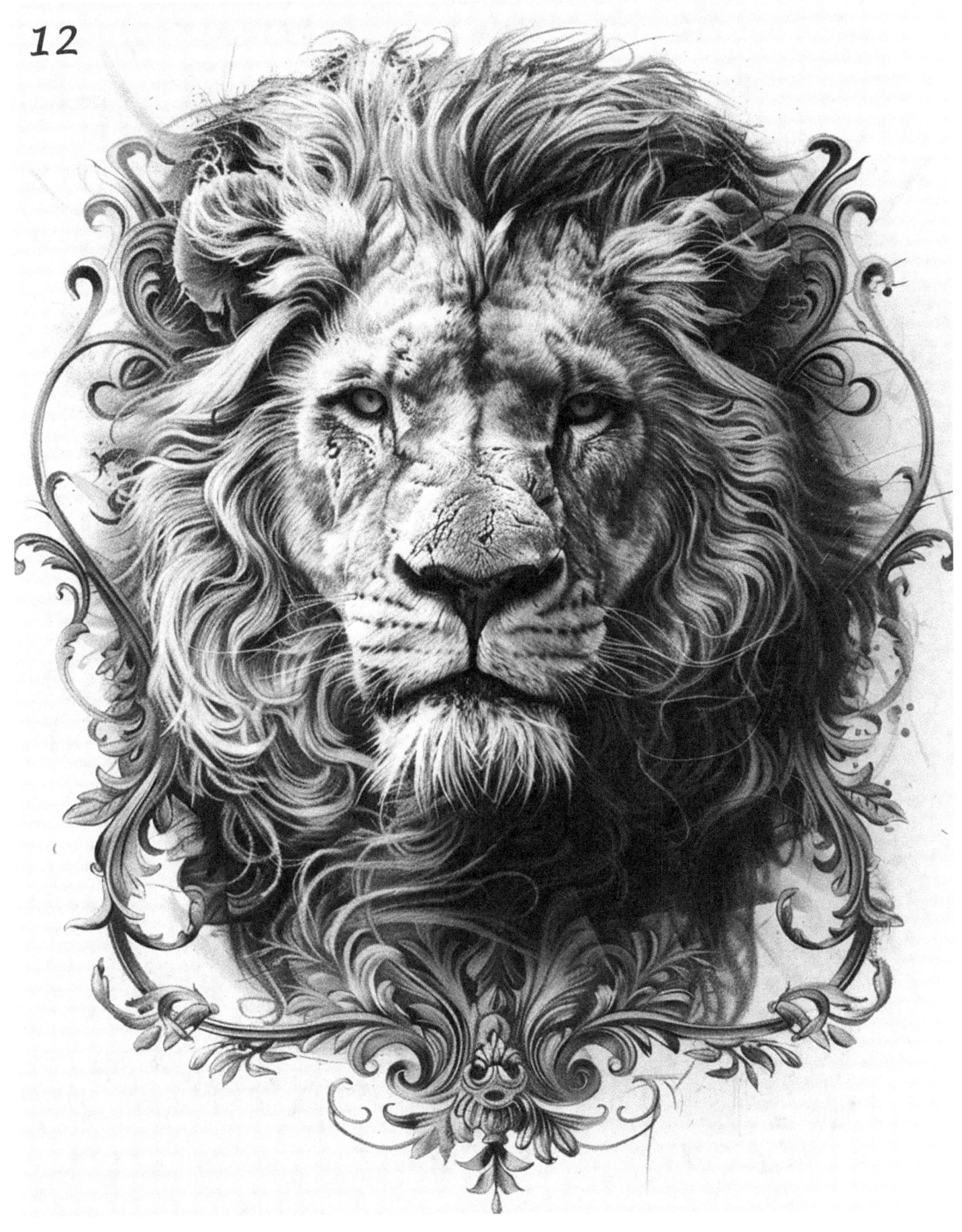

13

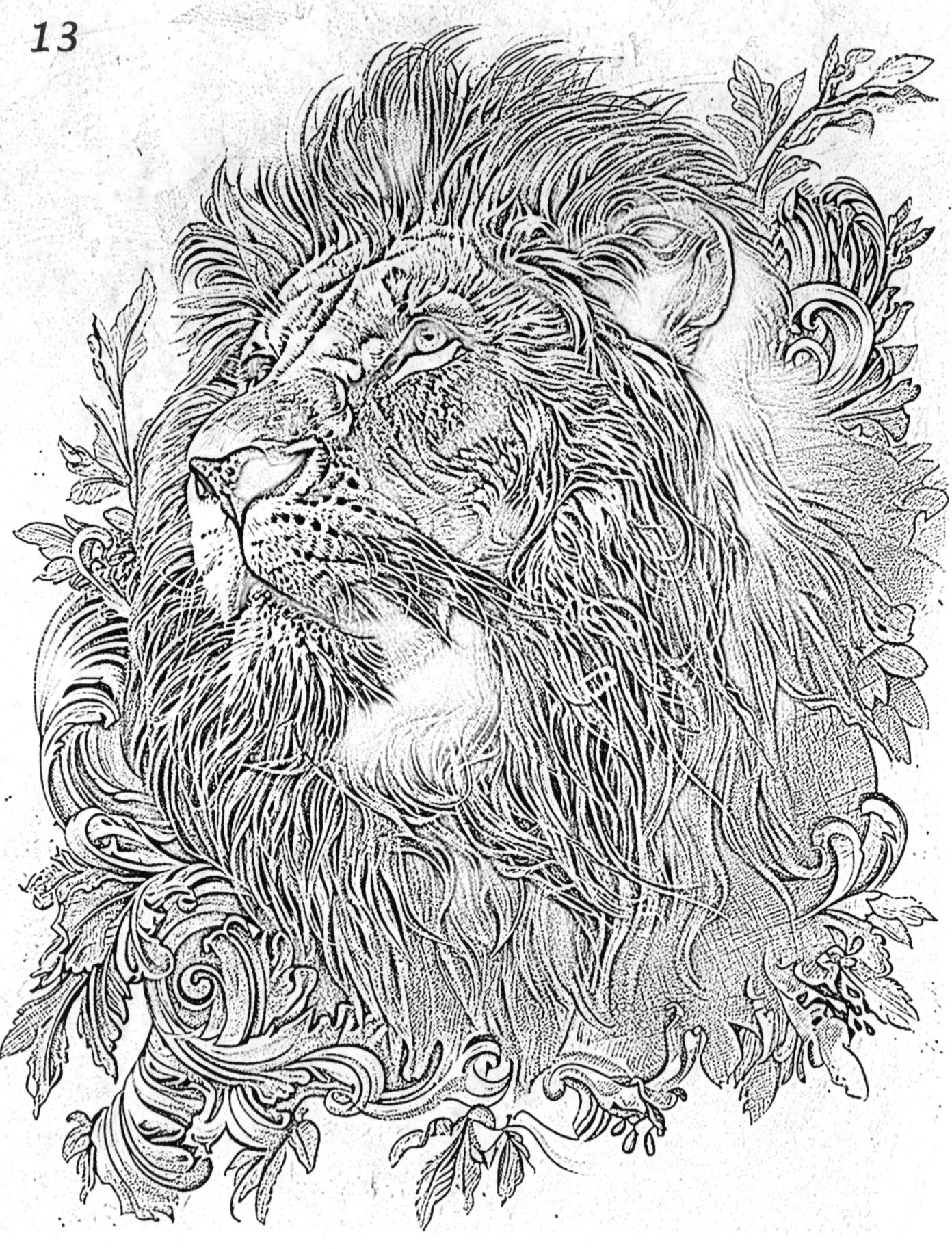

13

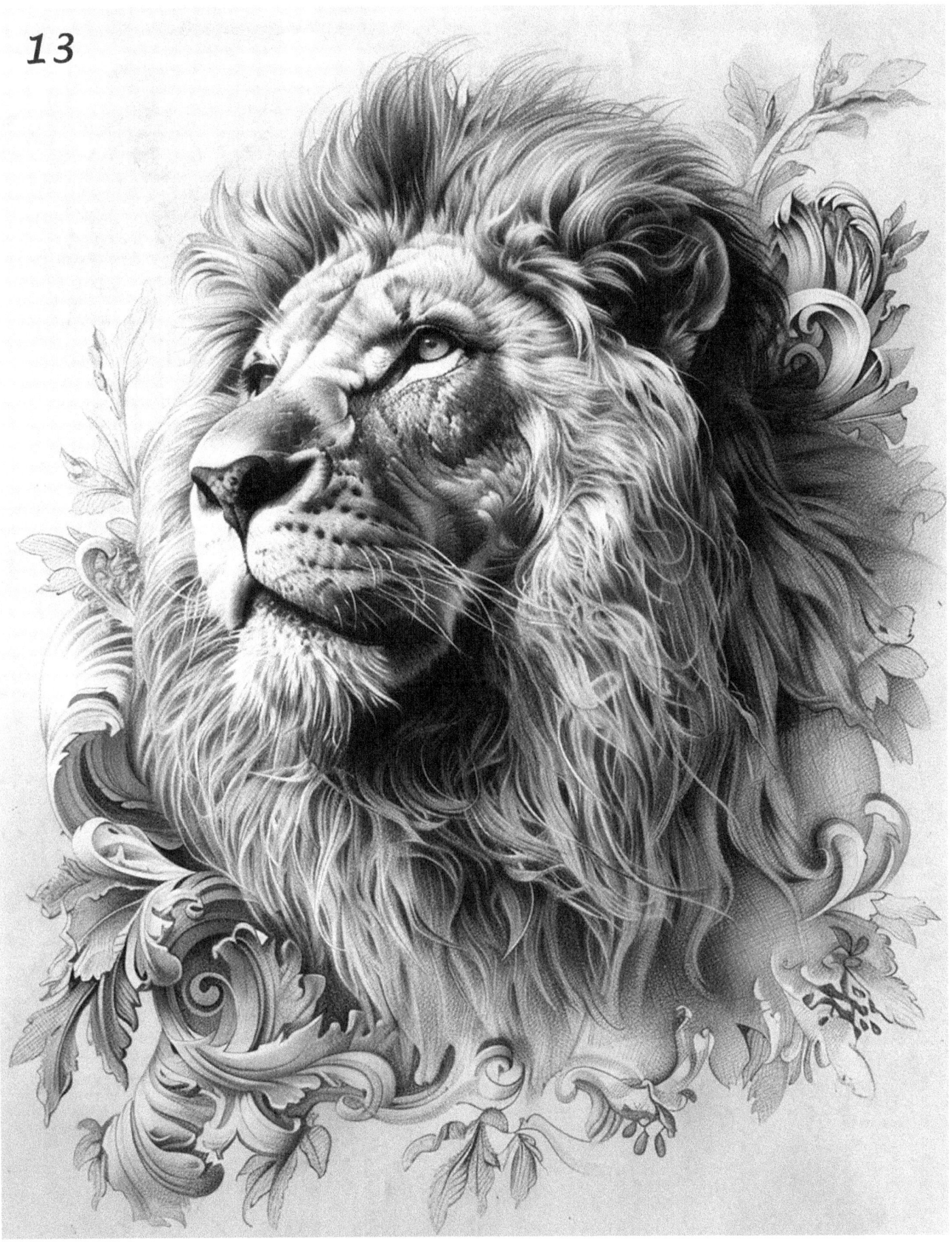

14

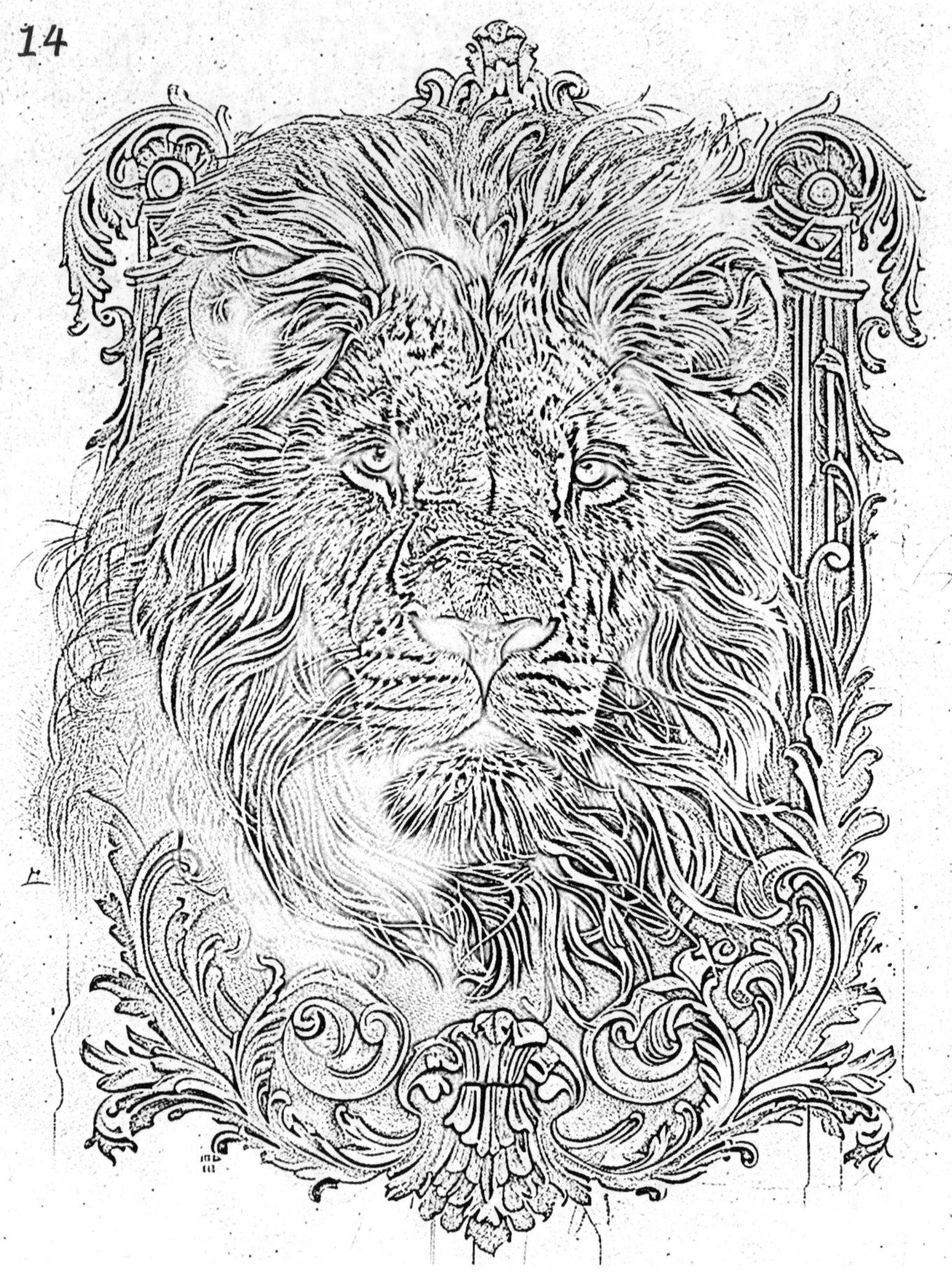

14

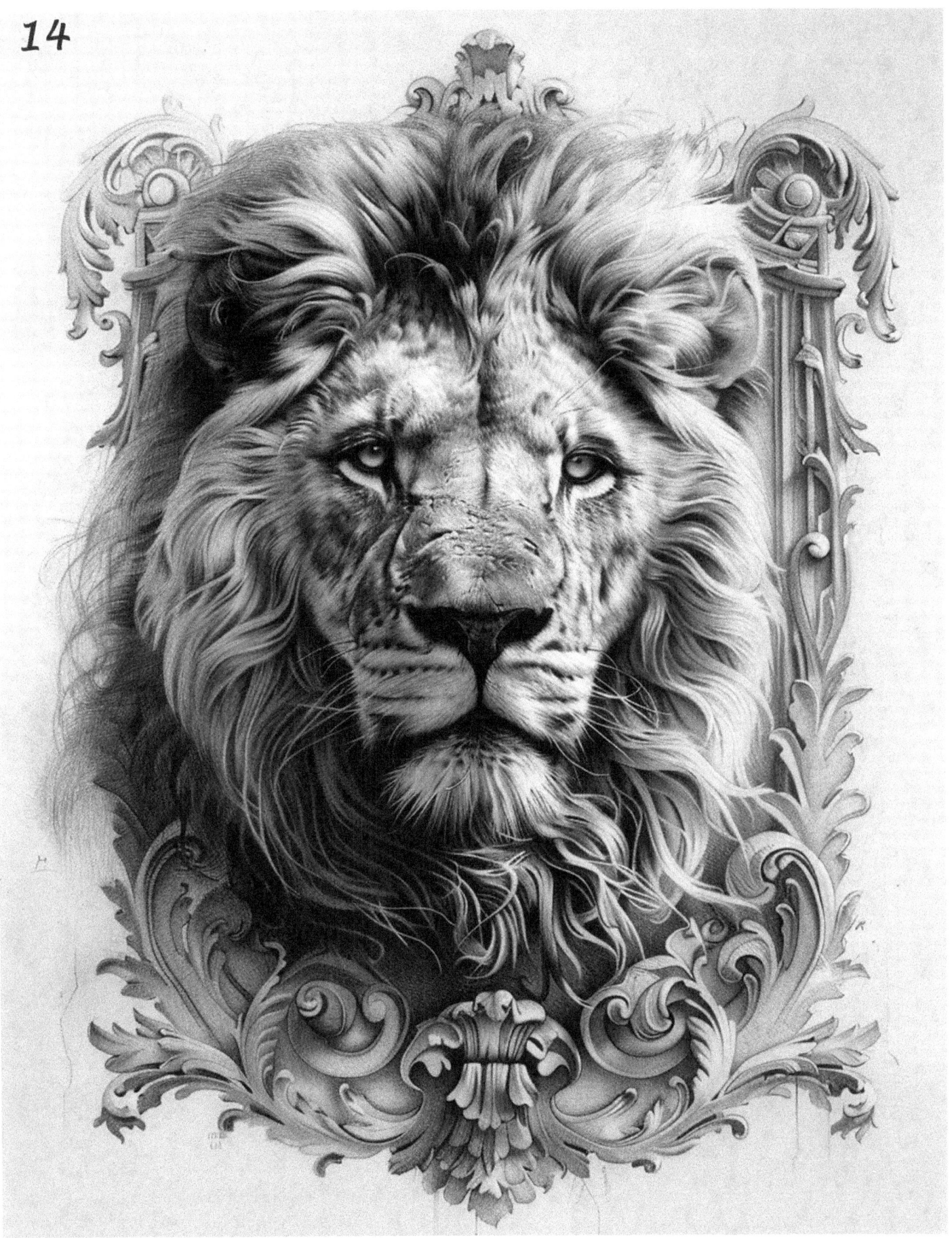

15

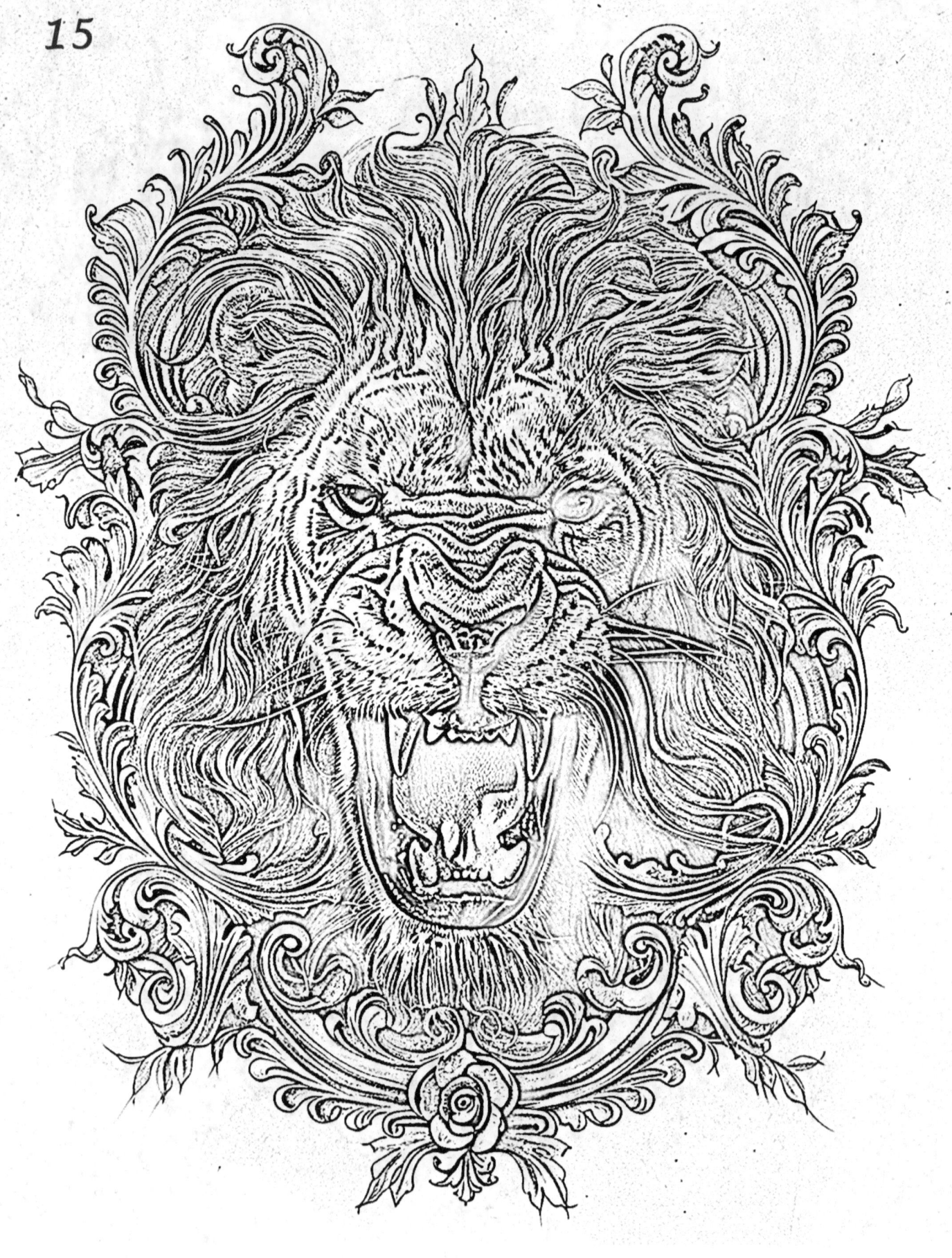

15

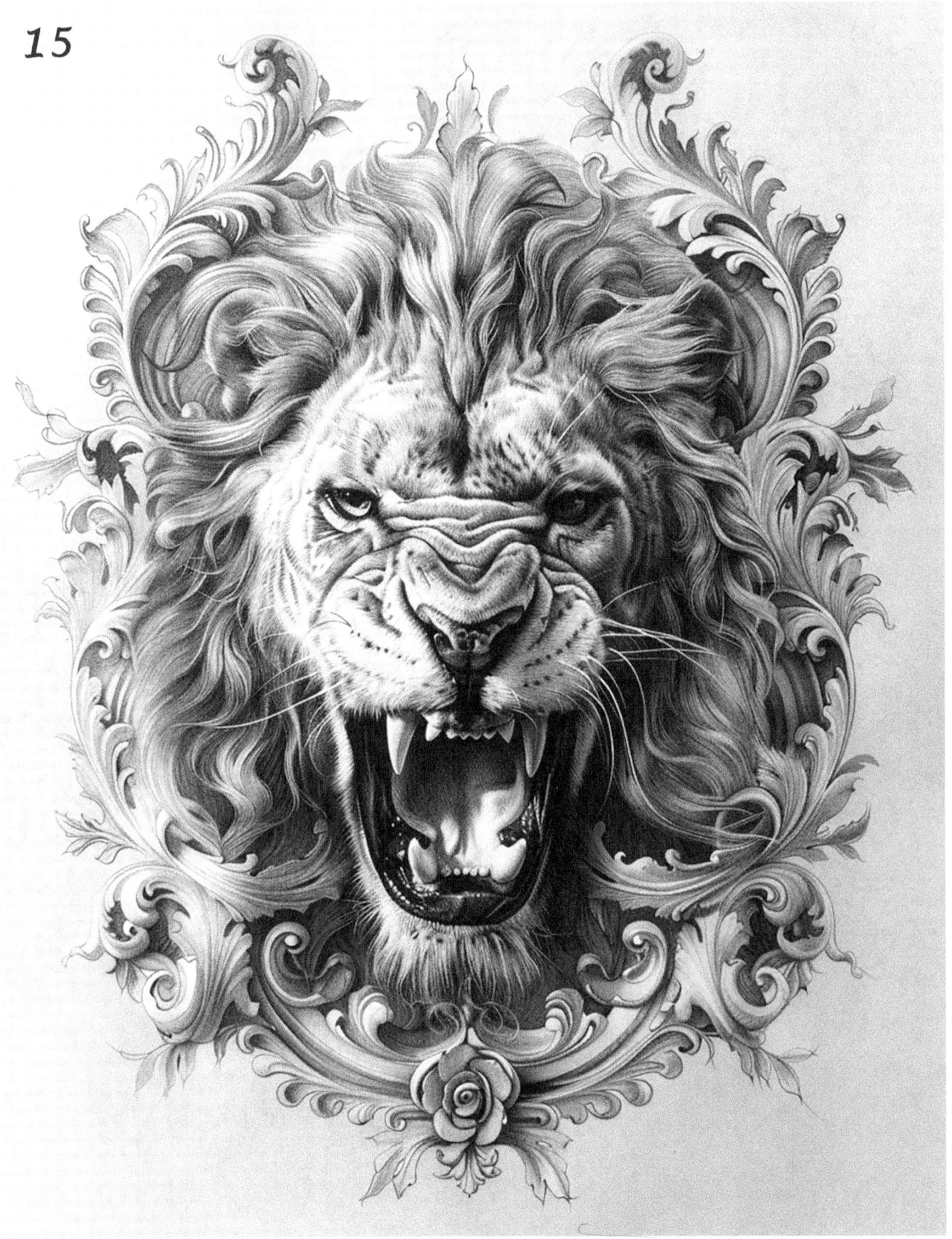

16

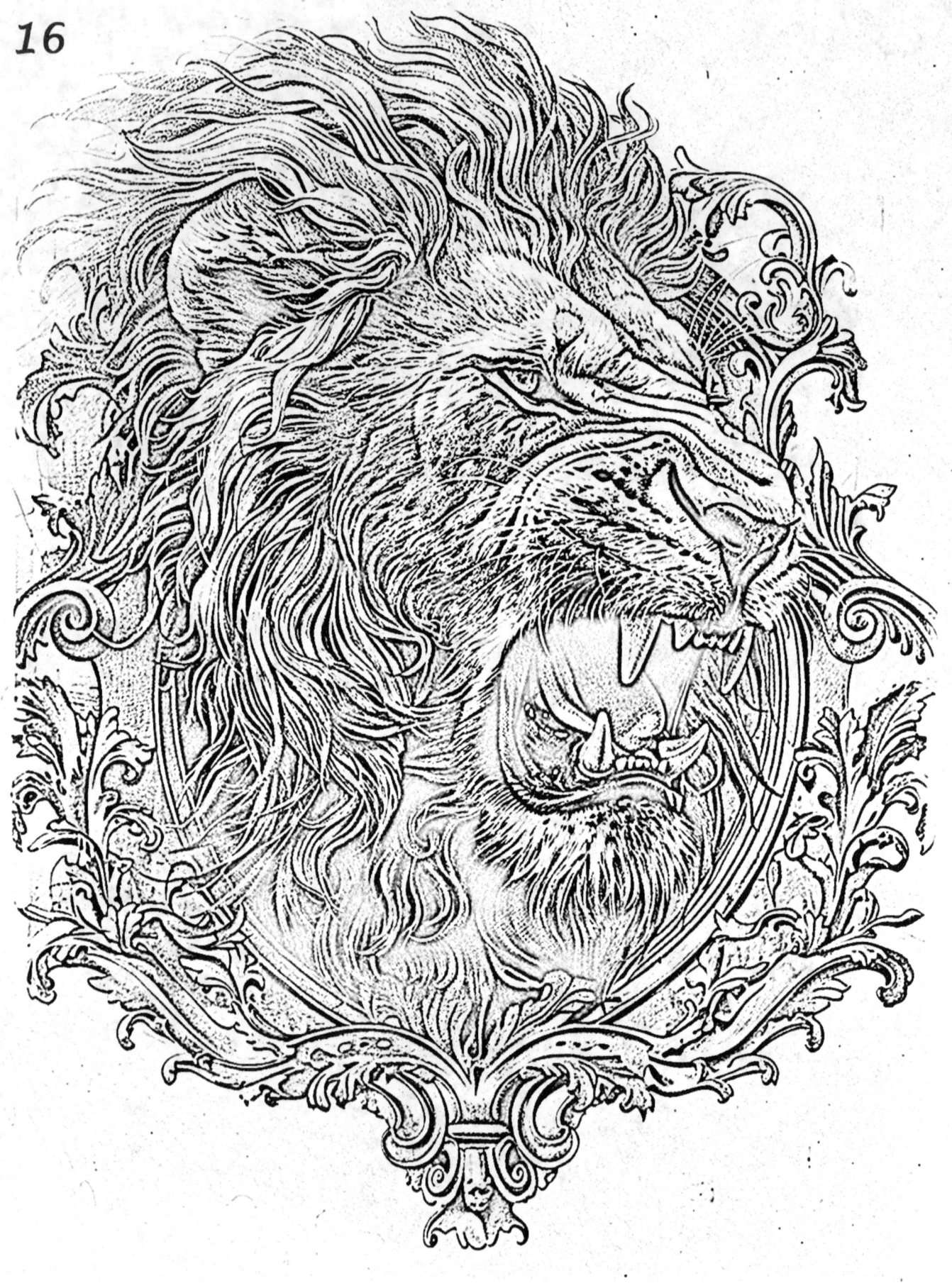

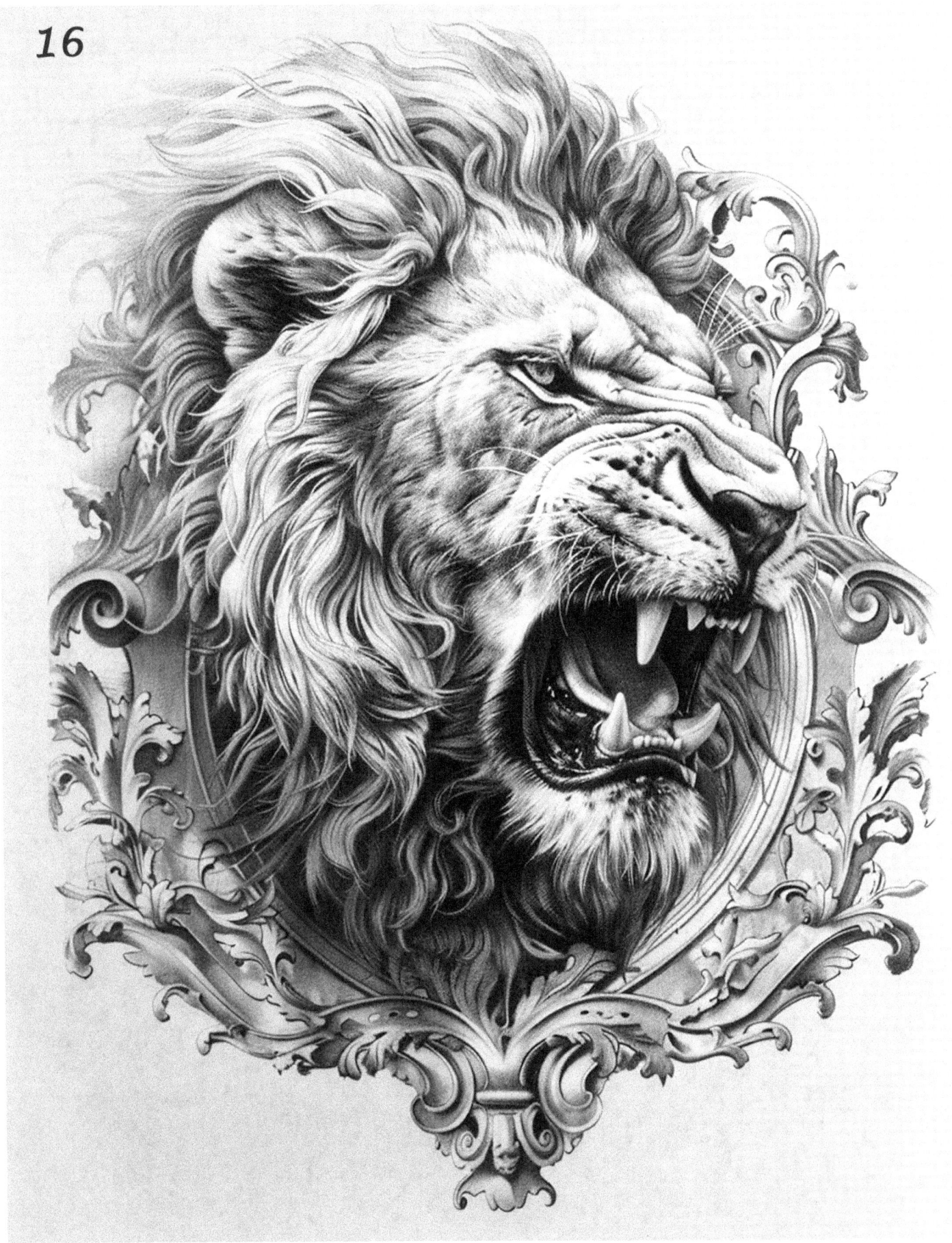

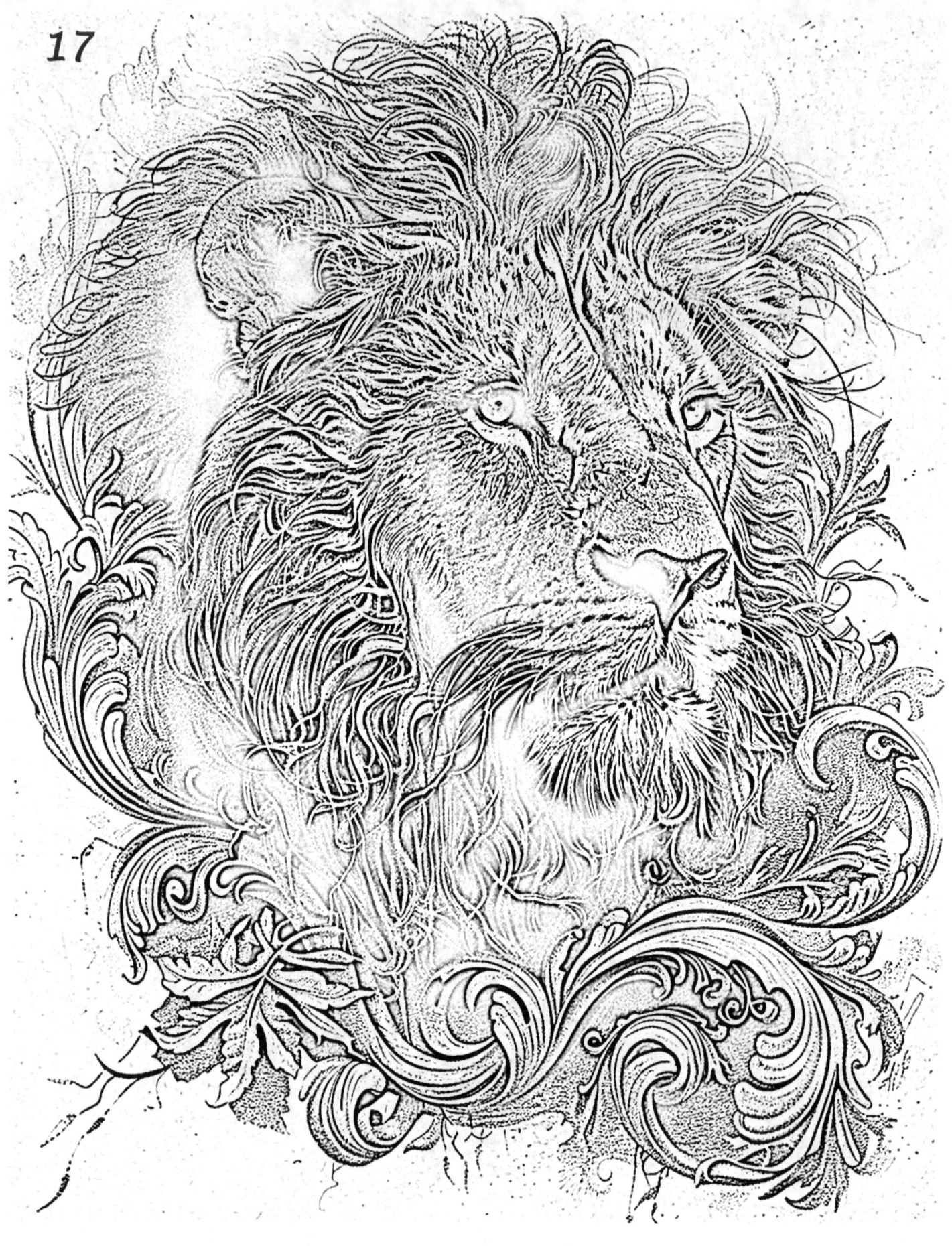

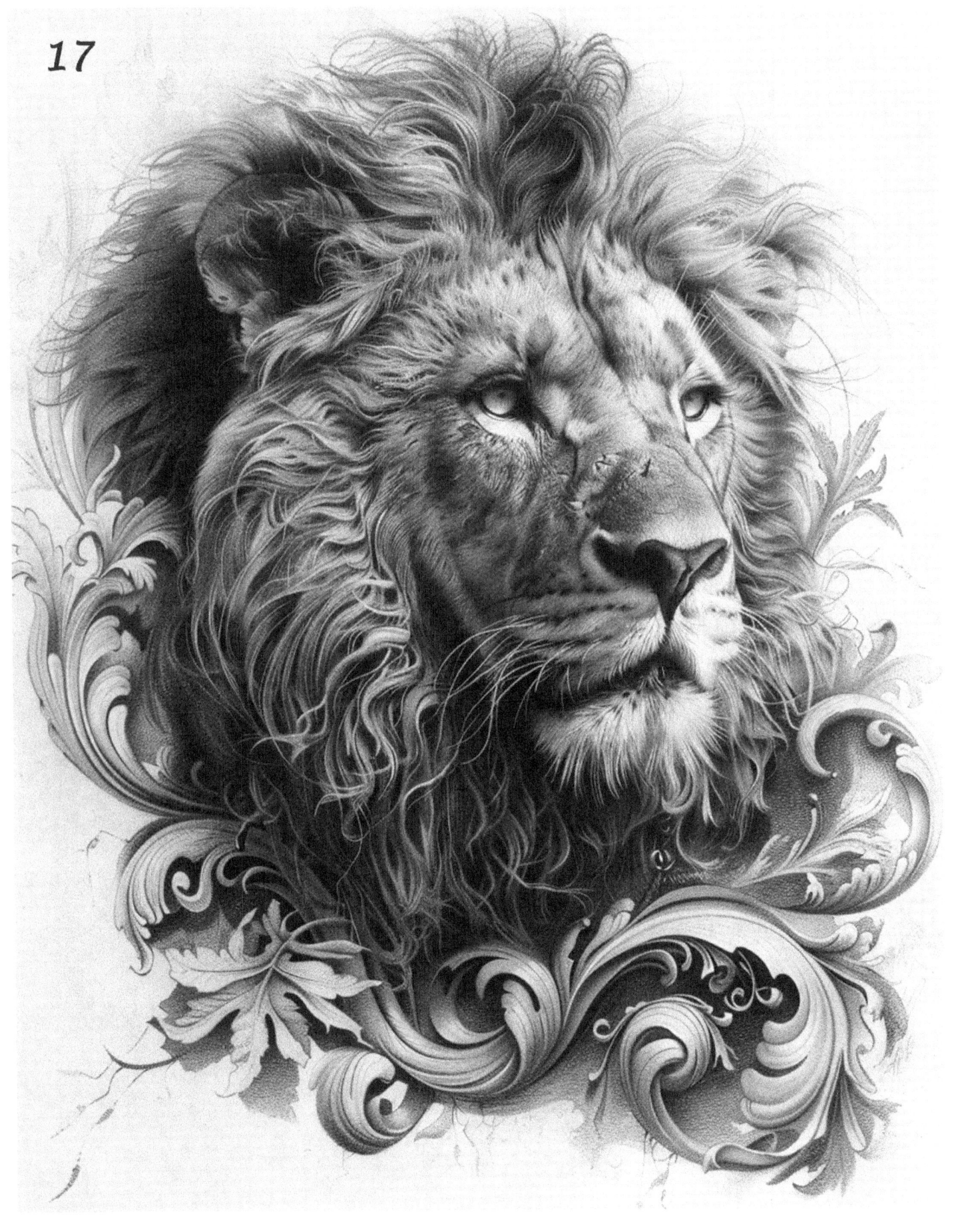

18

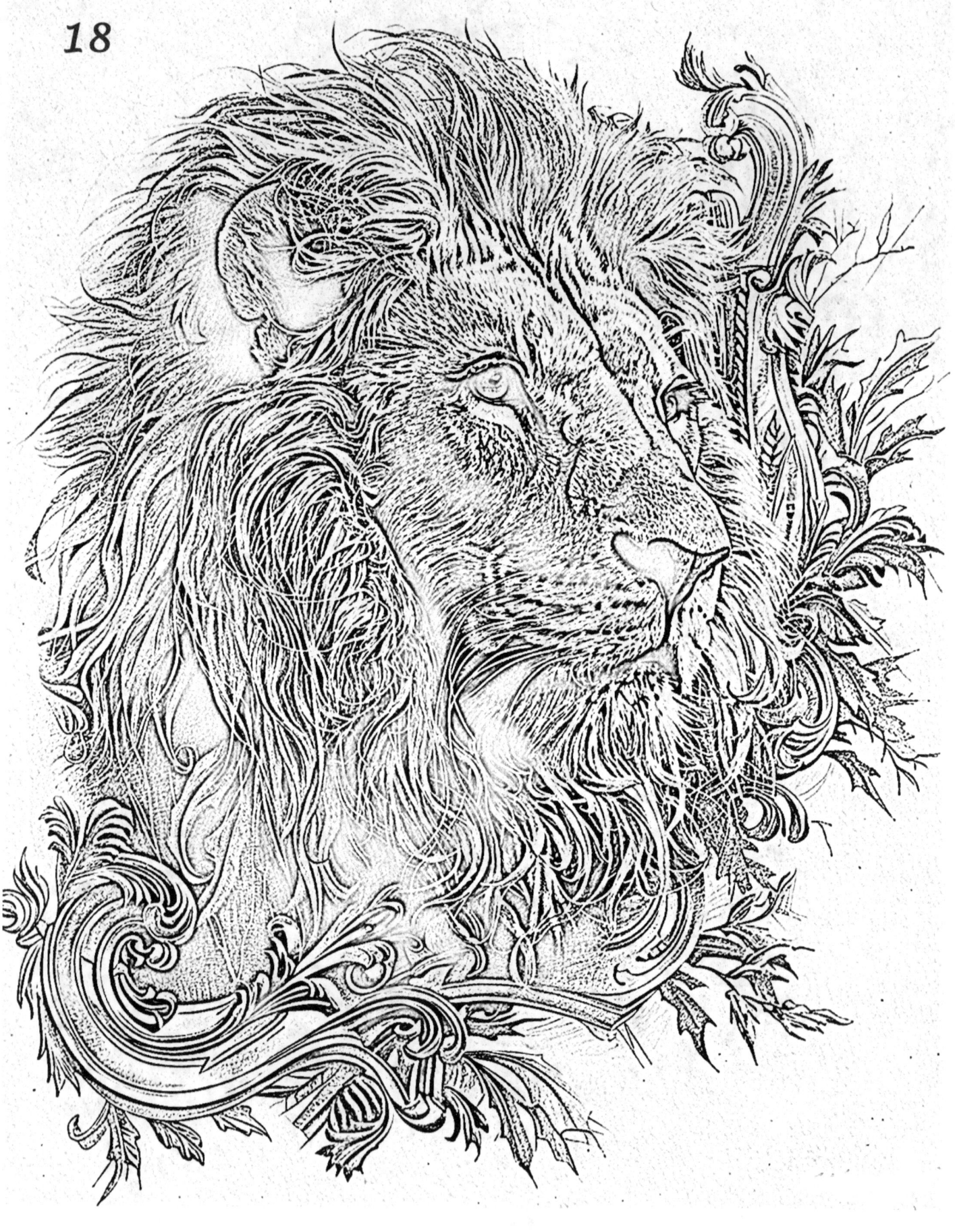

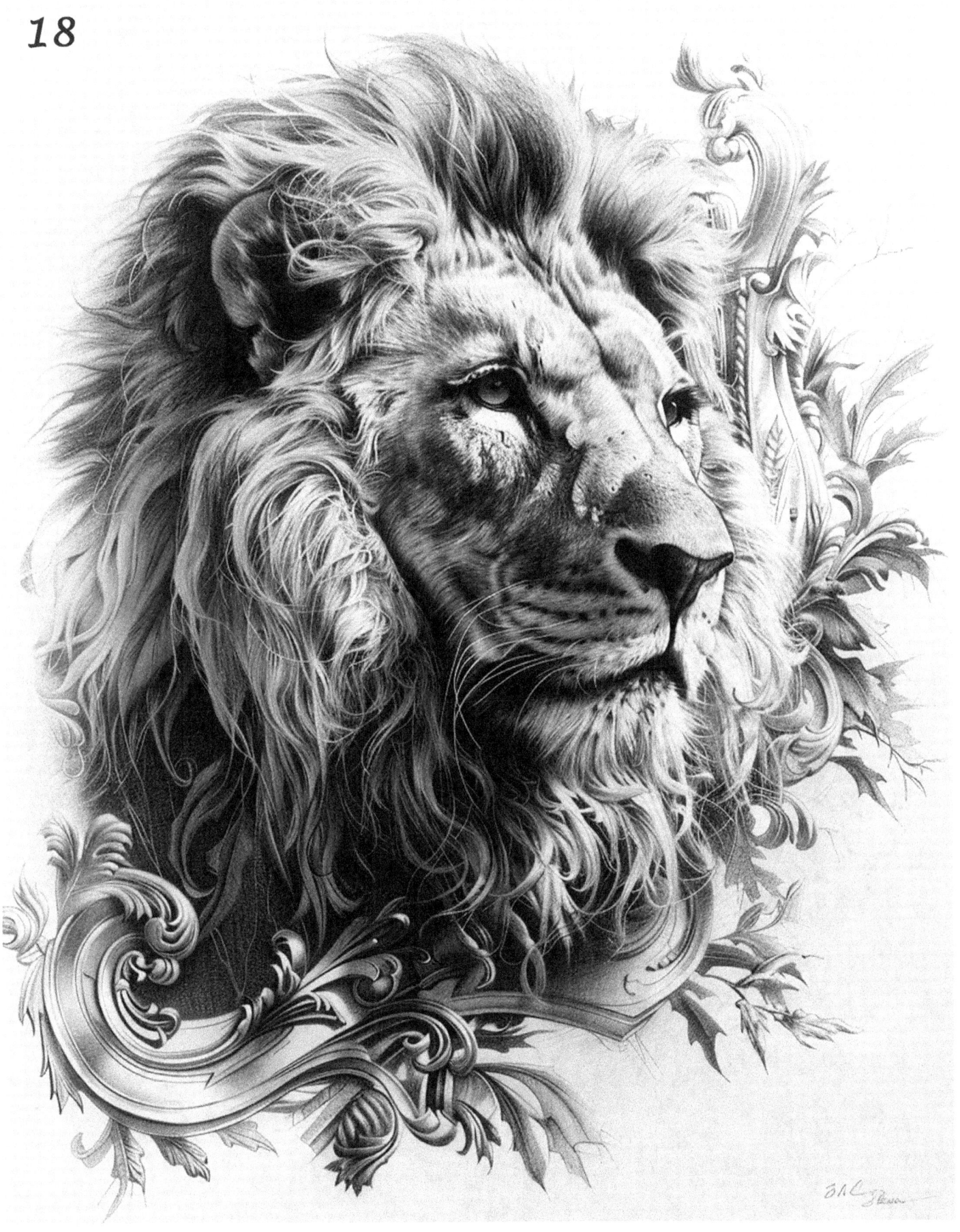

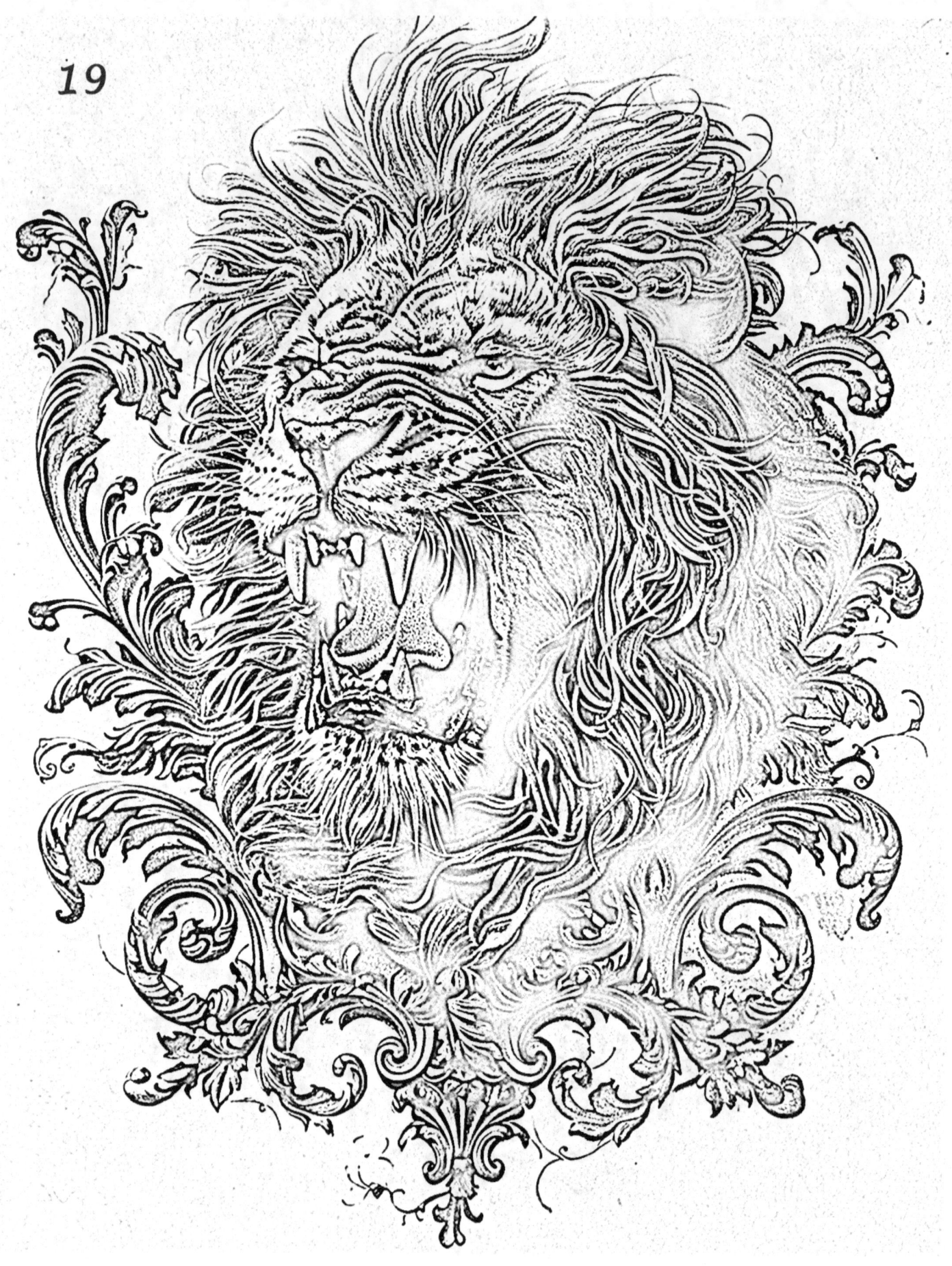

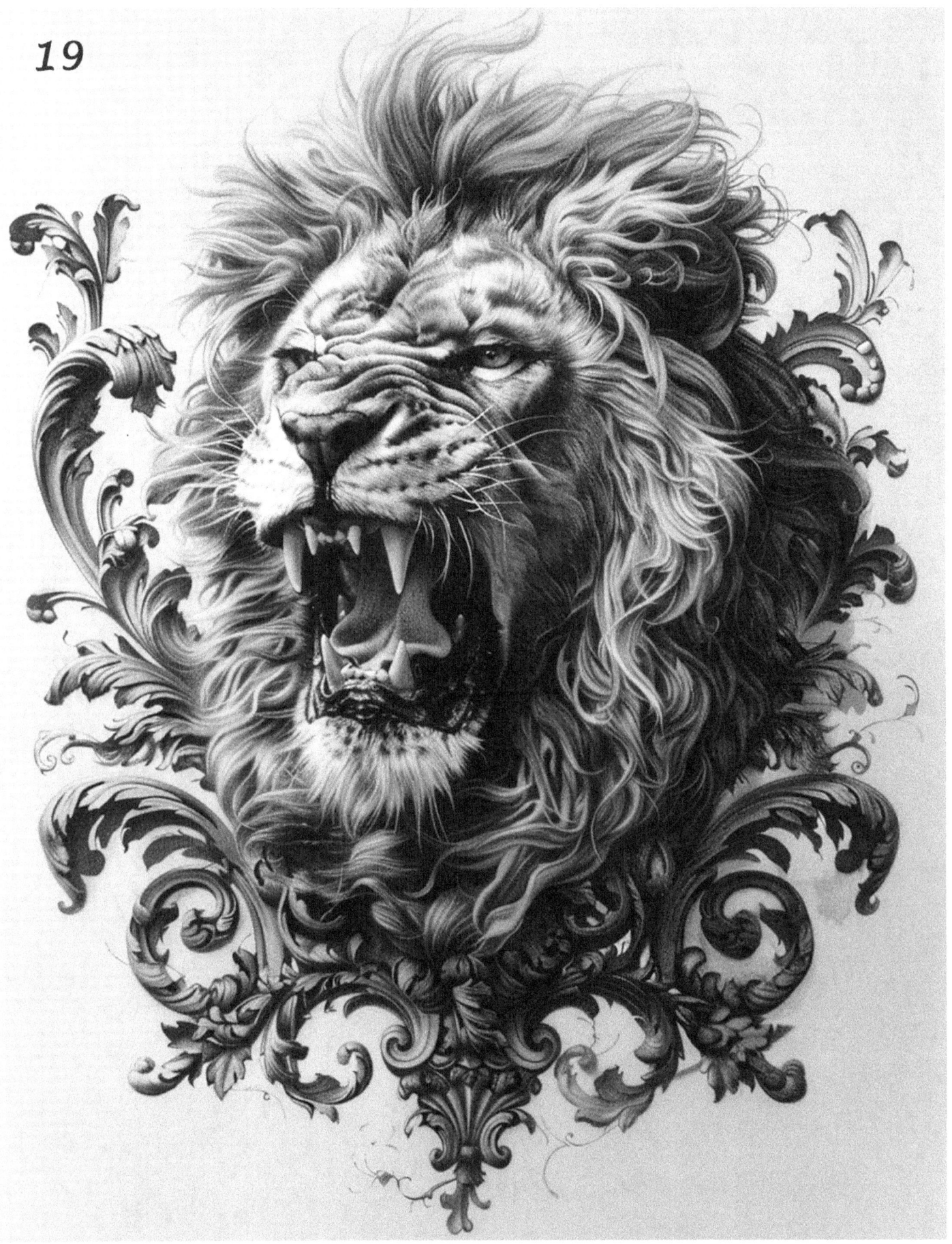

20

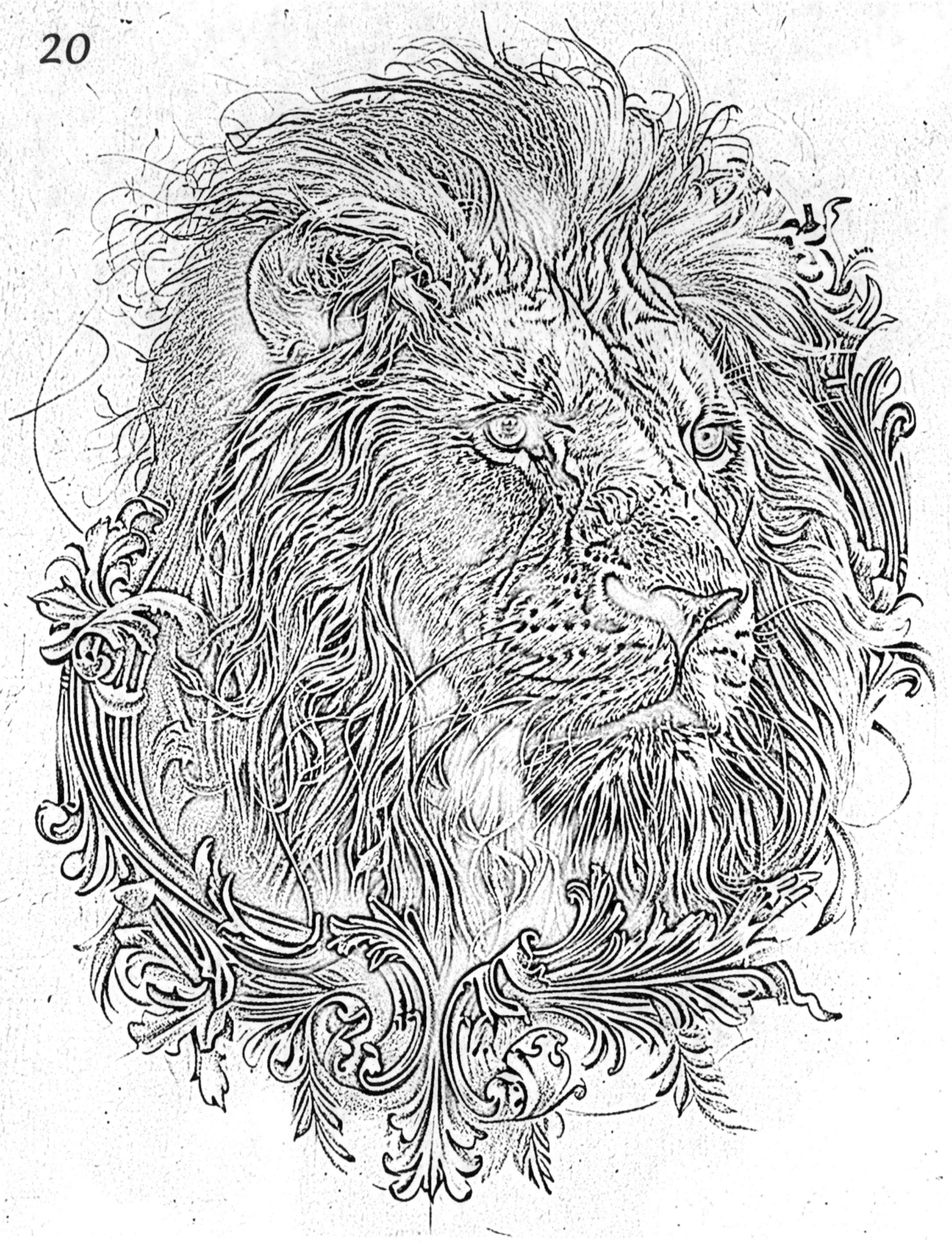

20

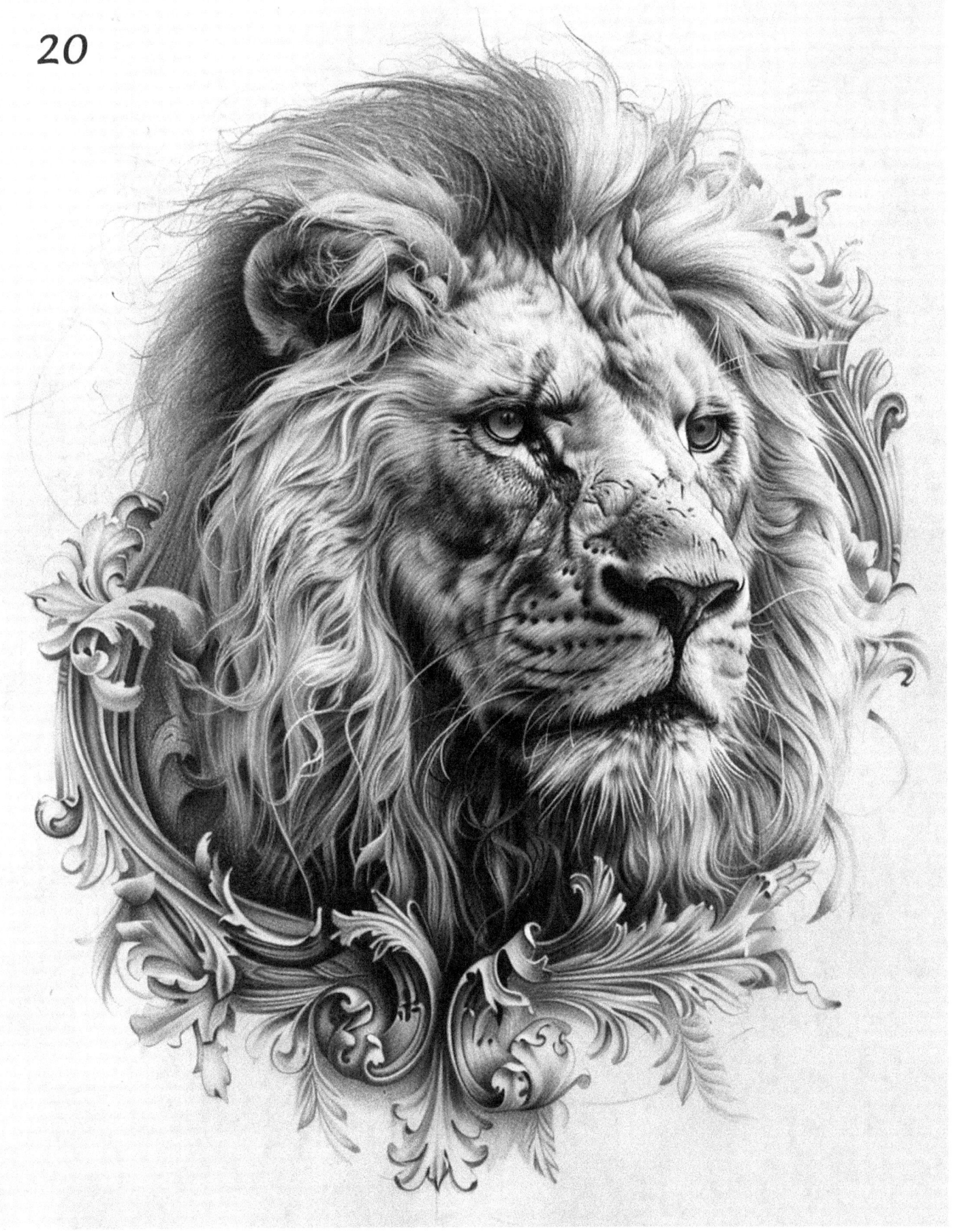

21

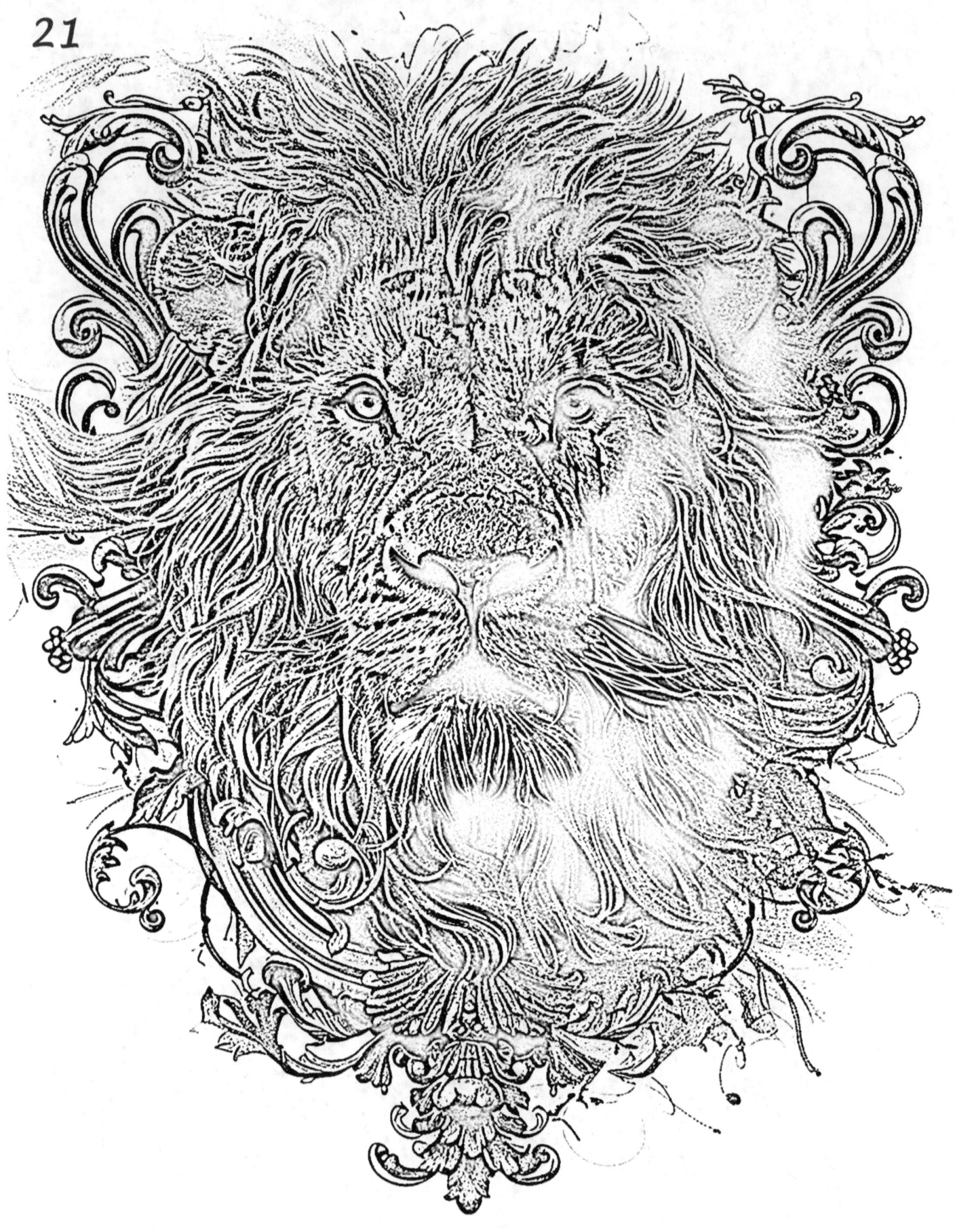

21

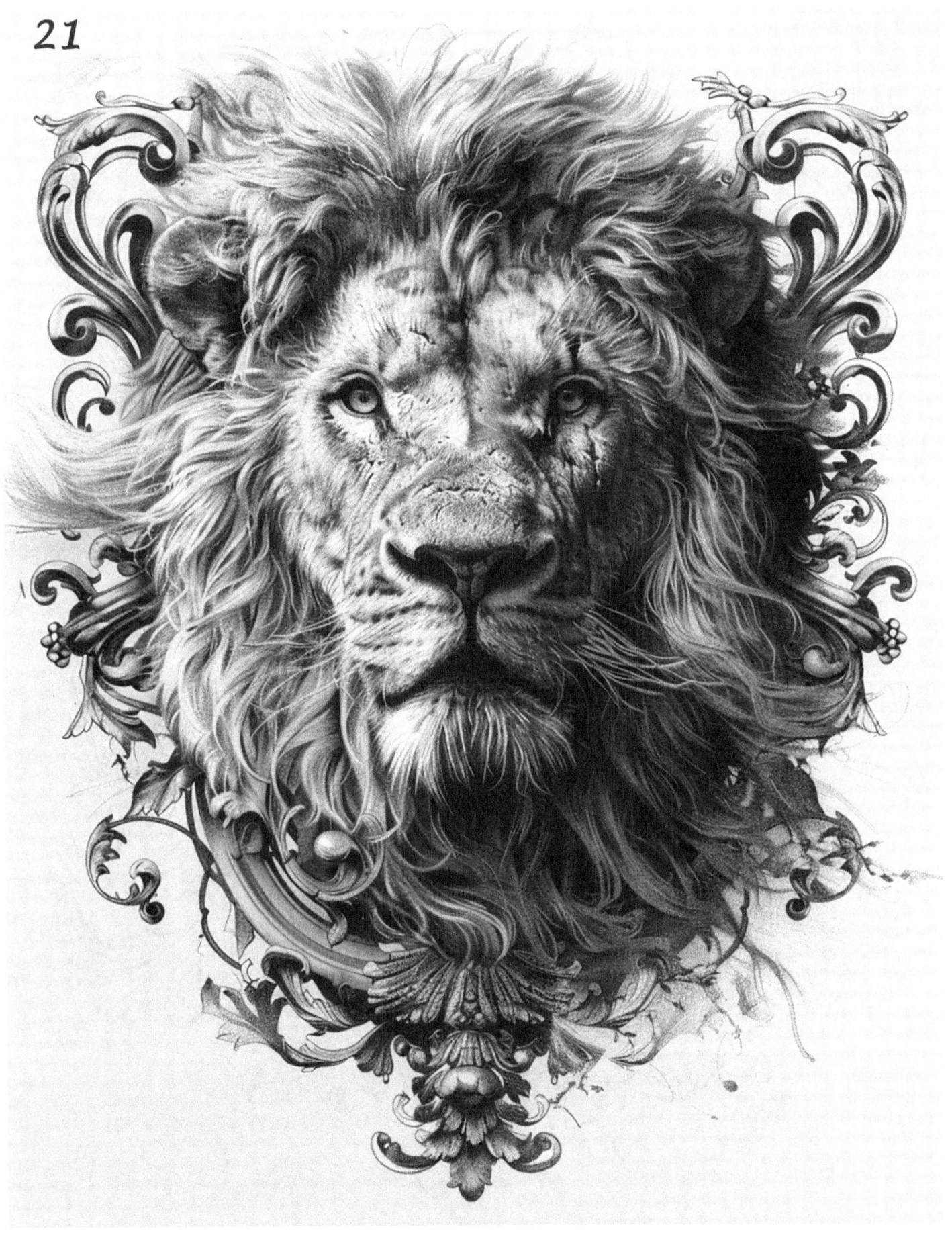

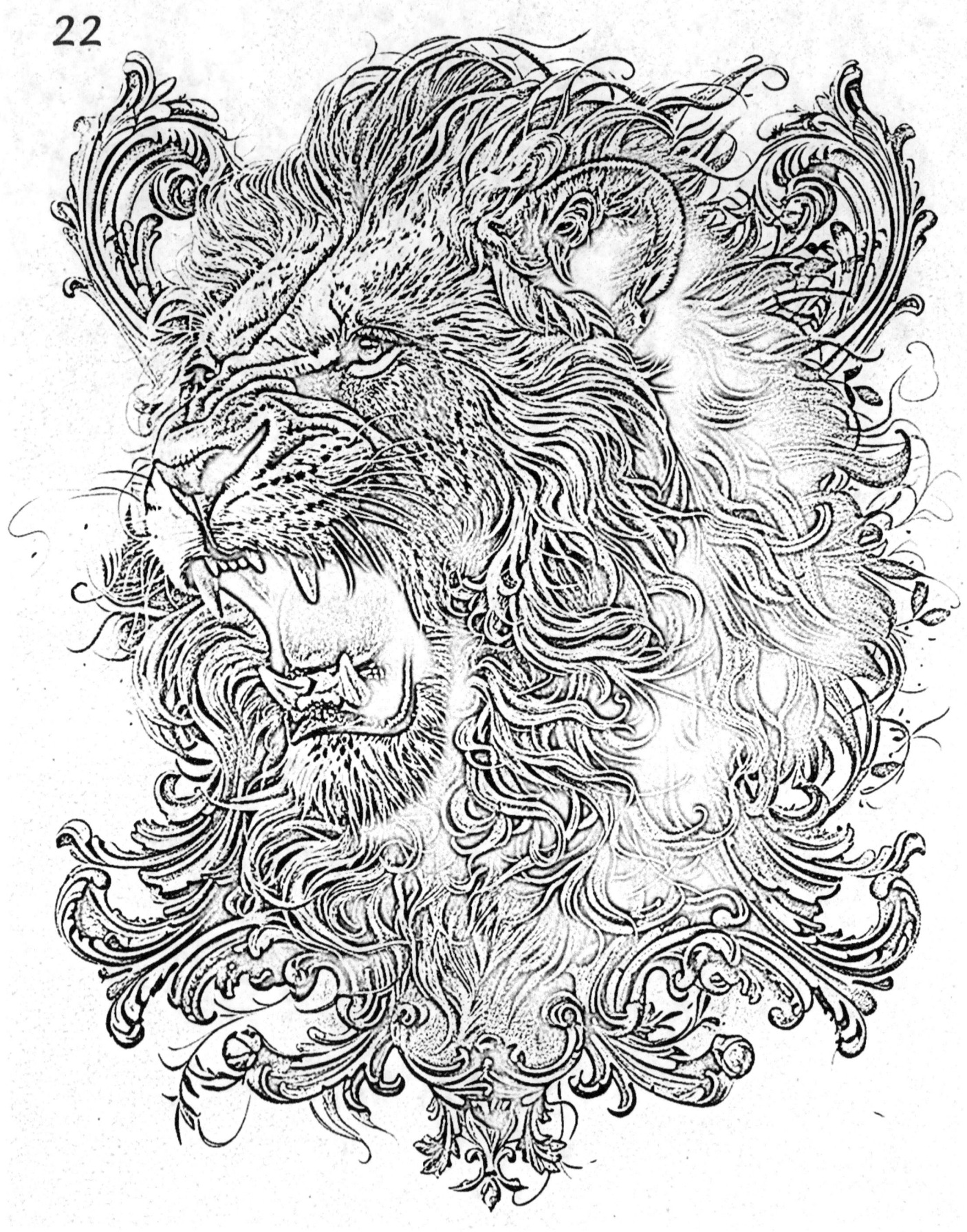

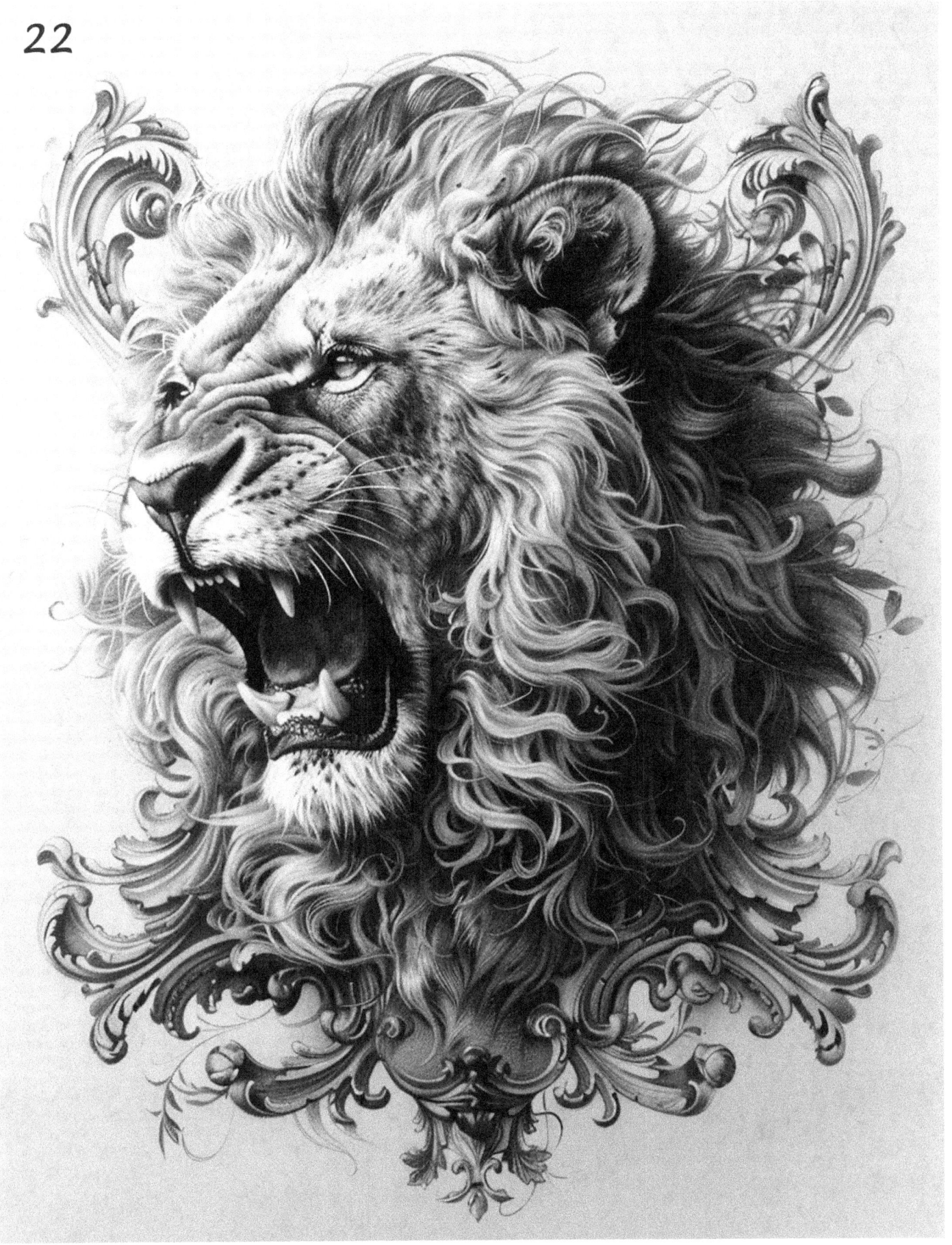

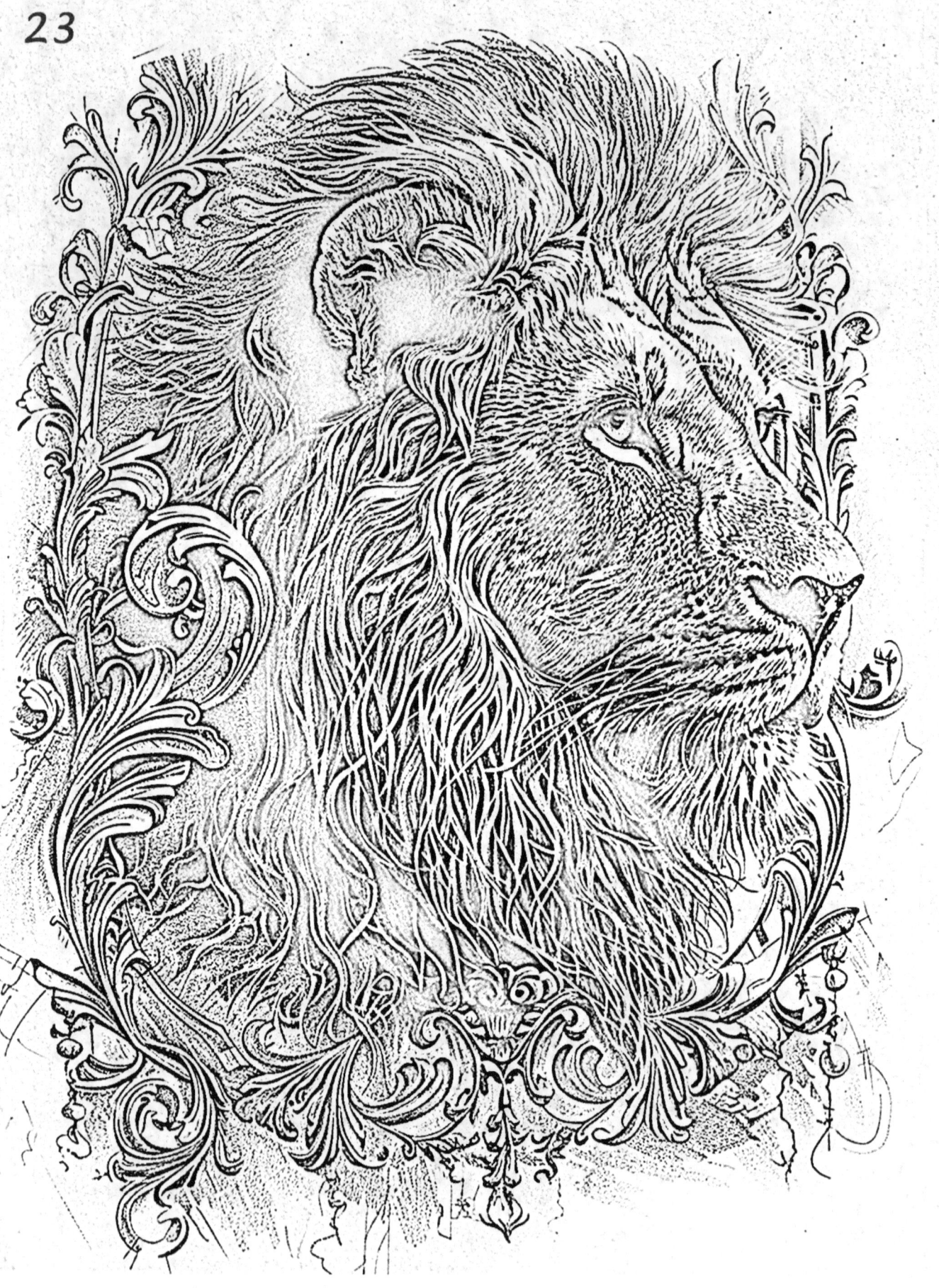

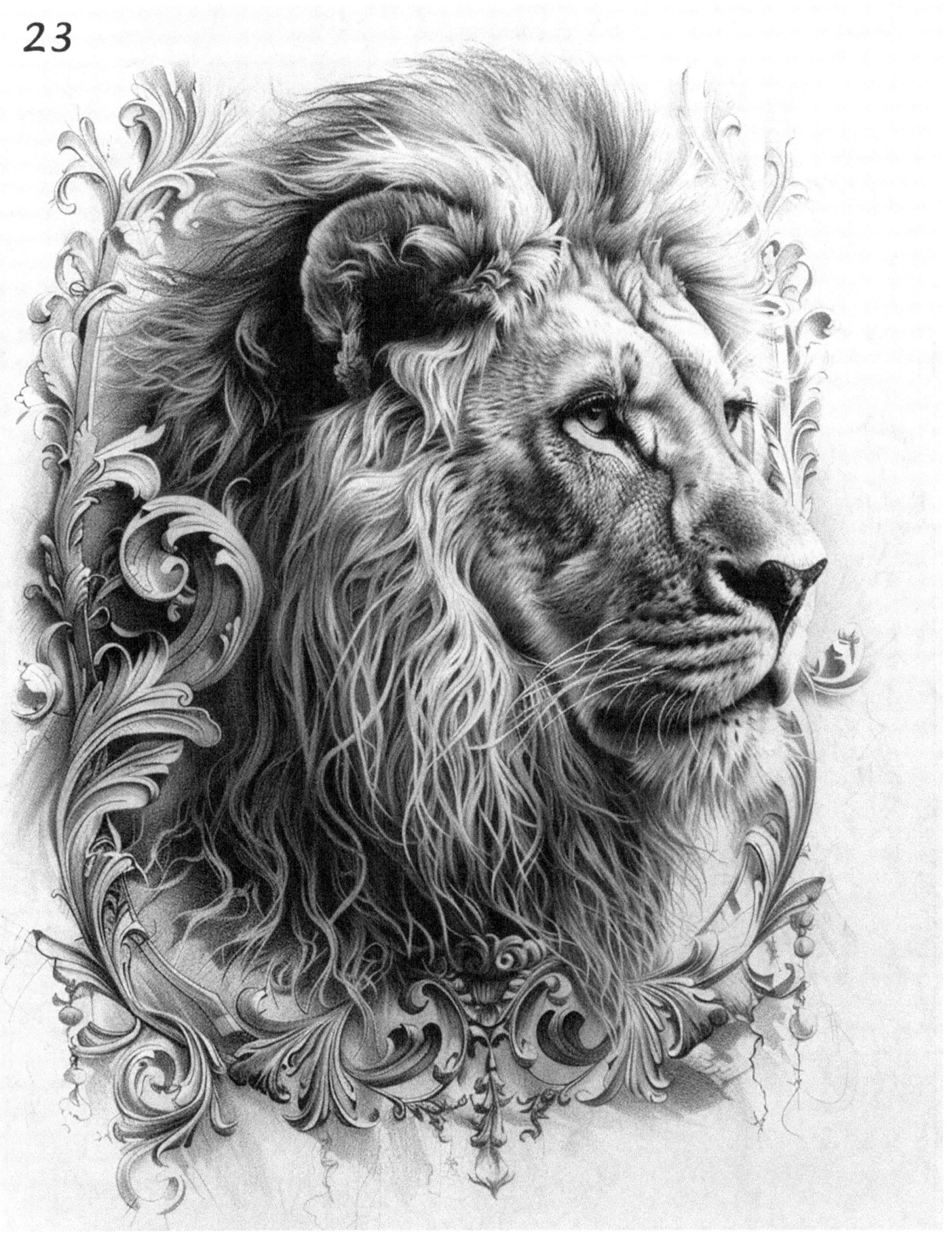

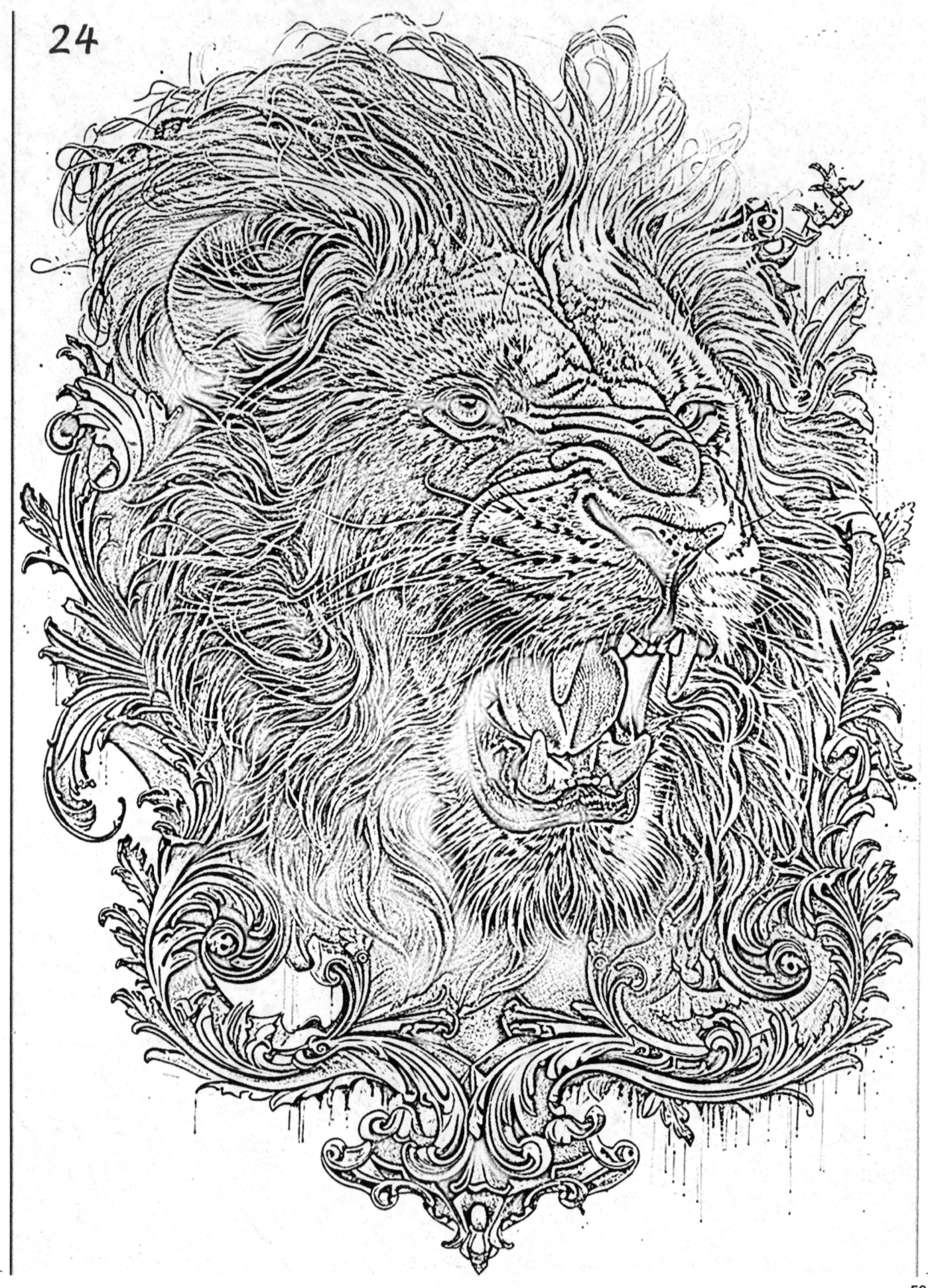

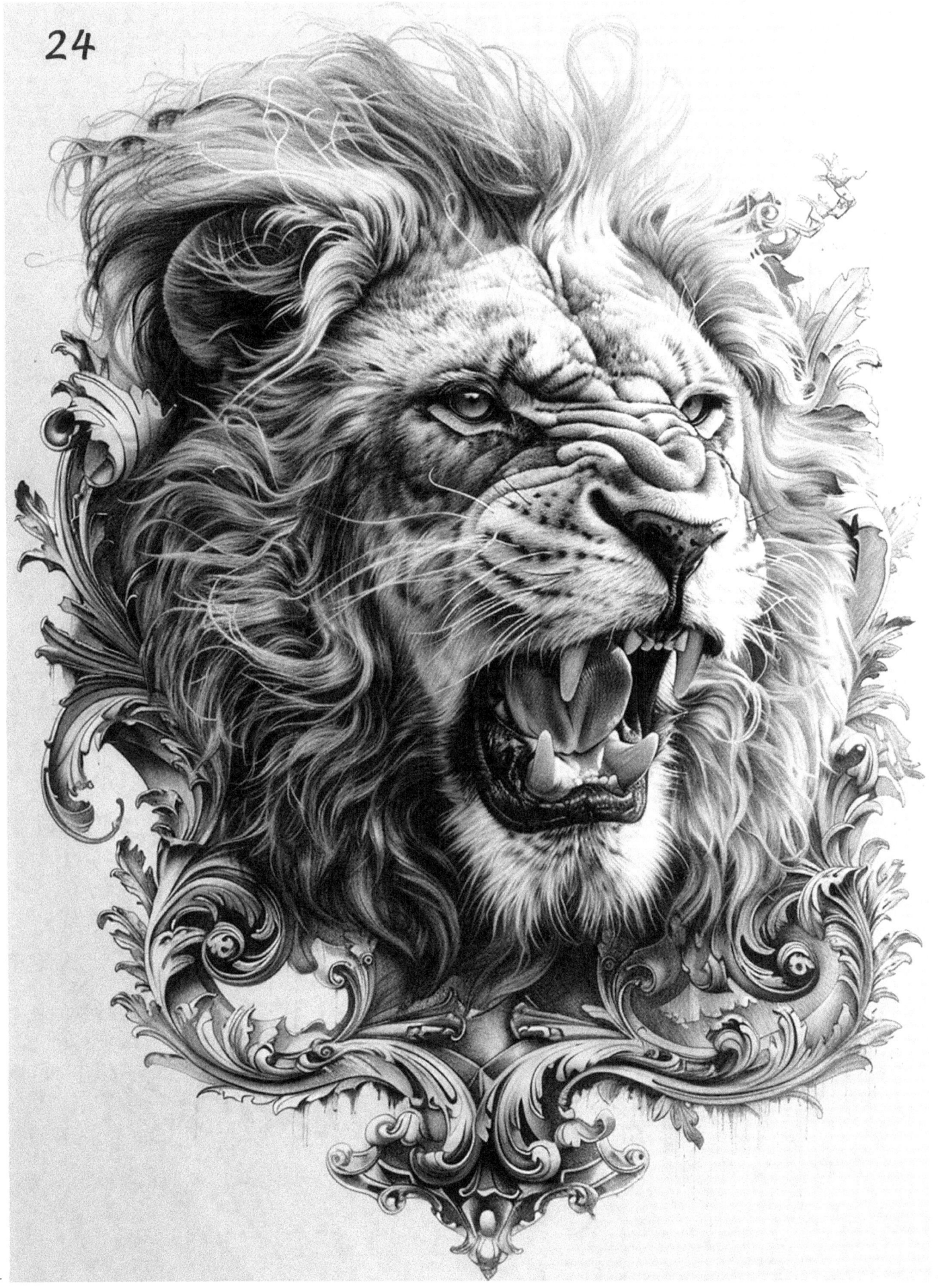

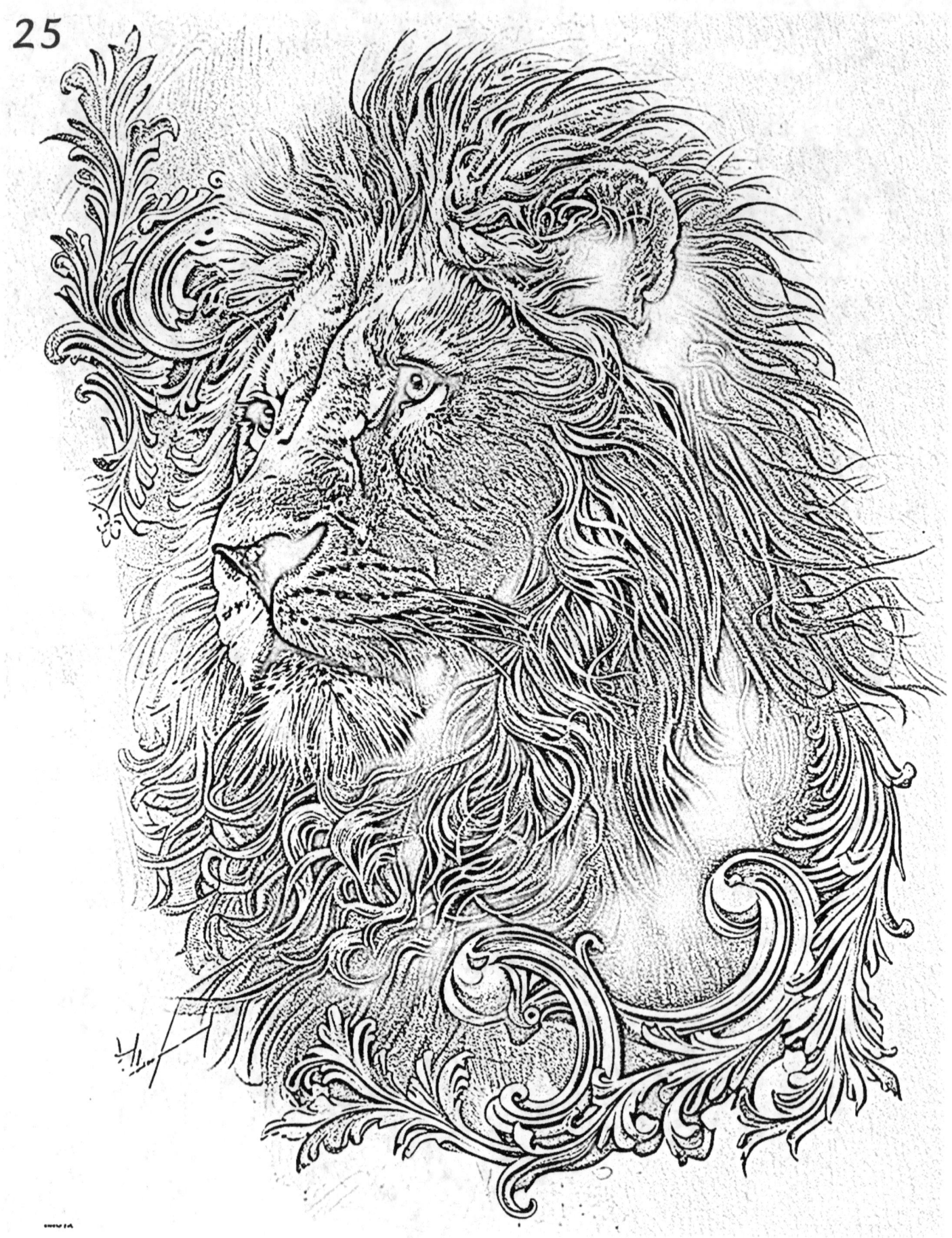

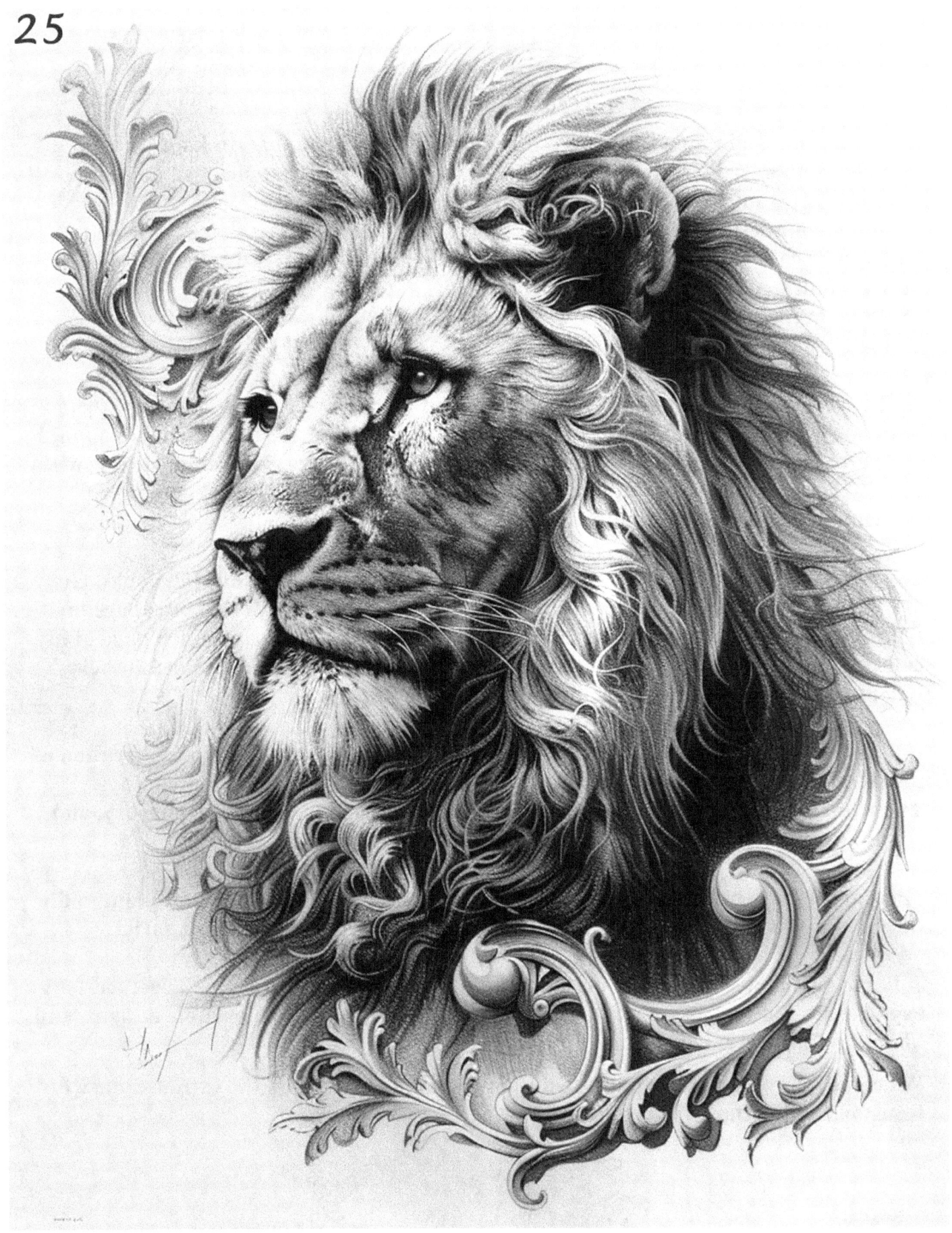

ABOUT THE AUTHOR

Immerse yourself in the captivating world of art, where imagination knows no bounds. With over three decades of experience as a painter, tattoo artist, and author, I have dedicated my life to the pursuit of artistic excellence.

Through countless hours of dedication, I have honed my skills in charcoal, pencils, and acrylic colors, specializing in the realms of realism, photorealism, and impressionism. My unique style blends elements of fantasy and impressionism, resulting in mesmerizing works of art that evoke deep emotions and leave a lasting impact.

In the realm of tattoo artistry, I have emerged as a trailblazer, revolutionizing the industry with my fresh and distinctive designs. Recognizing the need for innovation, I have created a new age of tattoo art that seamlessly combines my preferred style with eye-catching aesthetics. My designs not only captivate the eye but also empower individuals to express their individuality and uniqueness.

Expanding my creative horizons, I have delved into the world of coloring books. Gone are the days of simplistic designs with thick lines. I am on a mission to introduce the realms of realism and impressionism to the coloring book landscape. Each page of my coloring books offers intricate details and a chance for individuals to unleash their inner artist, resulting in remarkable and vibrant creations.

But my artistic endeavors don't stop there. I am currently engrossed in the creation of photo reference books that showcase wildlife and nature in unprecedented ways. These books will transport you to a world of vivid colors, breathtaking imagery, and seemingly impossible poses.

Prepare to be captivated by the untamed beauty of the natural world, brought to life through my keen eye for detail and my passion for pushing artistic boundaries.

Join me on an awe-inspiring journey where creativity knows no limits. Together, let's explore new dimensions of artistry, where fresh perspectives, remarkable designs, and boundless inspiration await.

Welcome to my world of art, where dreams become reality, and the extraordinary is transformed into tangible beauty

Scan the QR code below in order to download the PDF.

You will need WINRAR (or equivelant program) to open the archive. Enter the password :

LionsRoyalPower3!

If download does not work please contact us at our Facebook page
https://www.facebook.com/DivineTattooDesign/

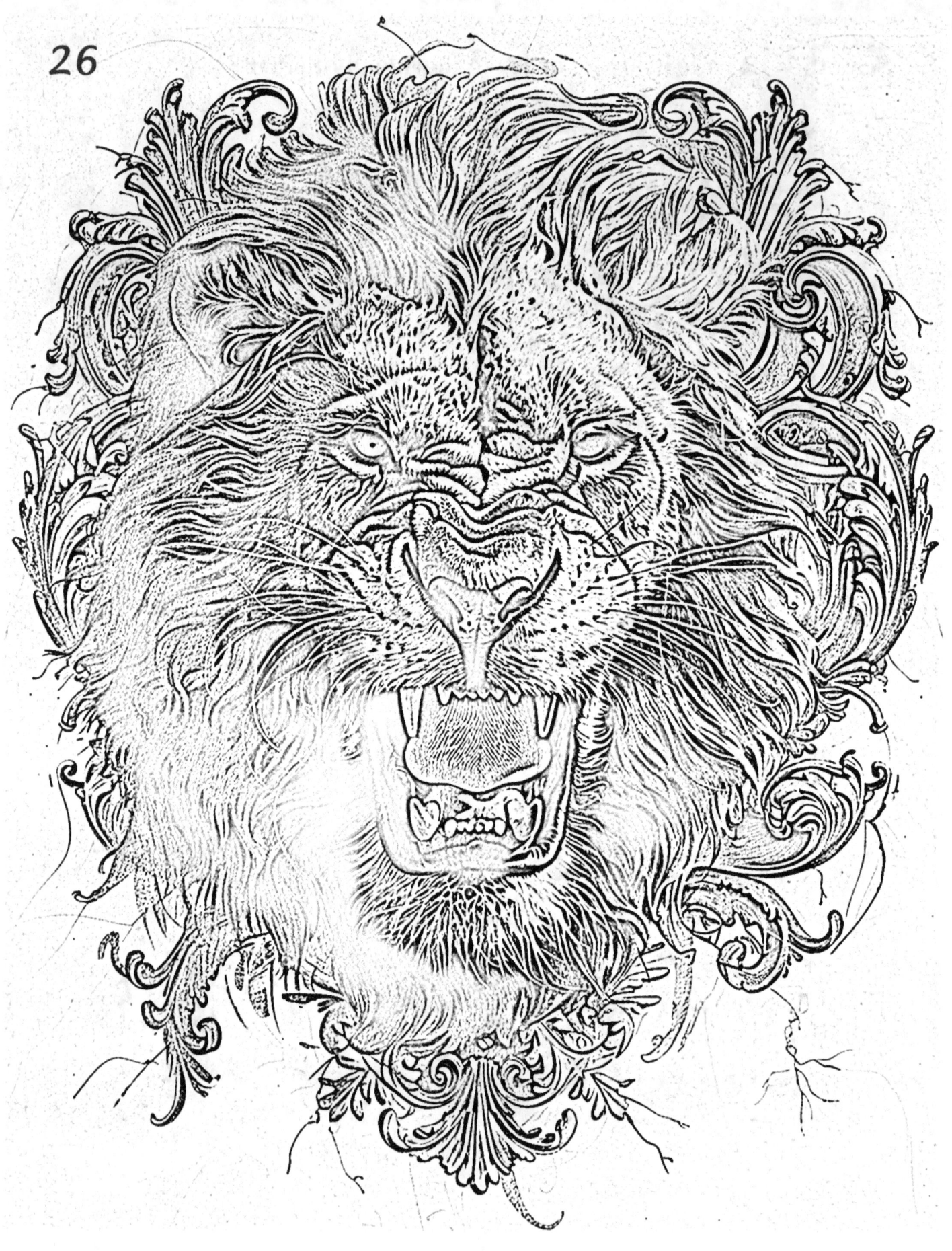

26

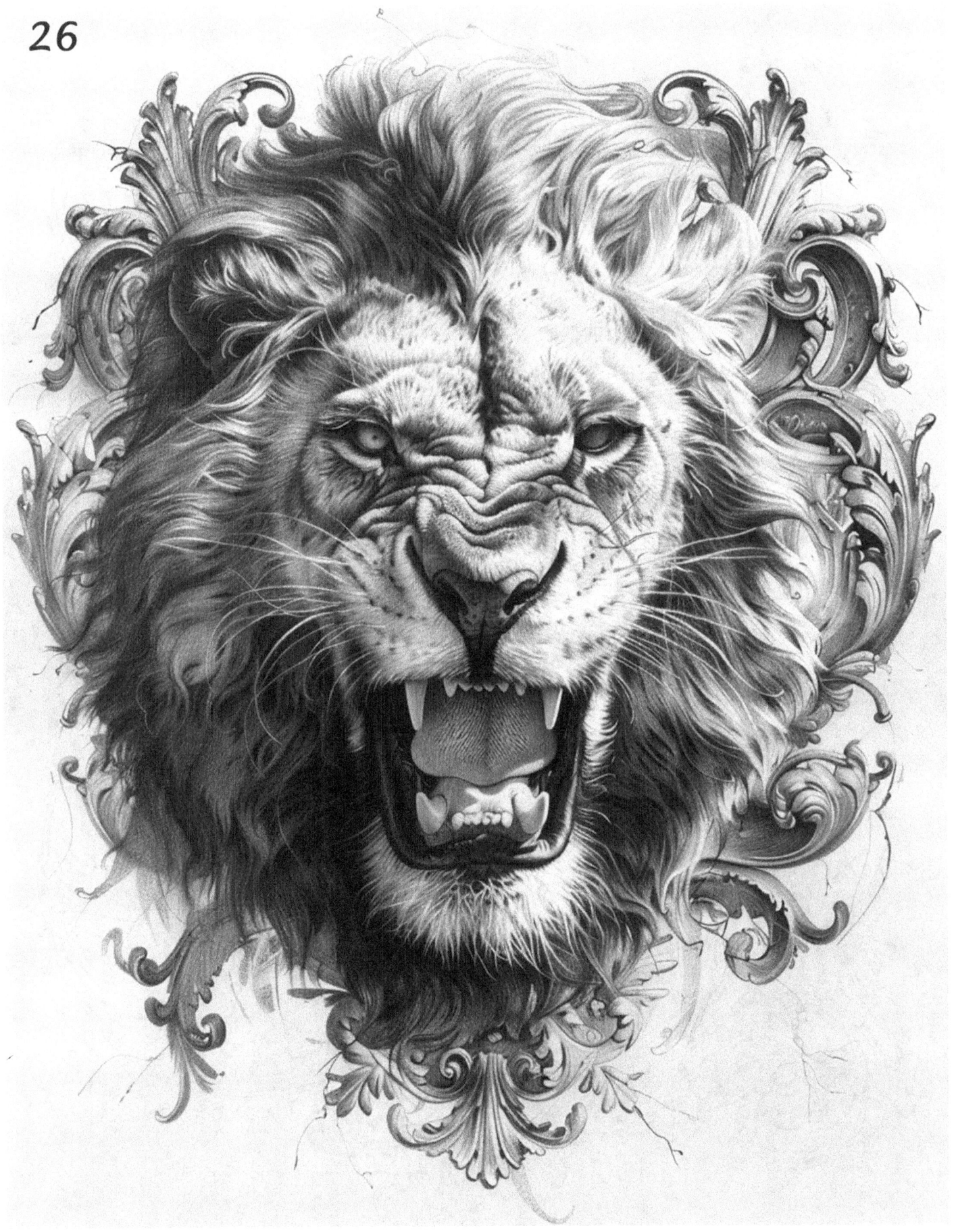

27

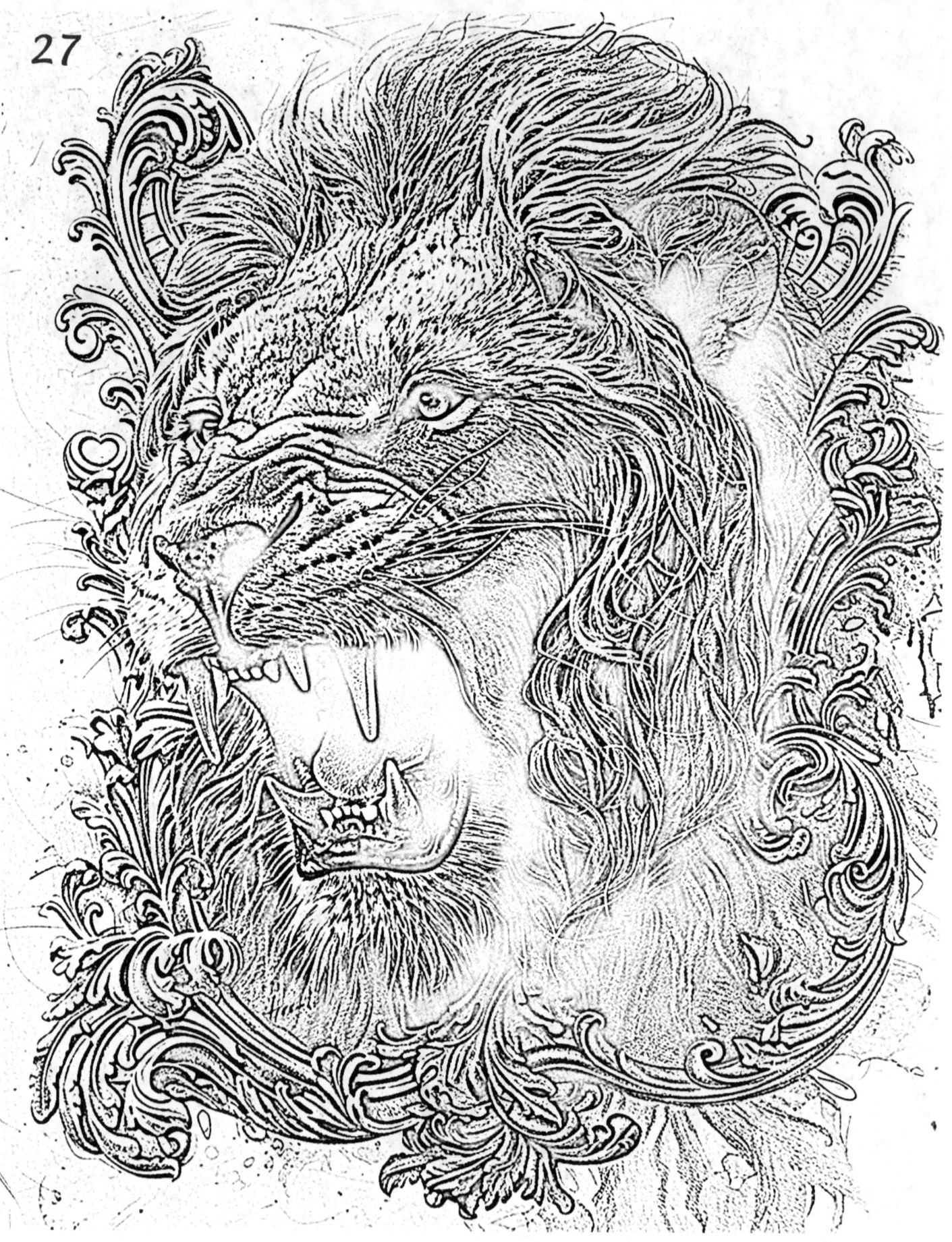

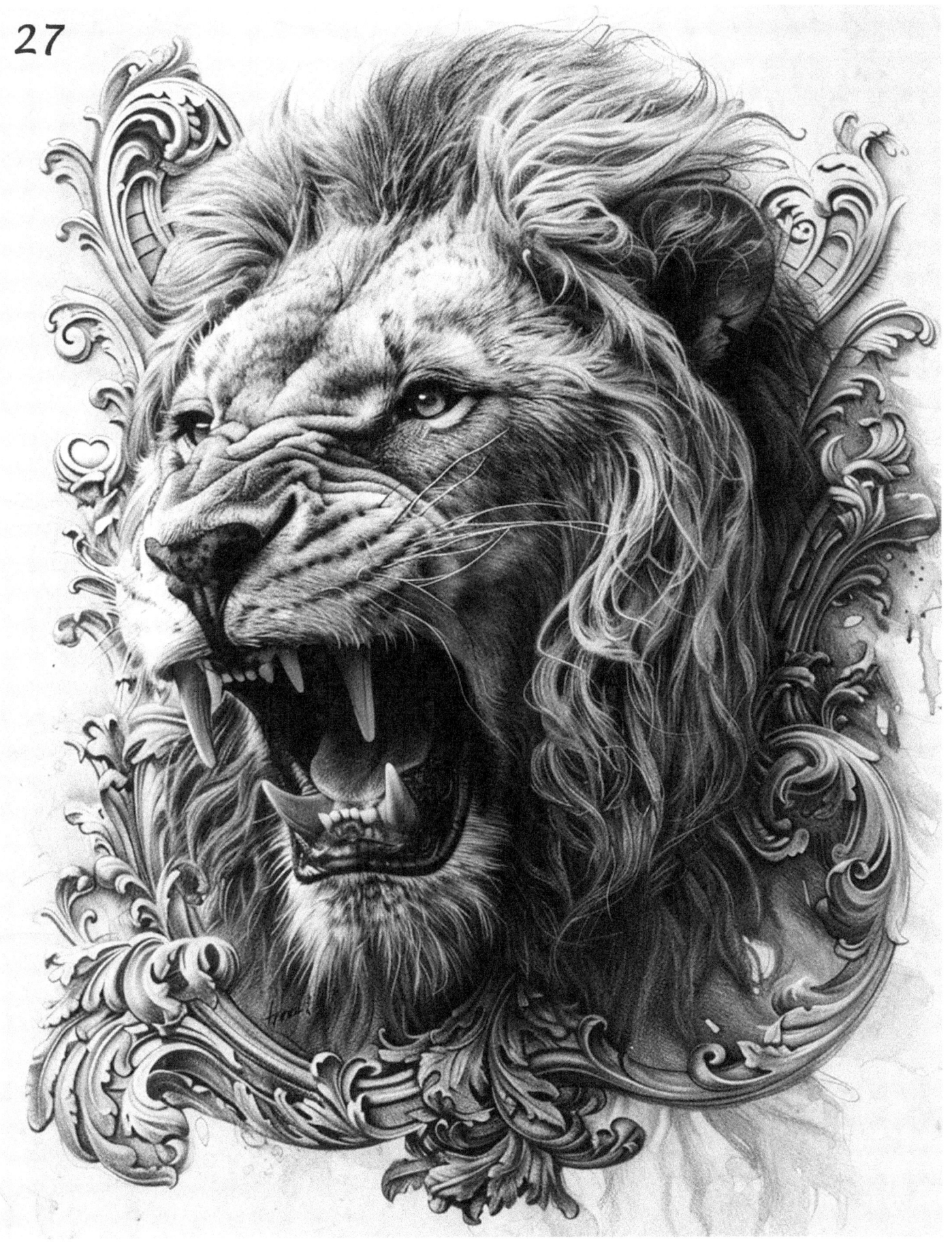

28

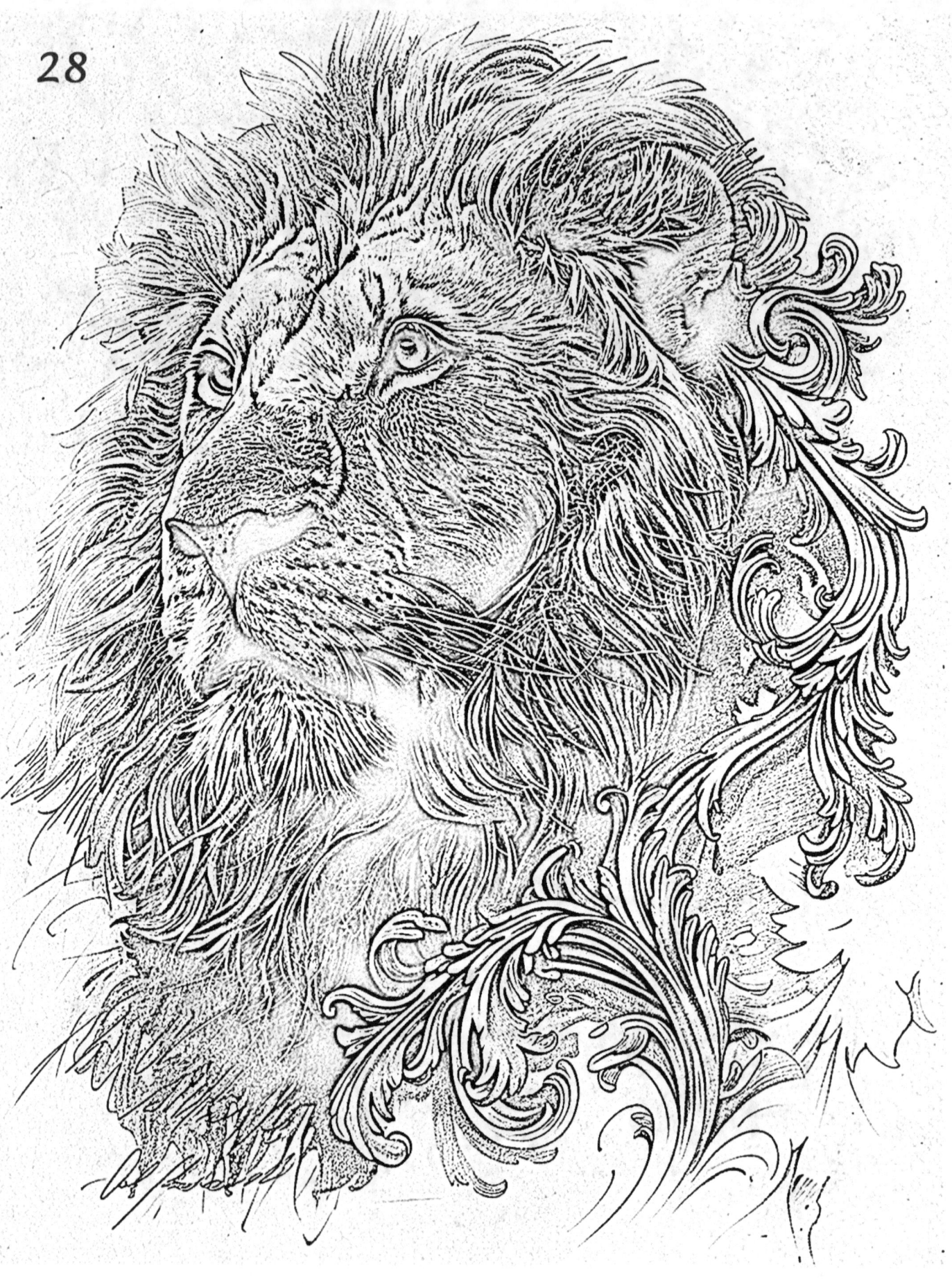

28

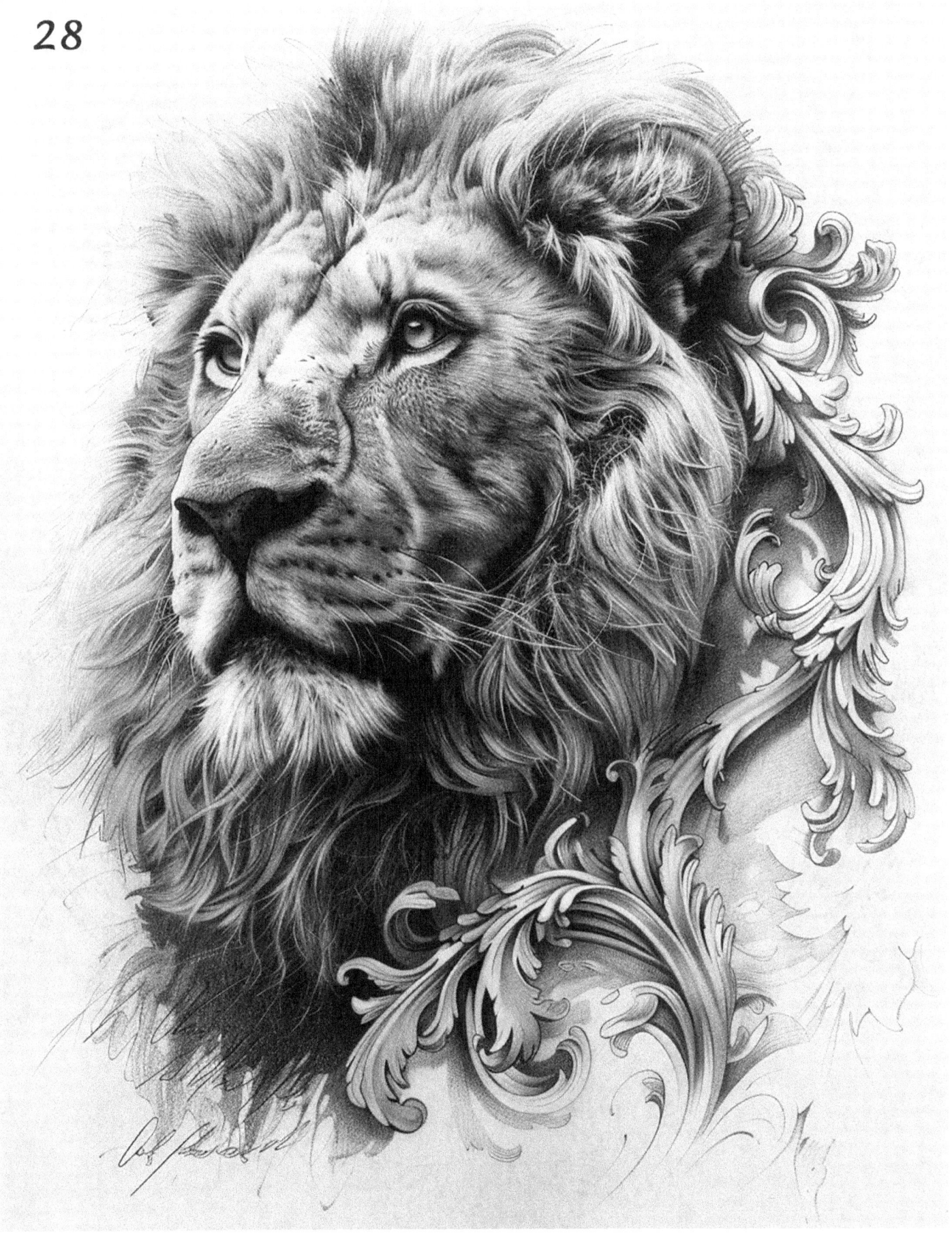

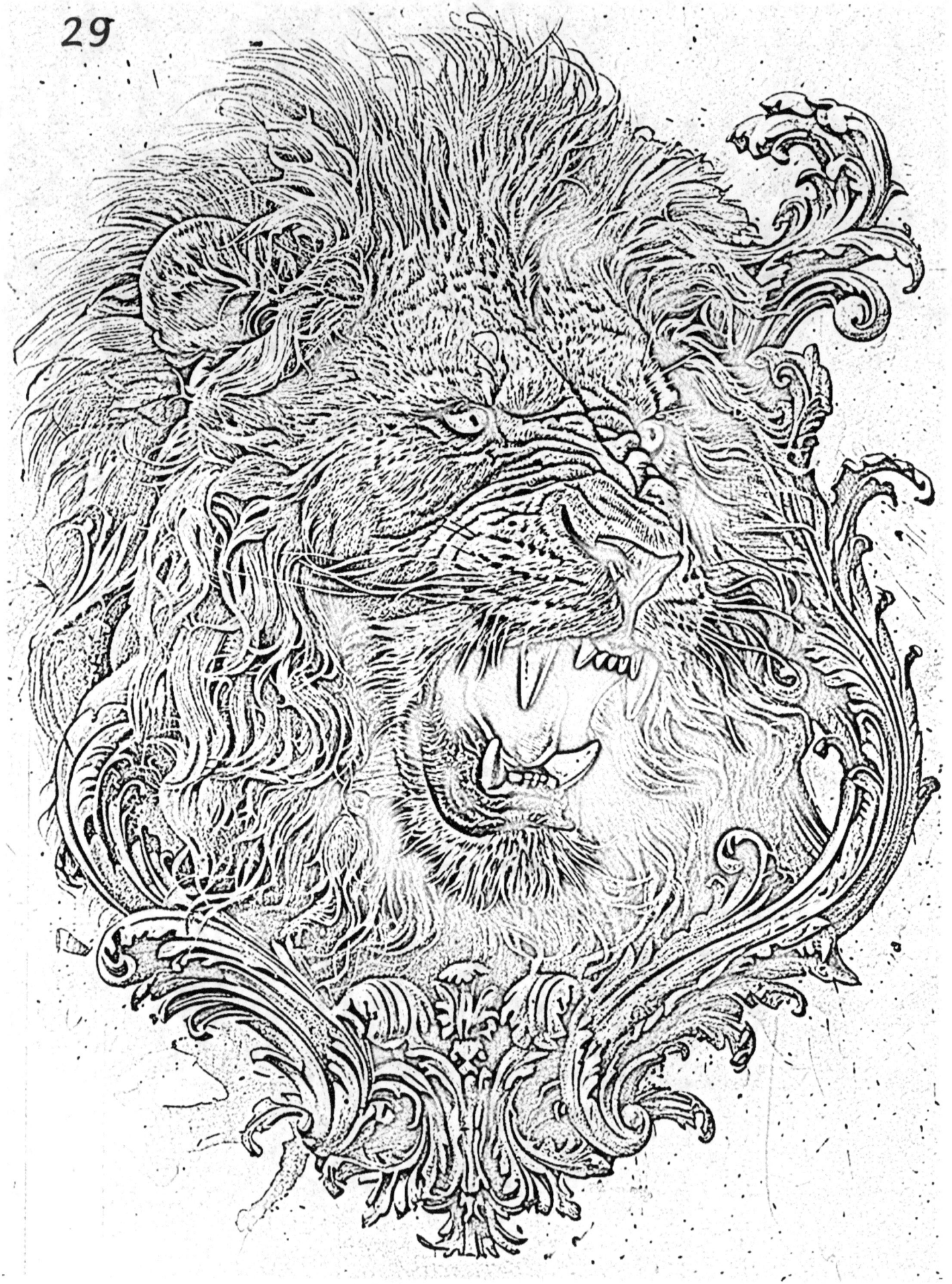

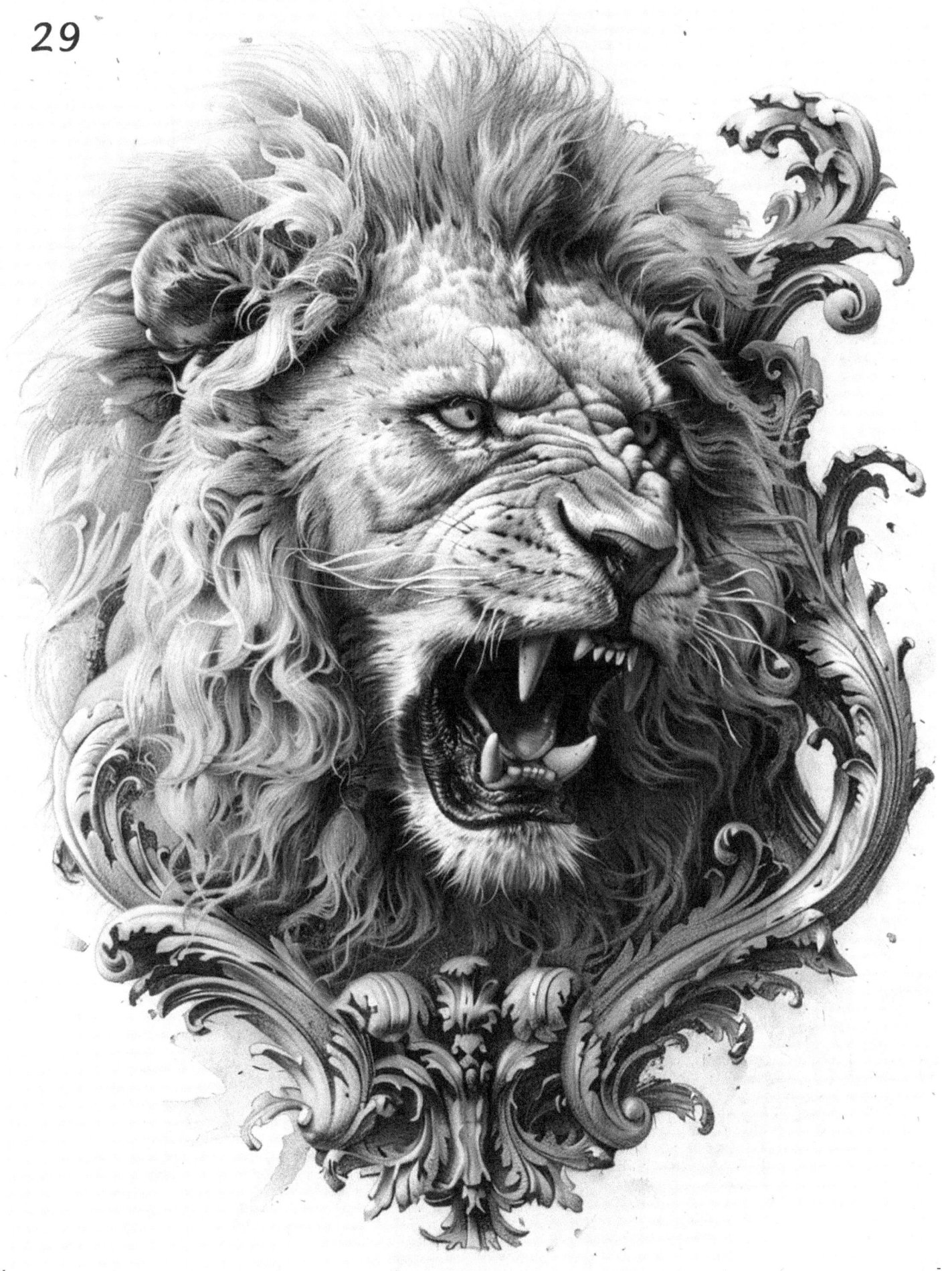

30

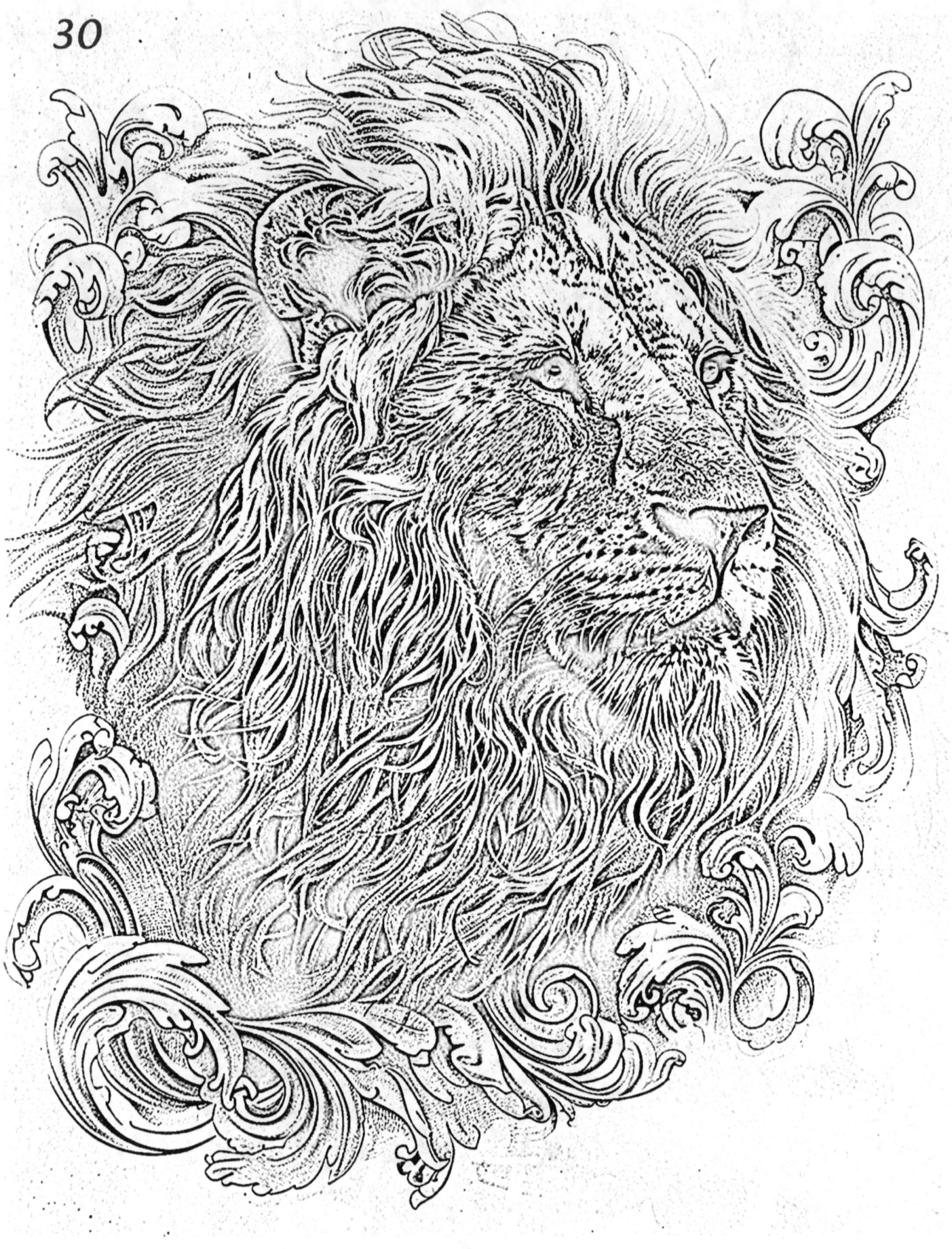

30

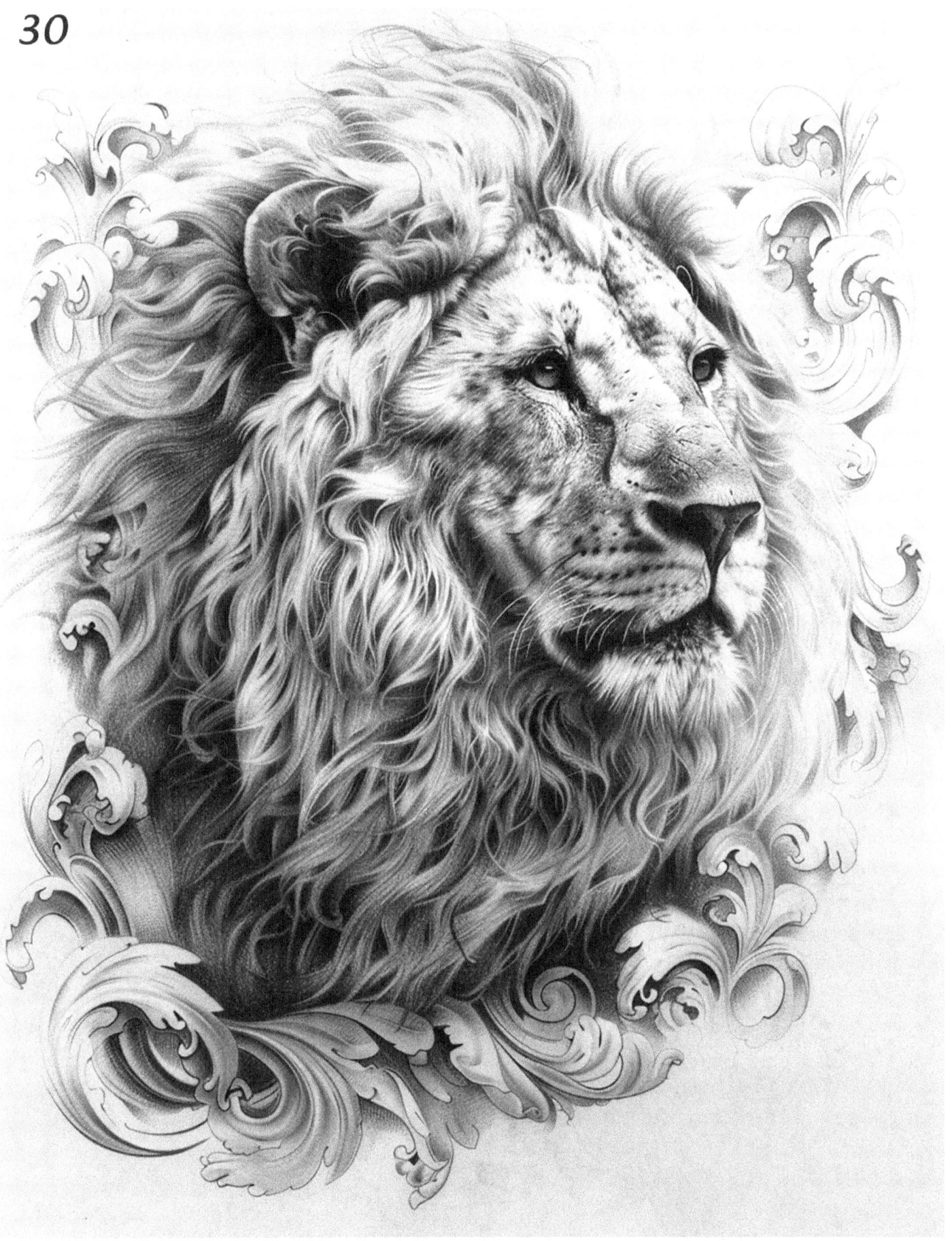

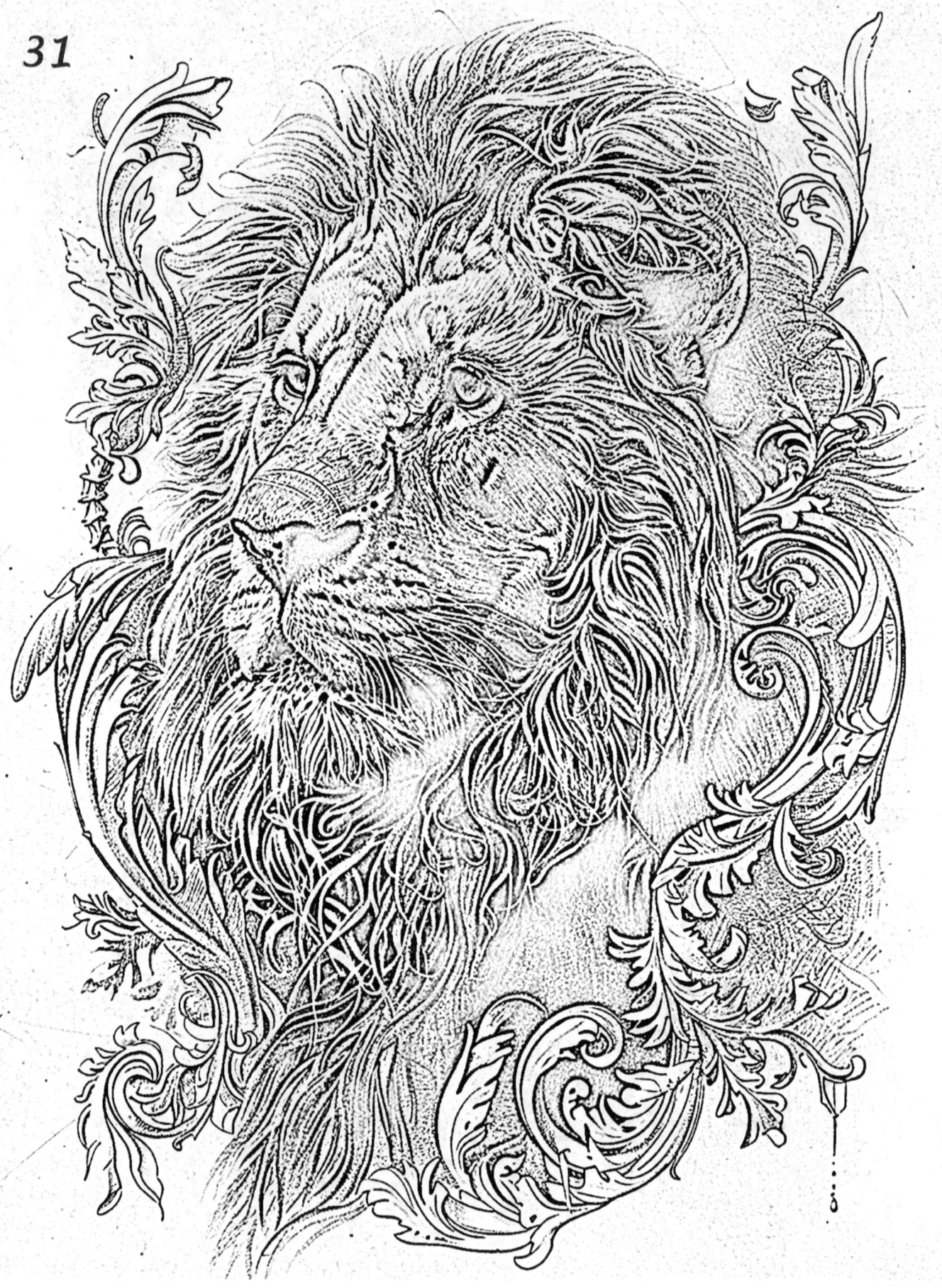

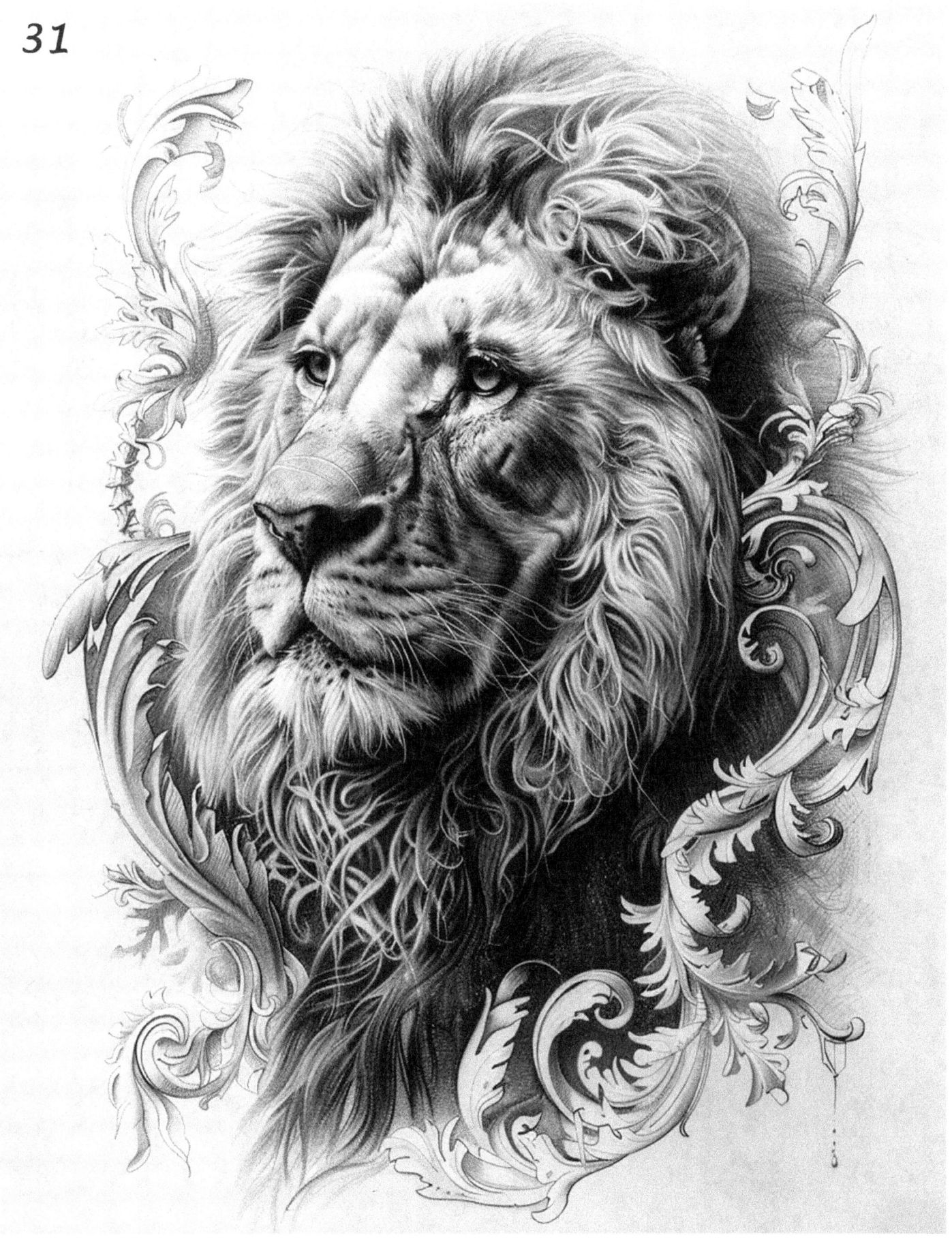

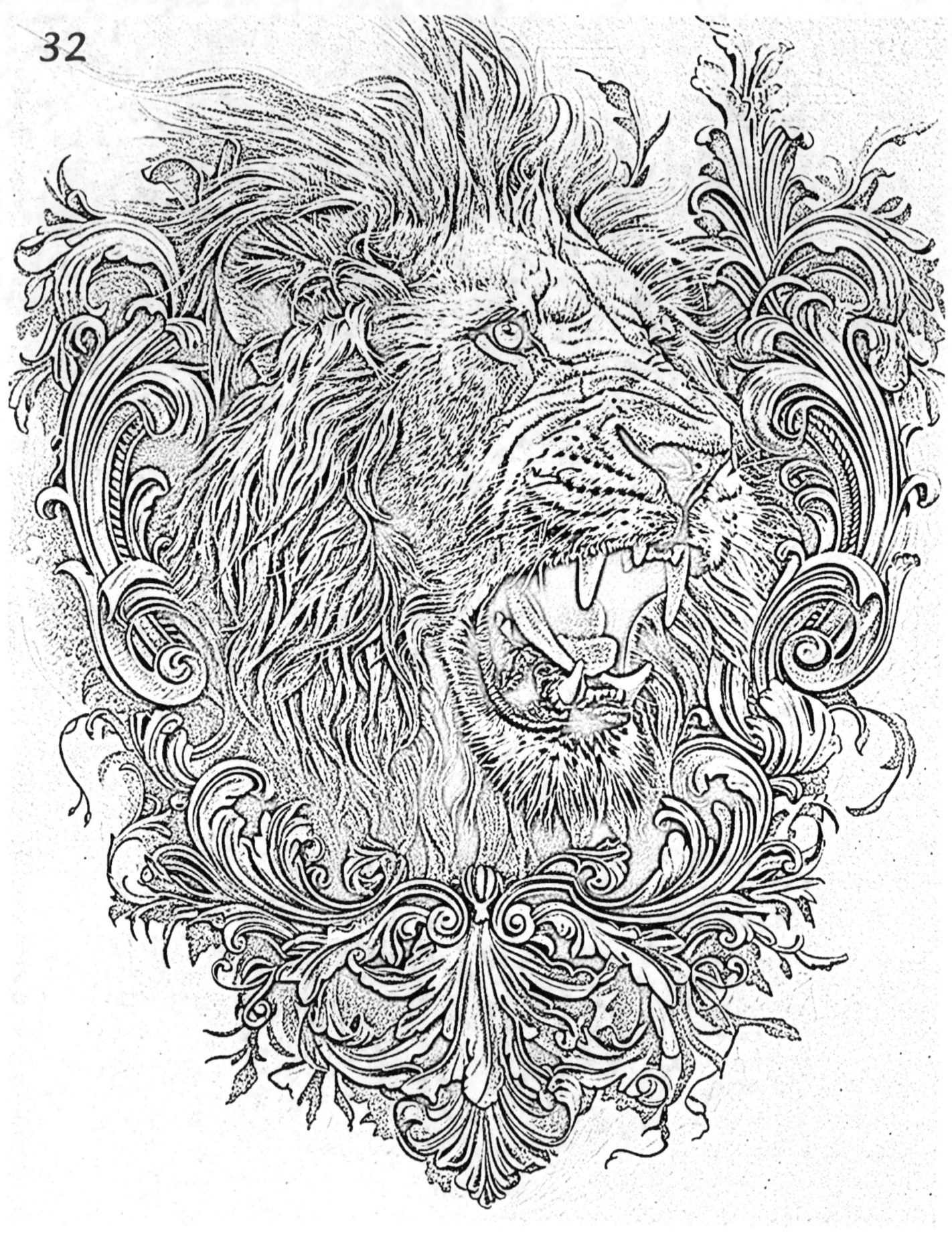

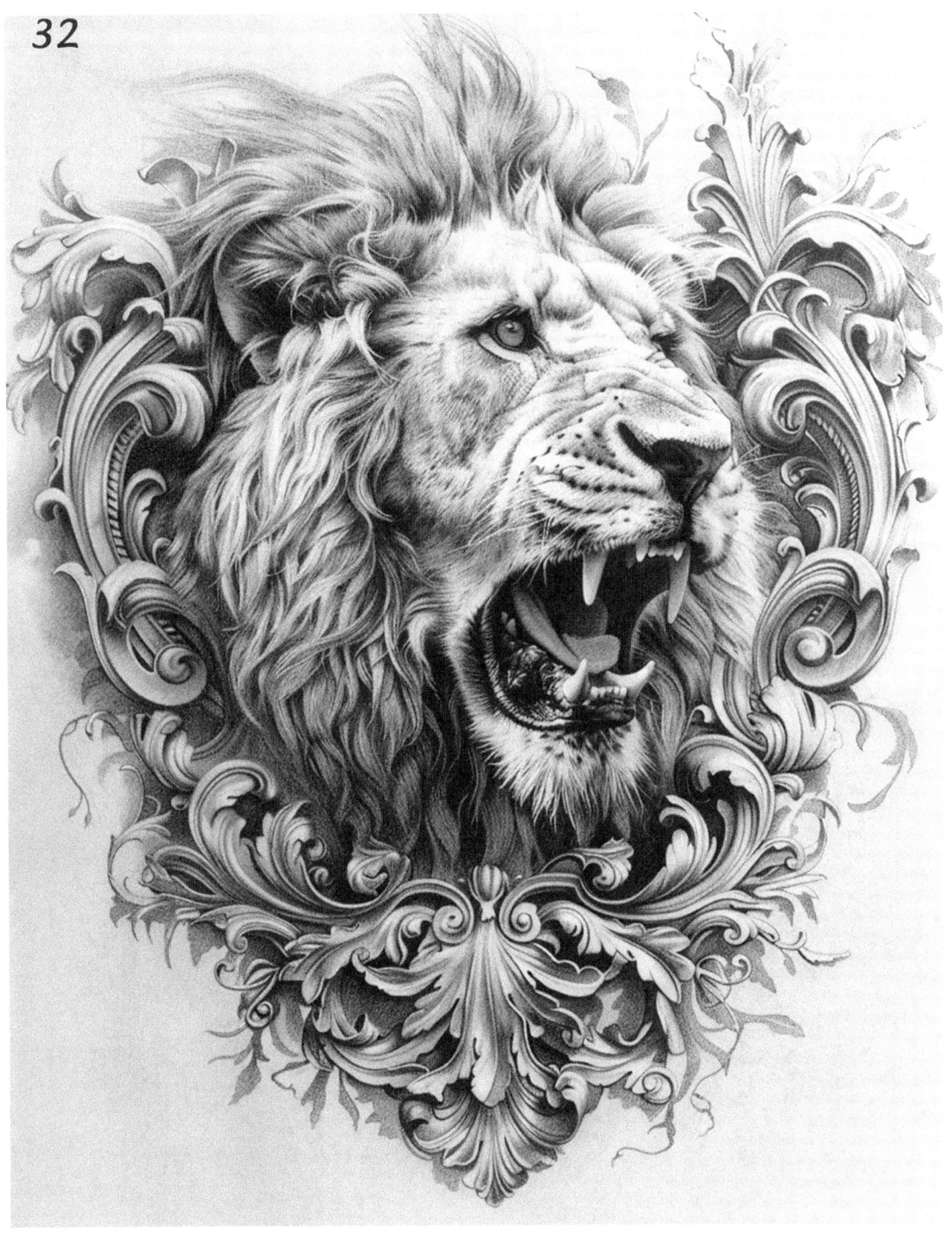

33

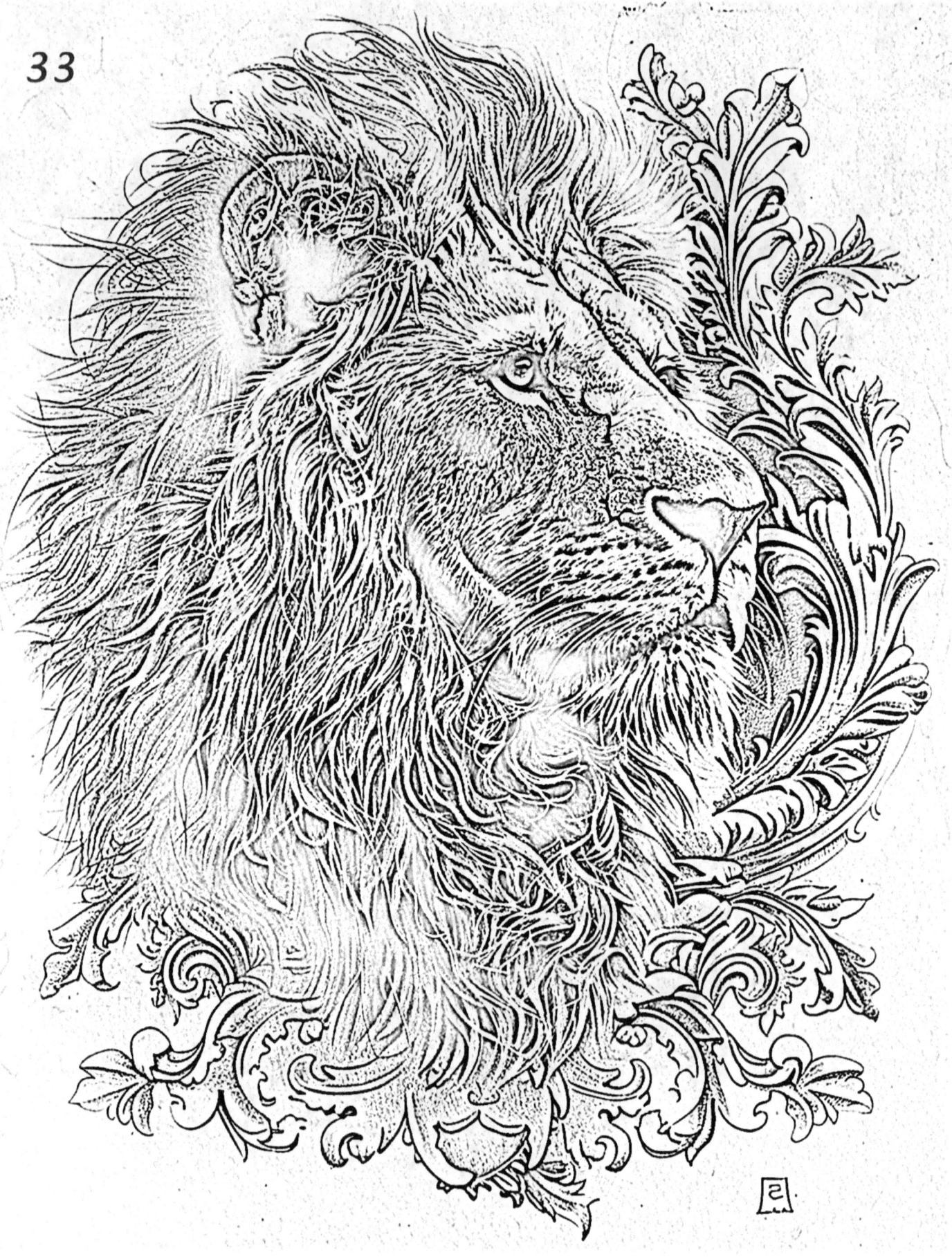

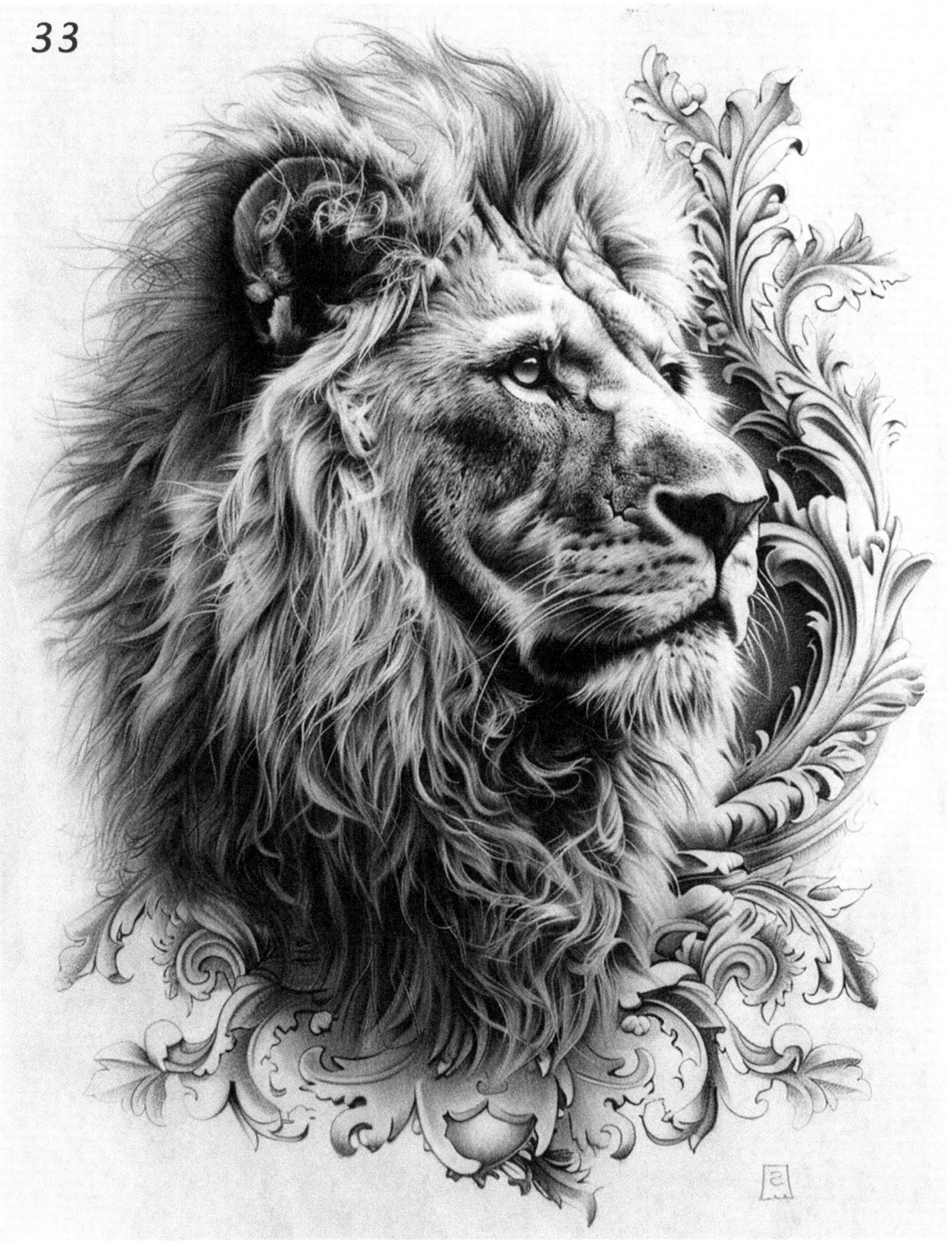

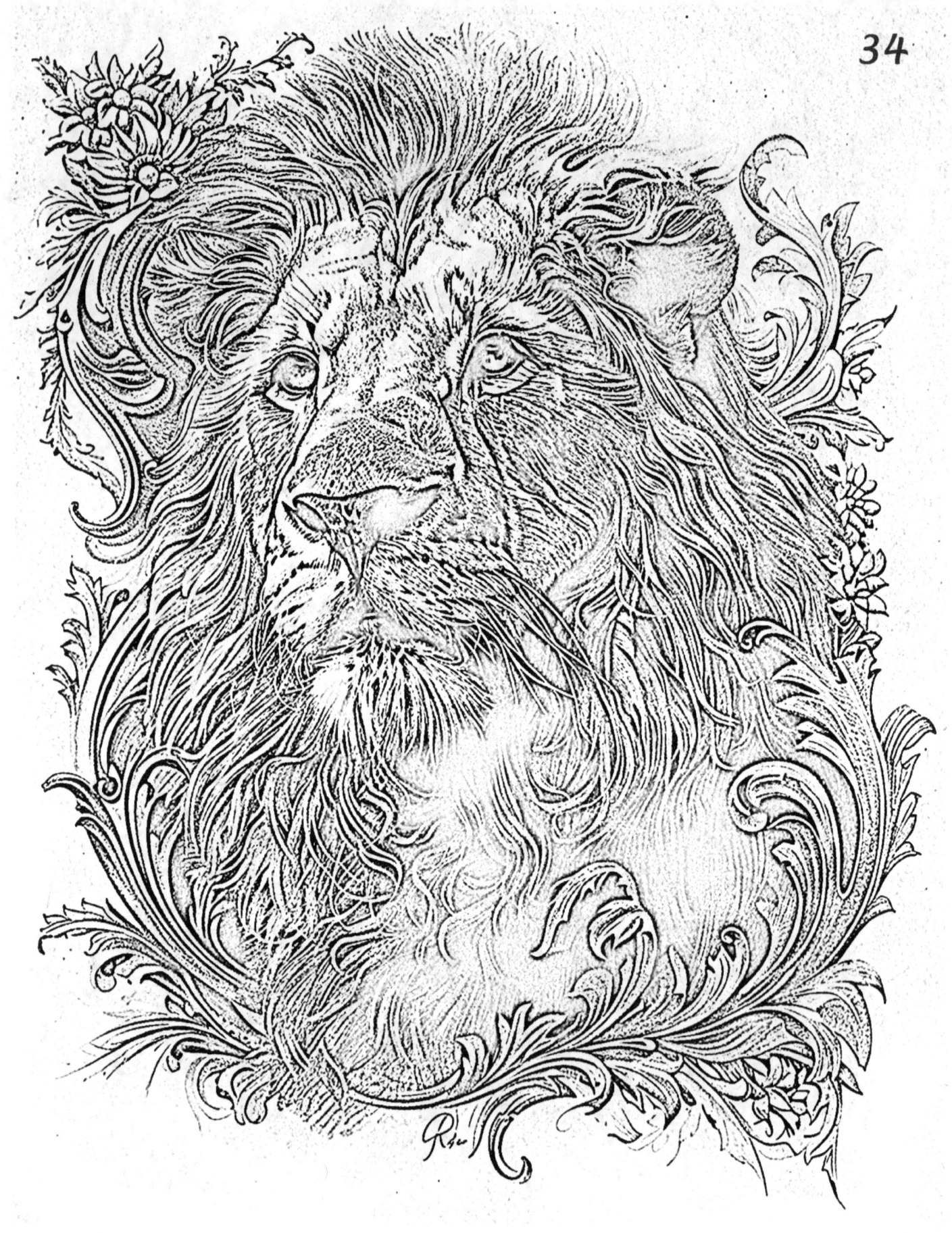

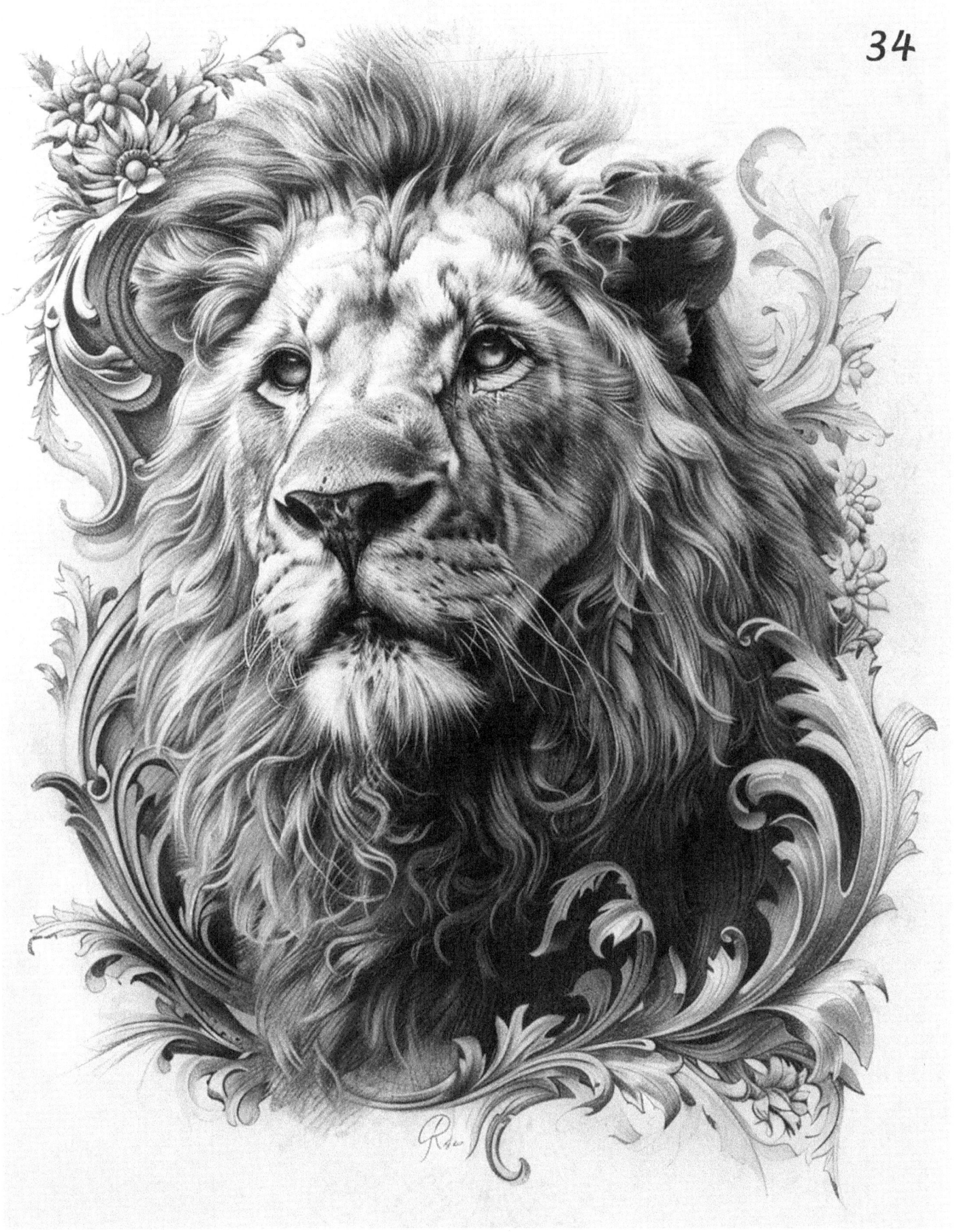

35

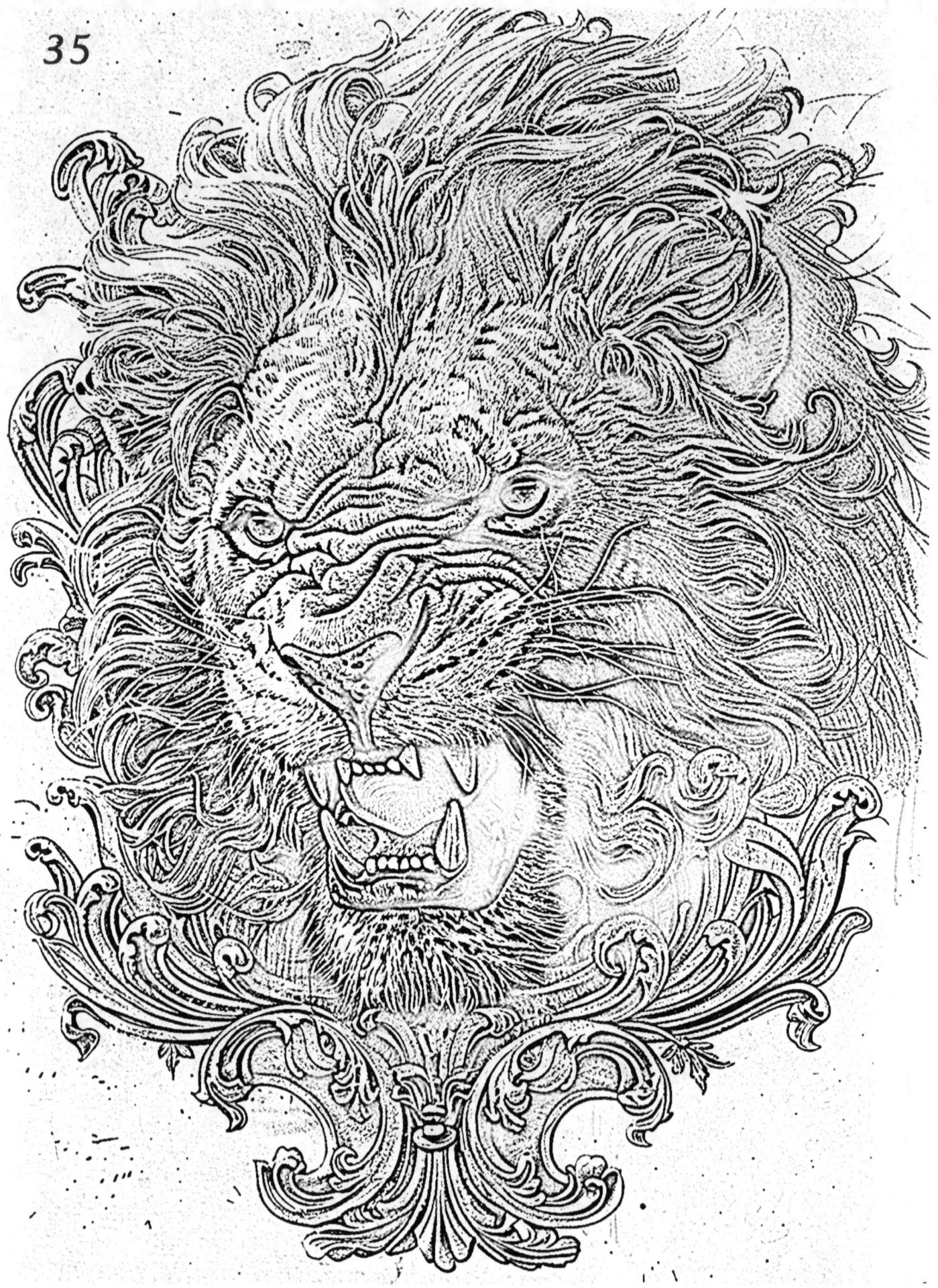

35

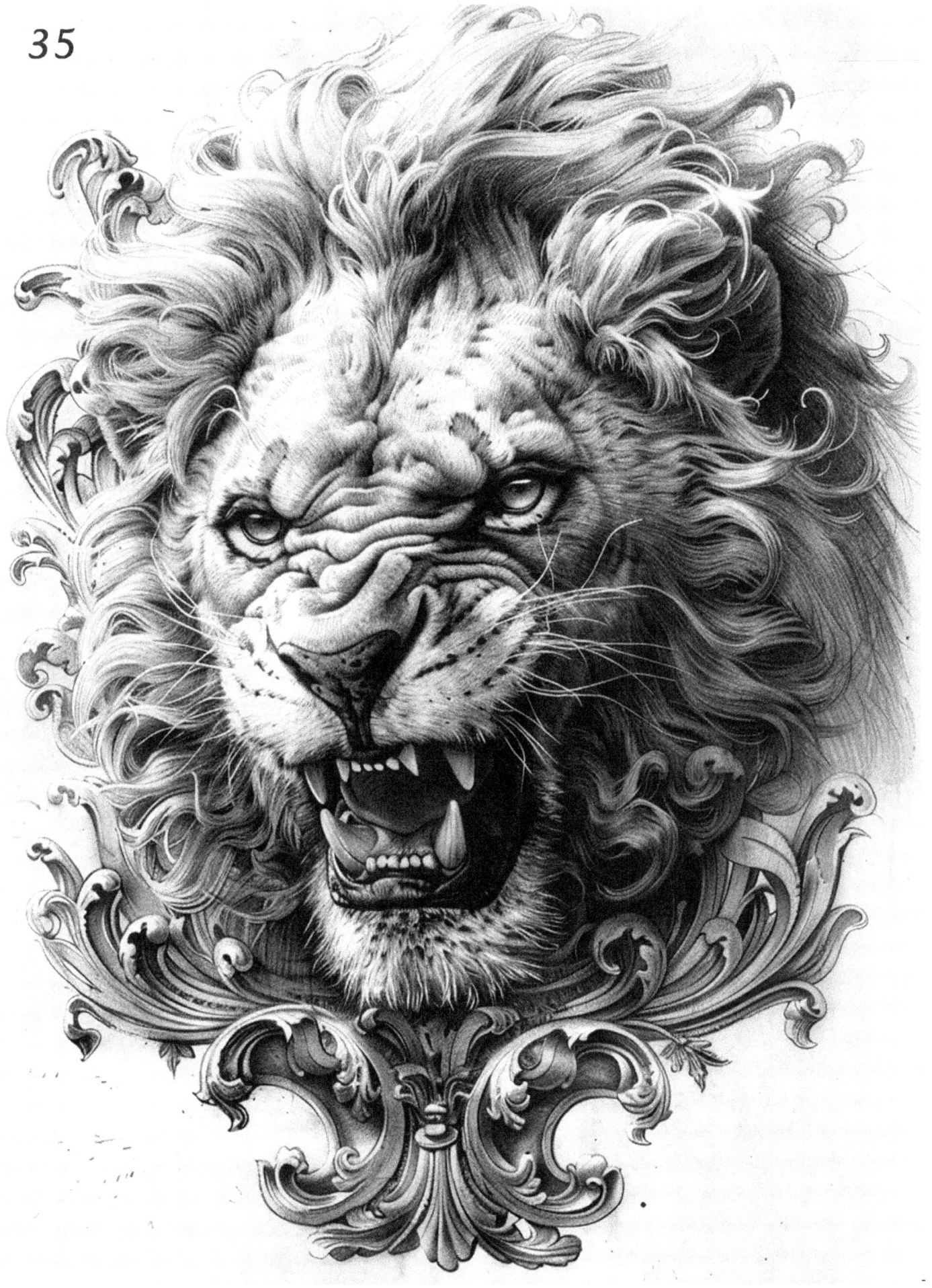

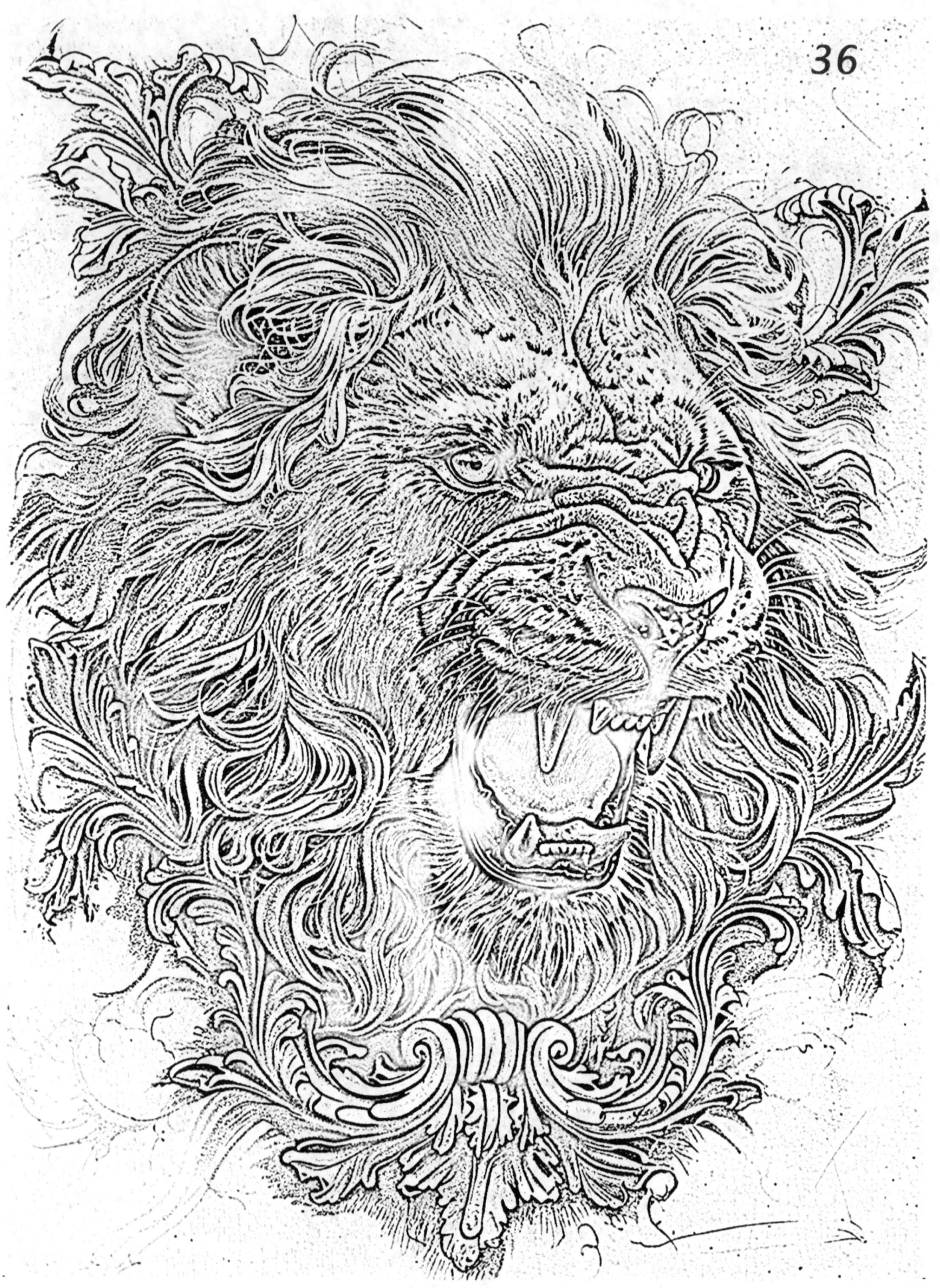

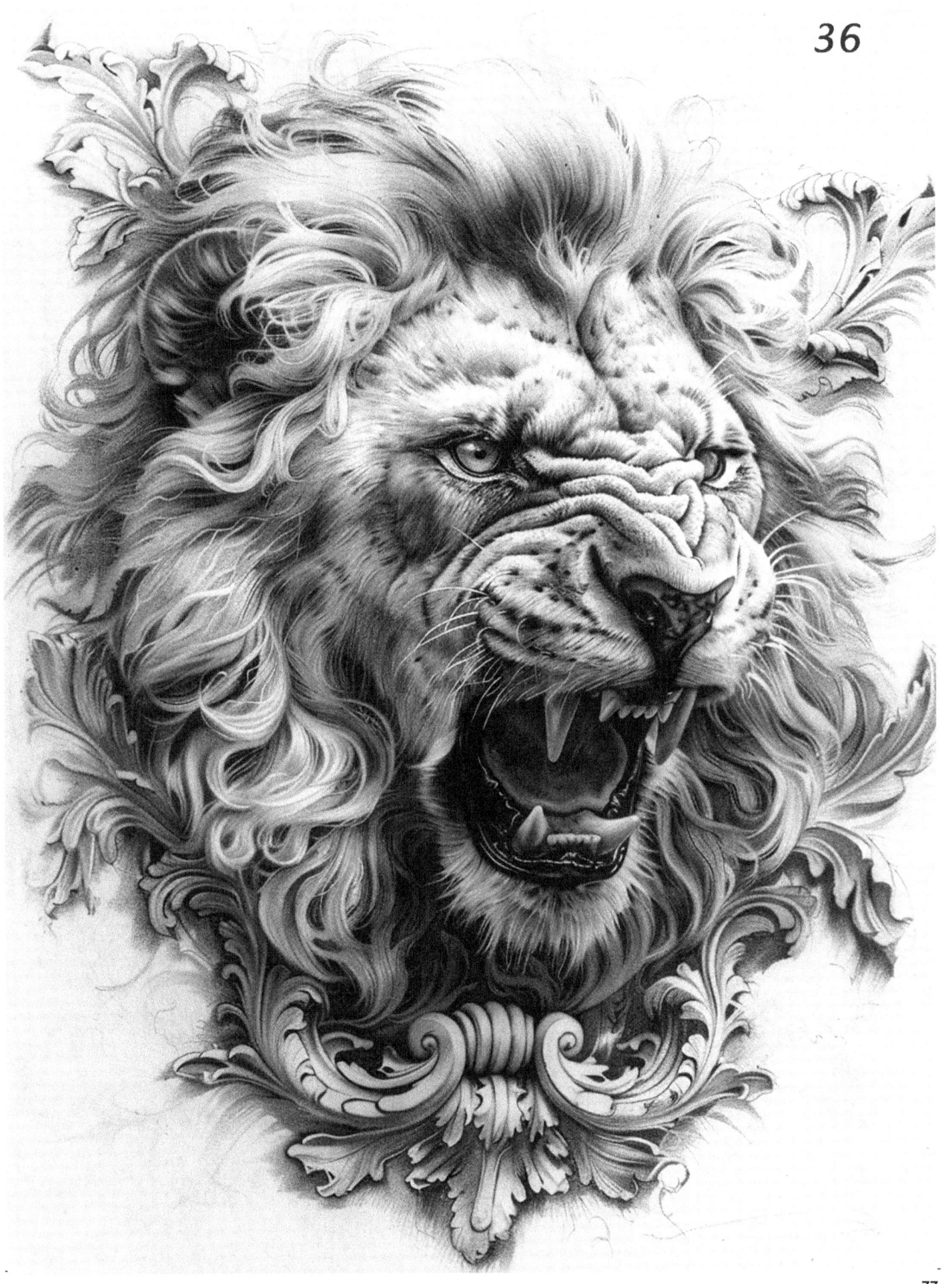

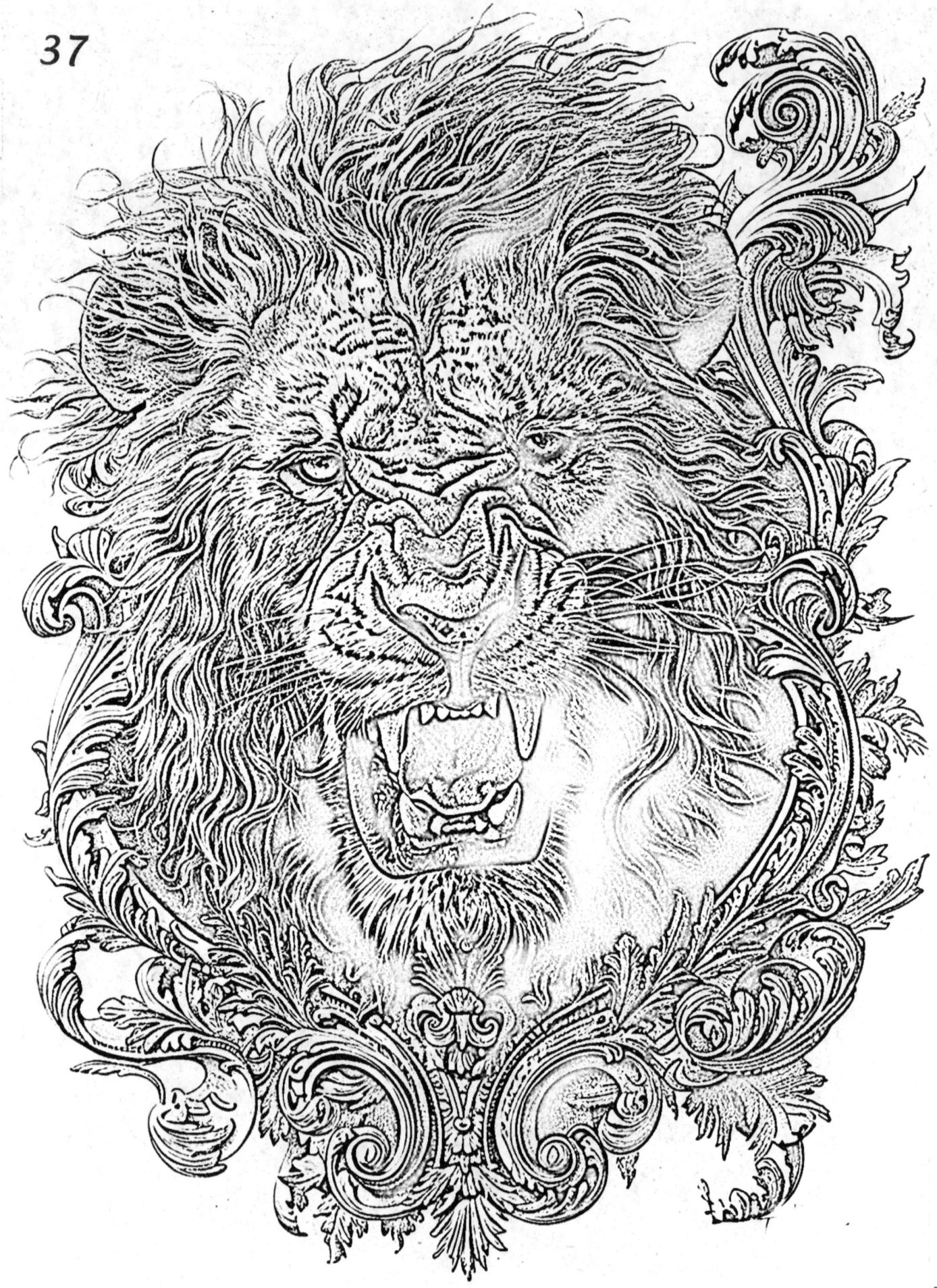

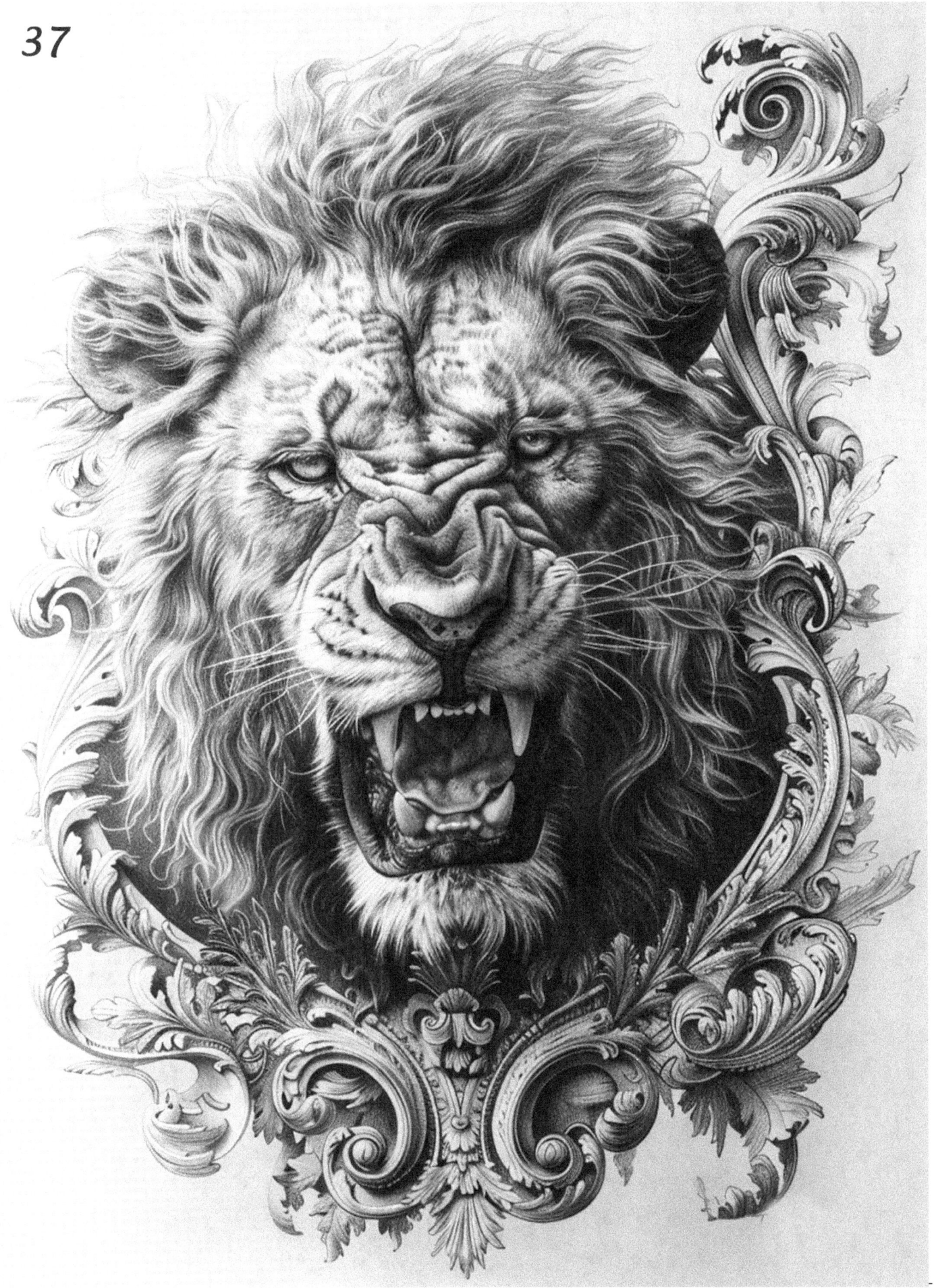

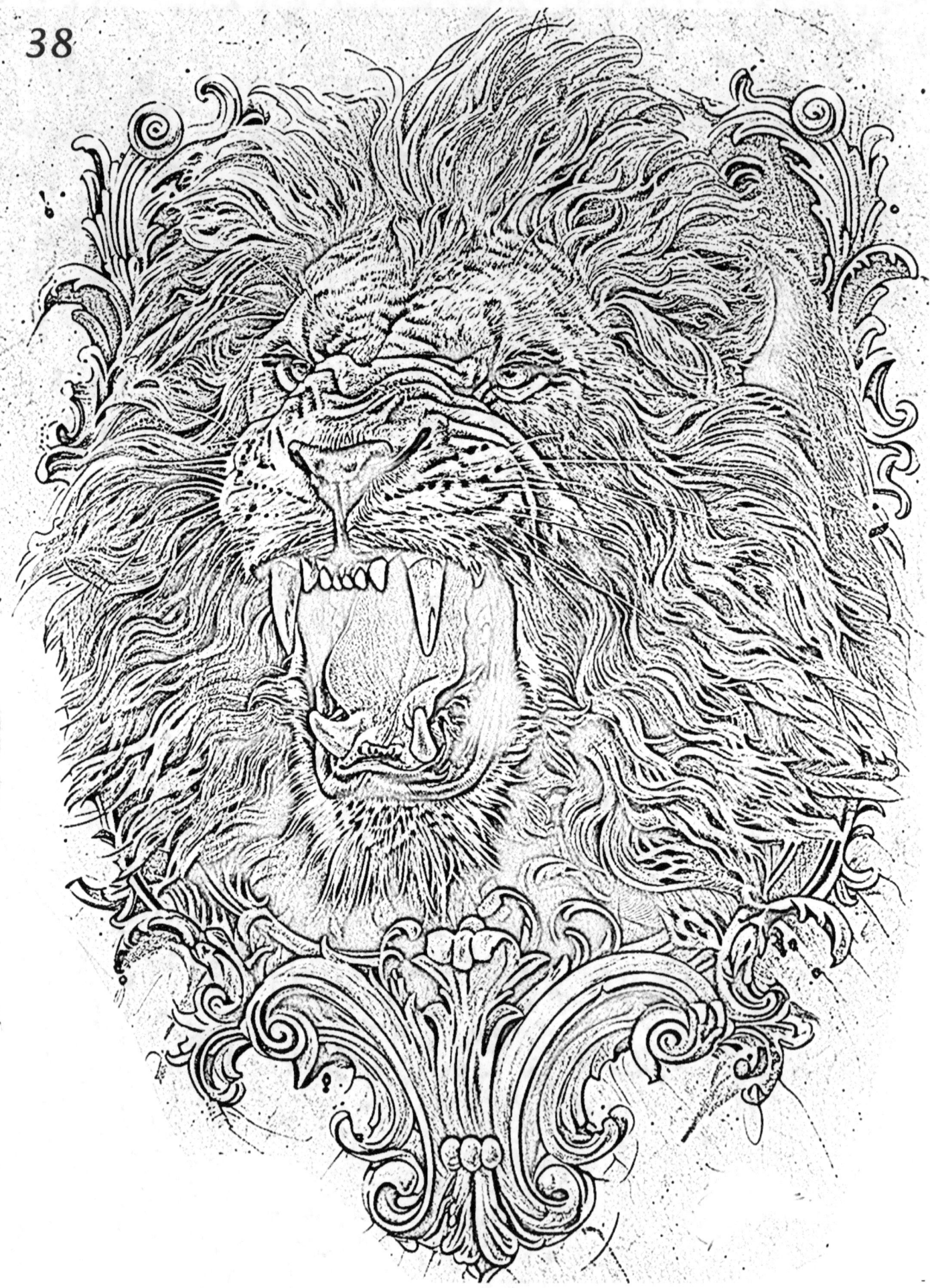

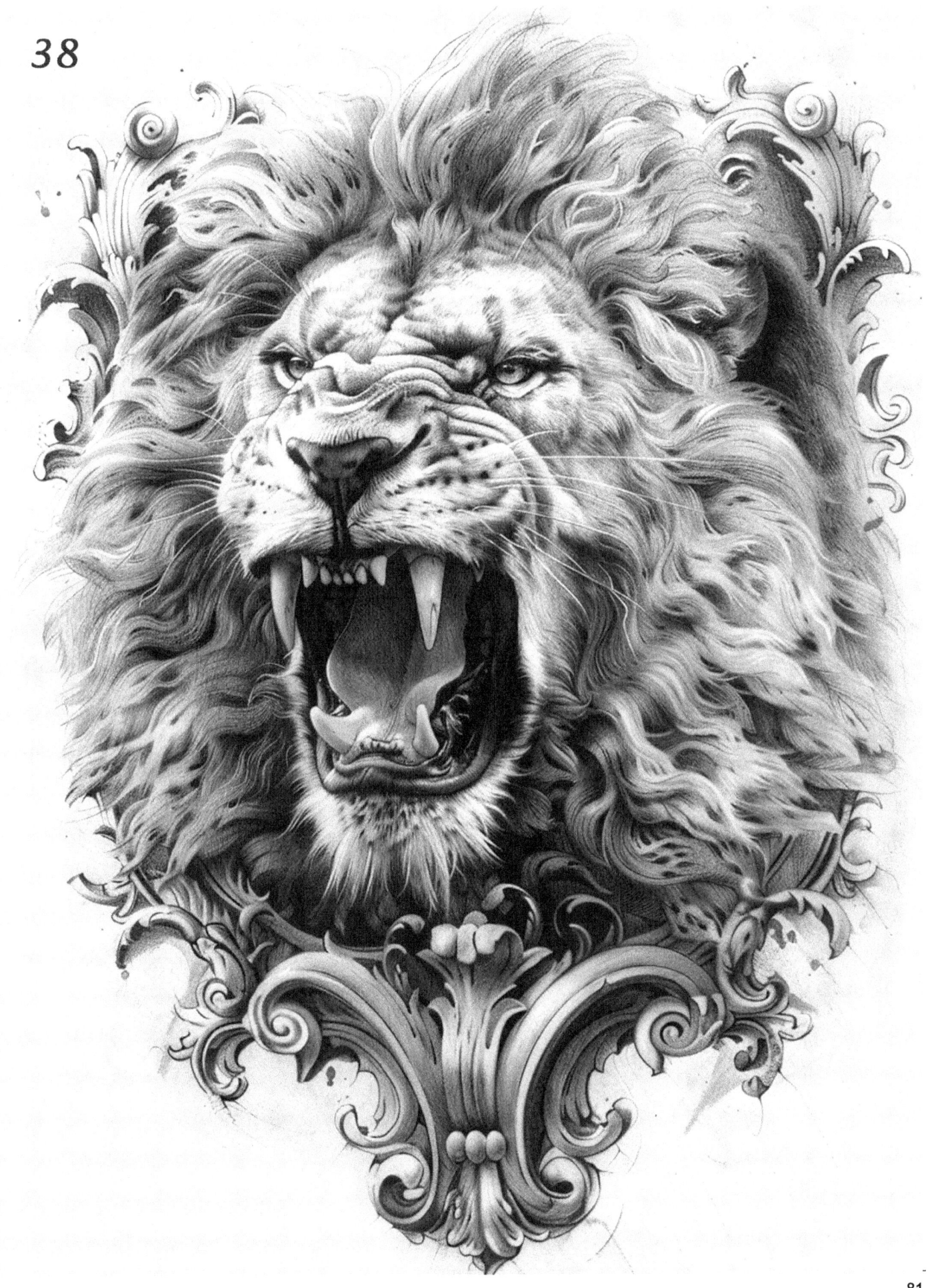

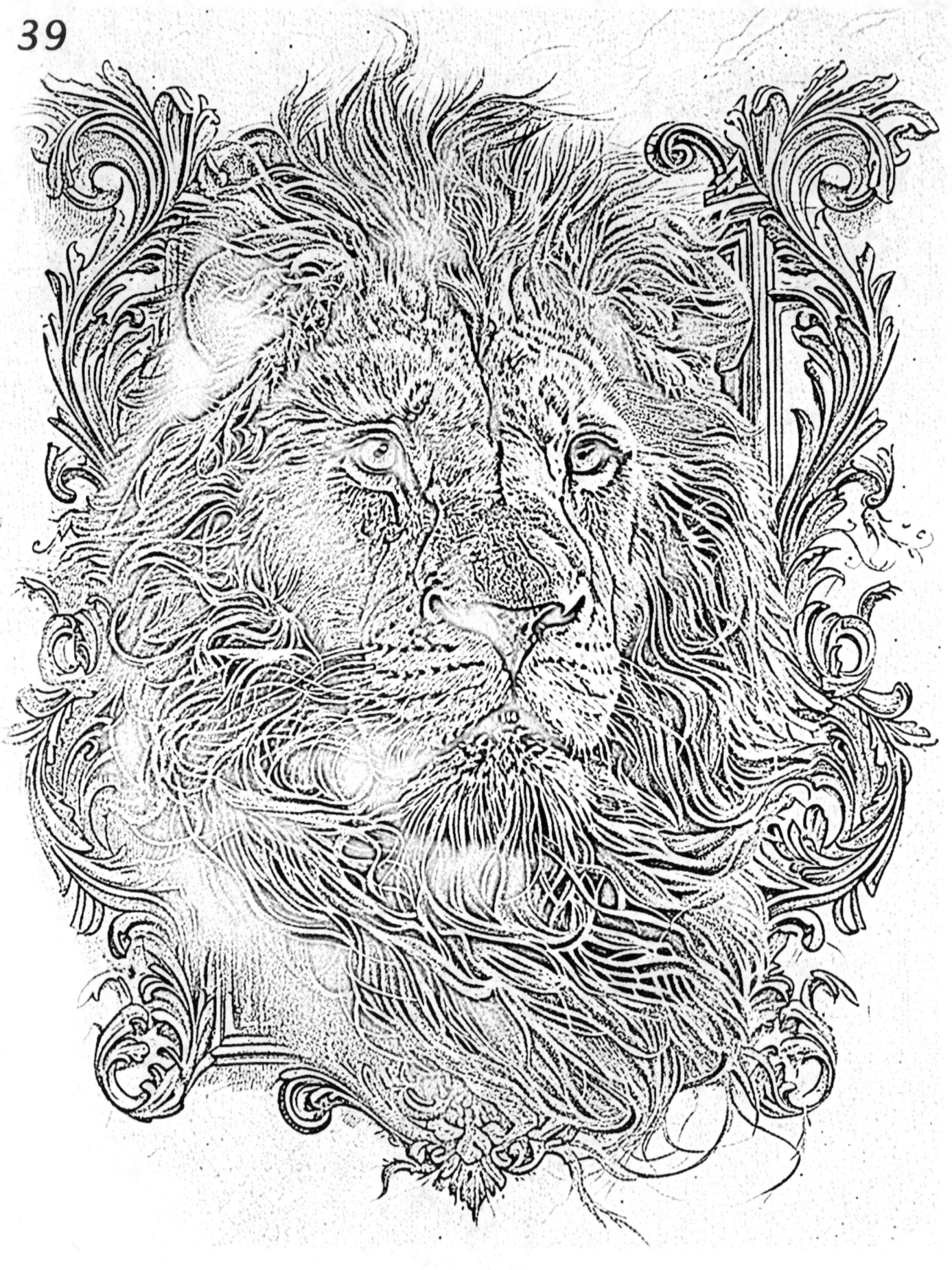

39

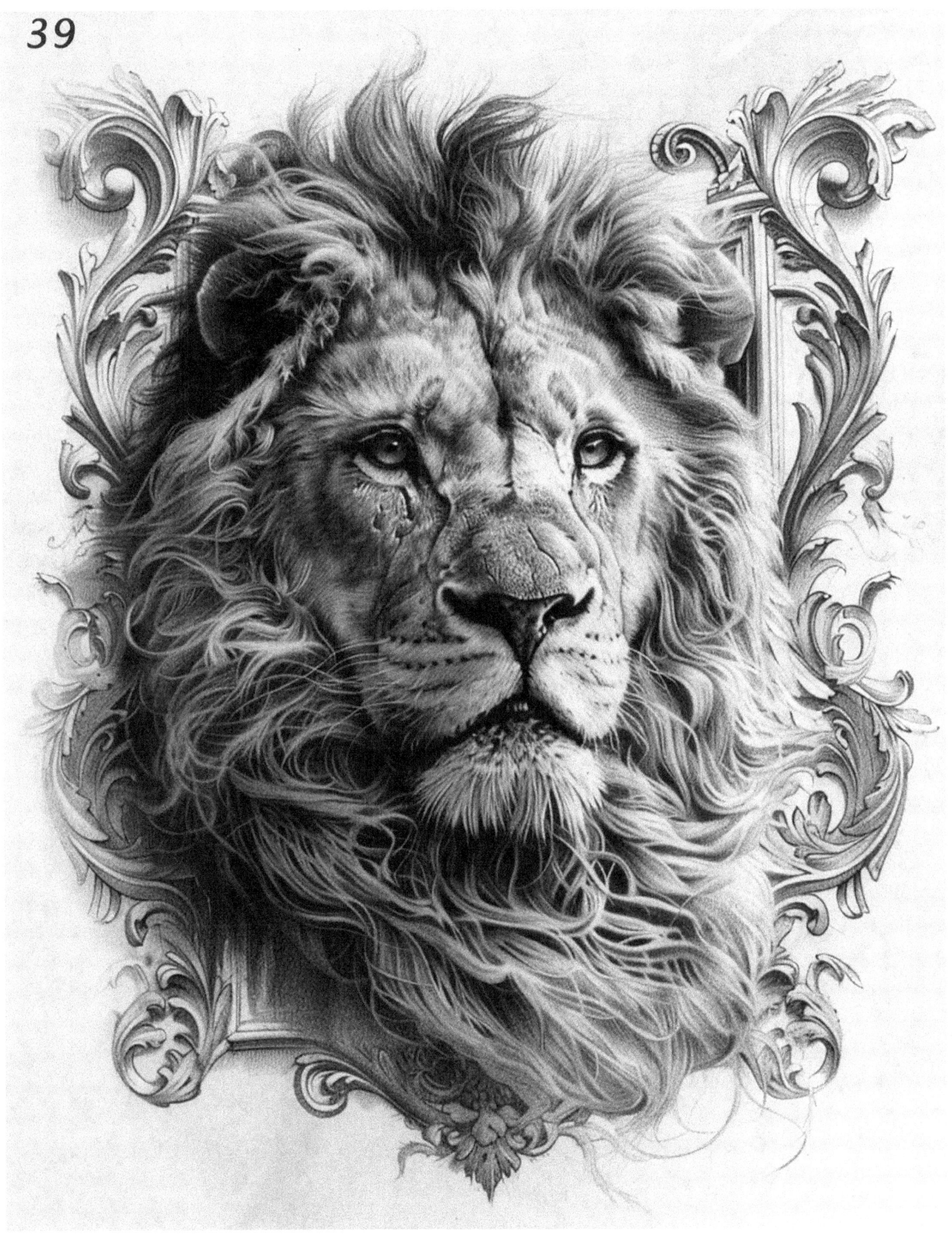

40

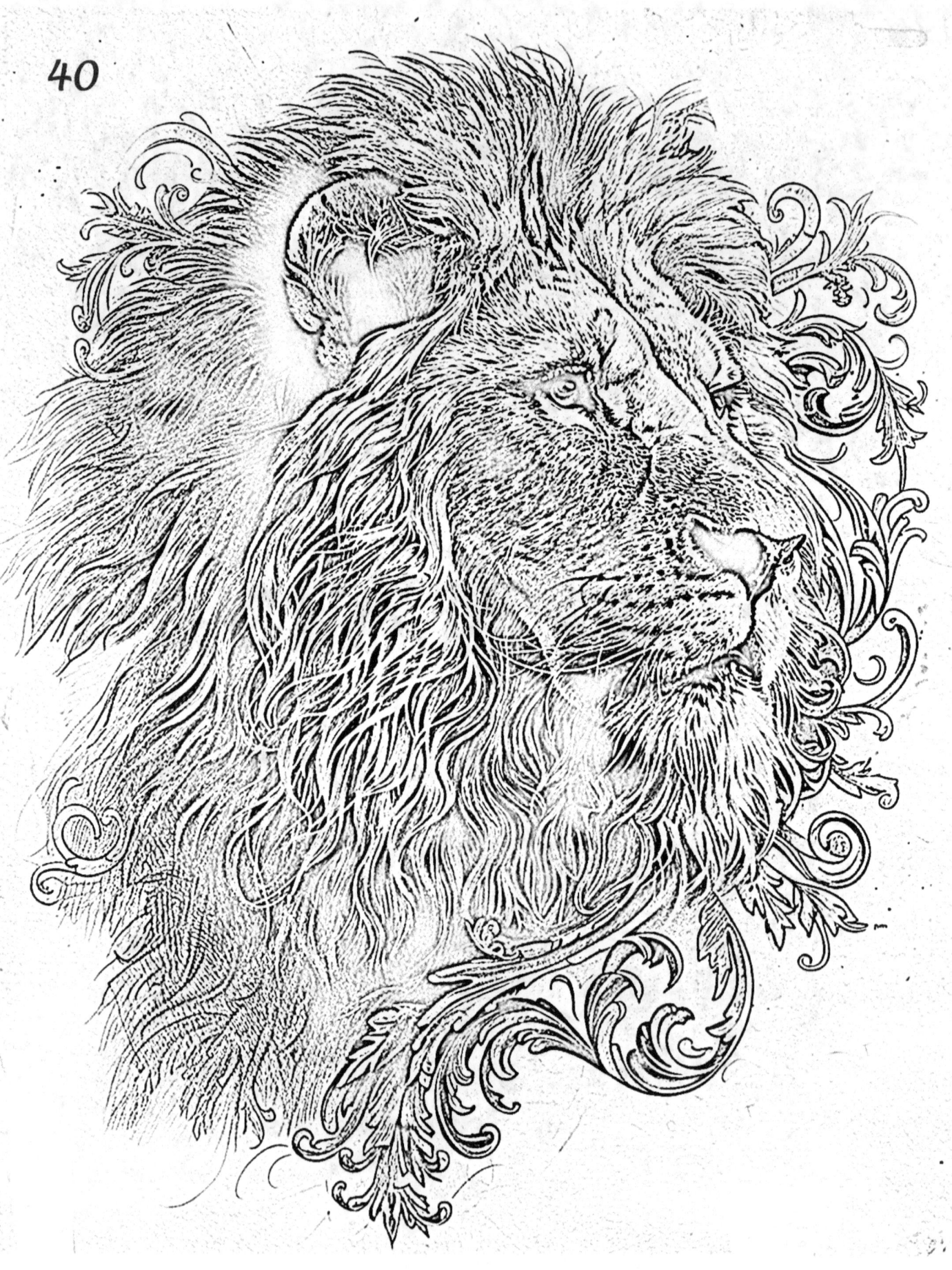

40

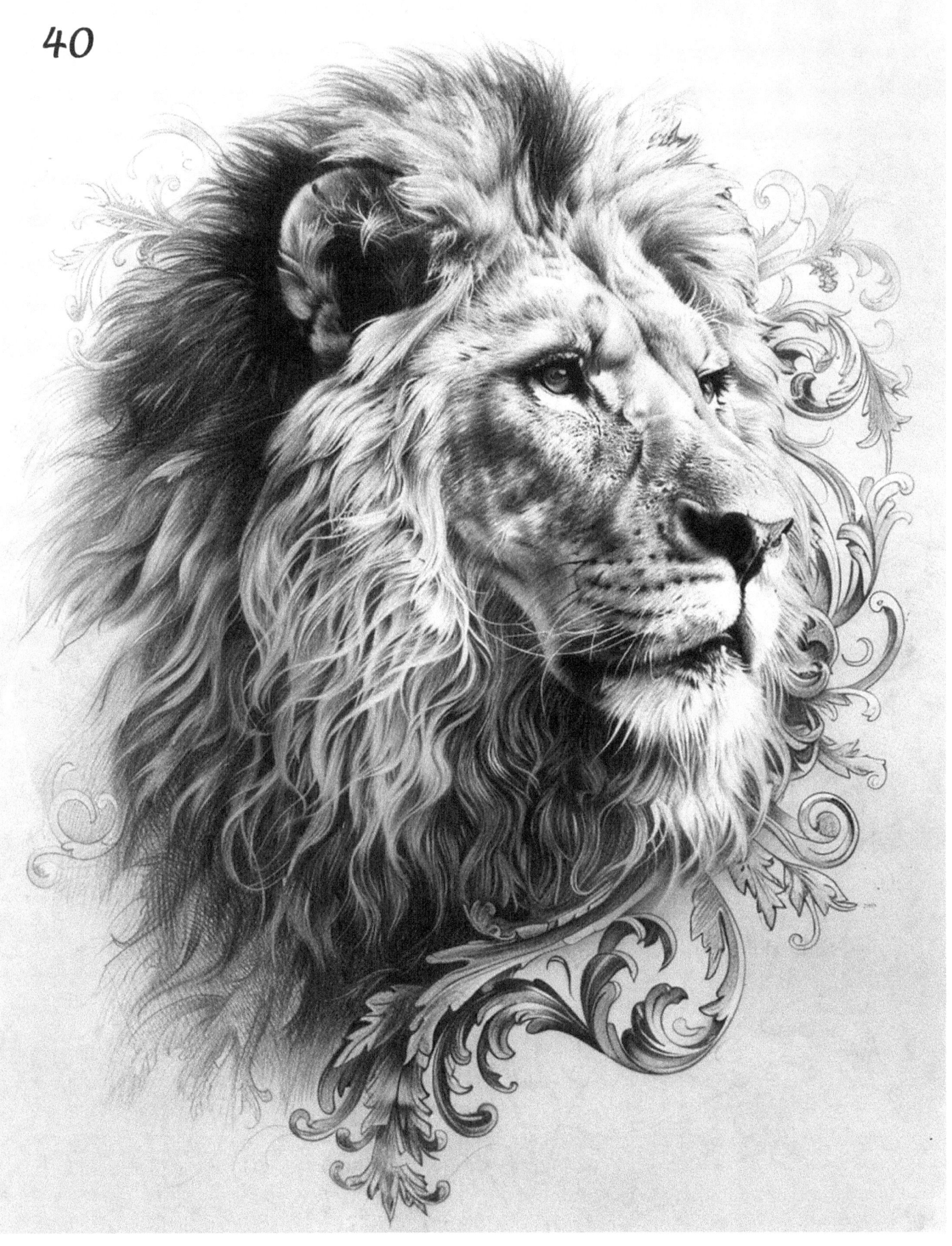

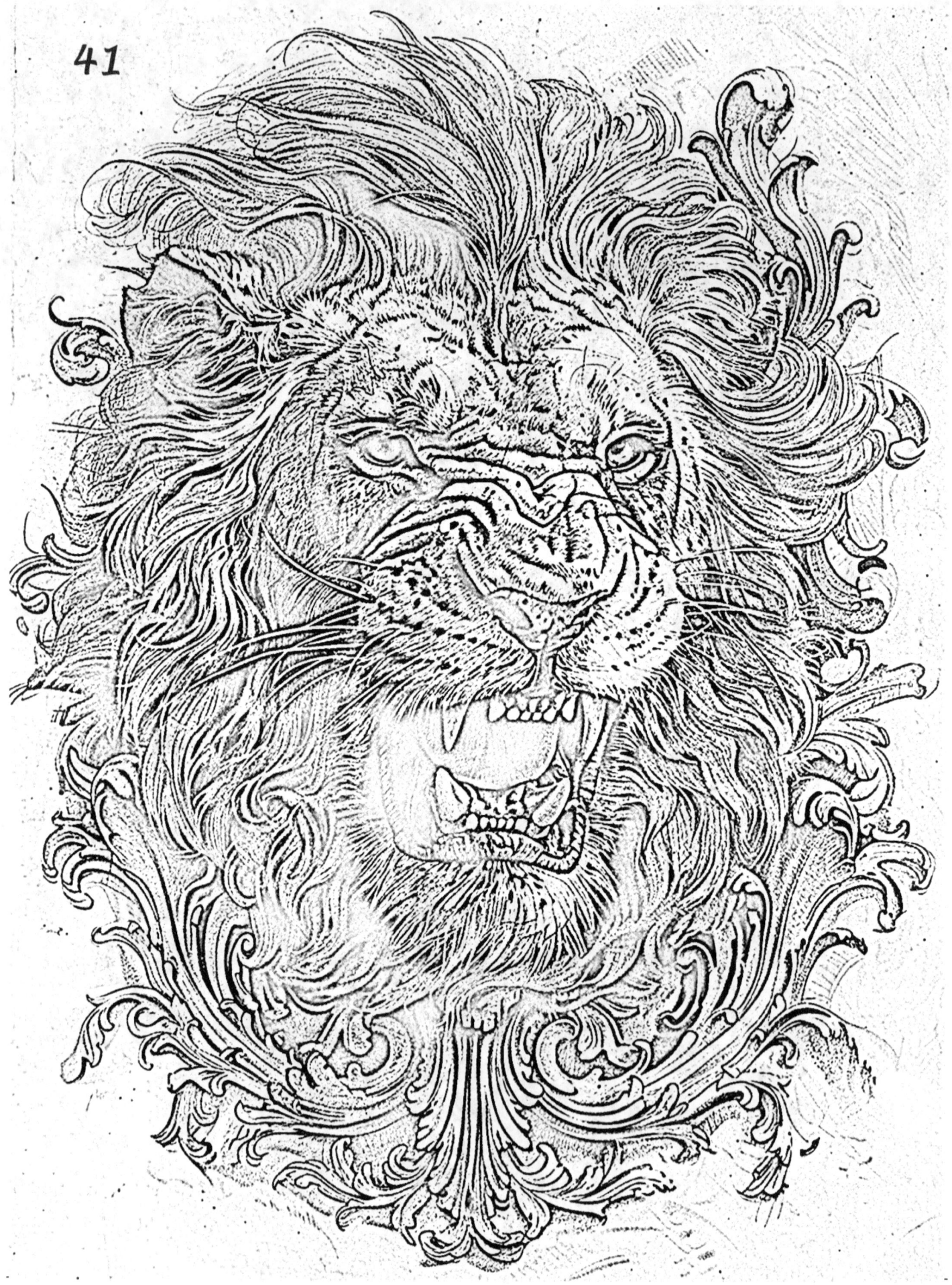

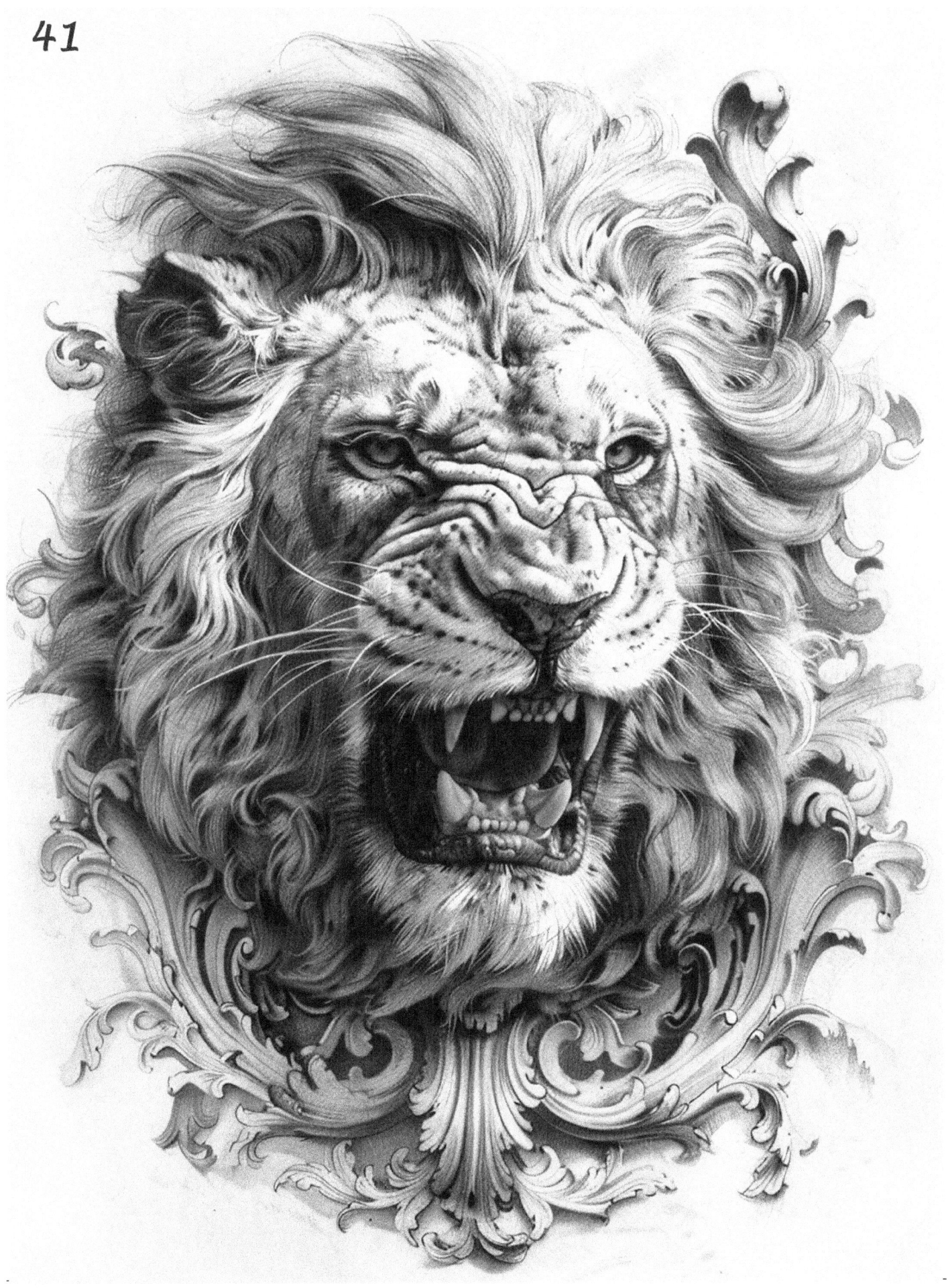

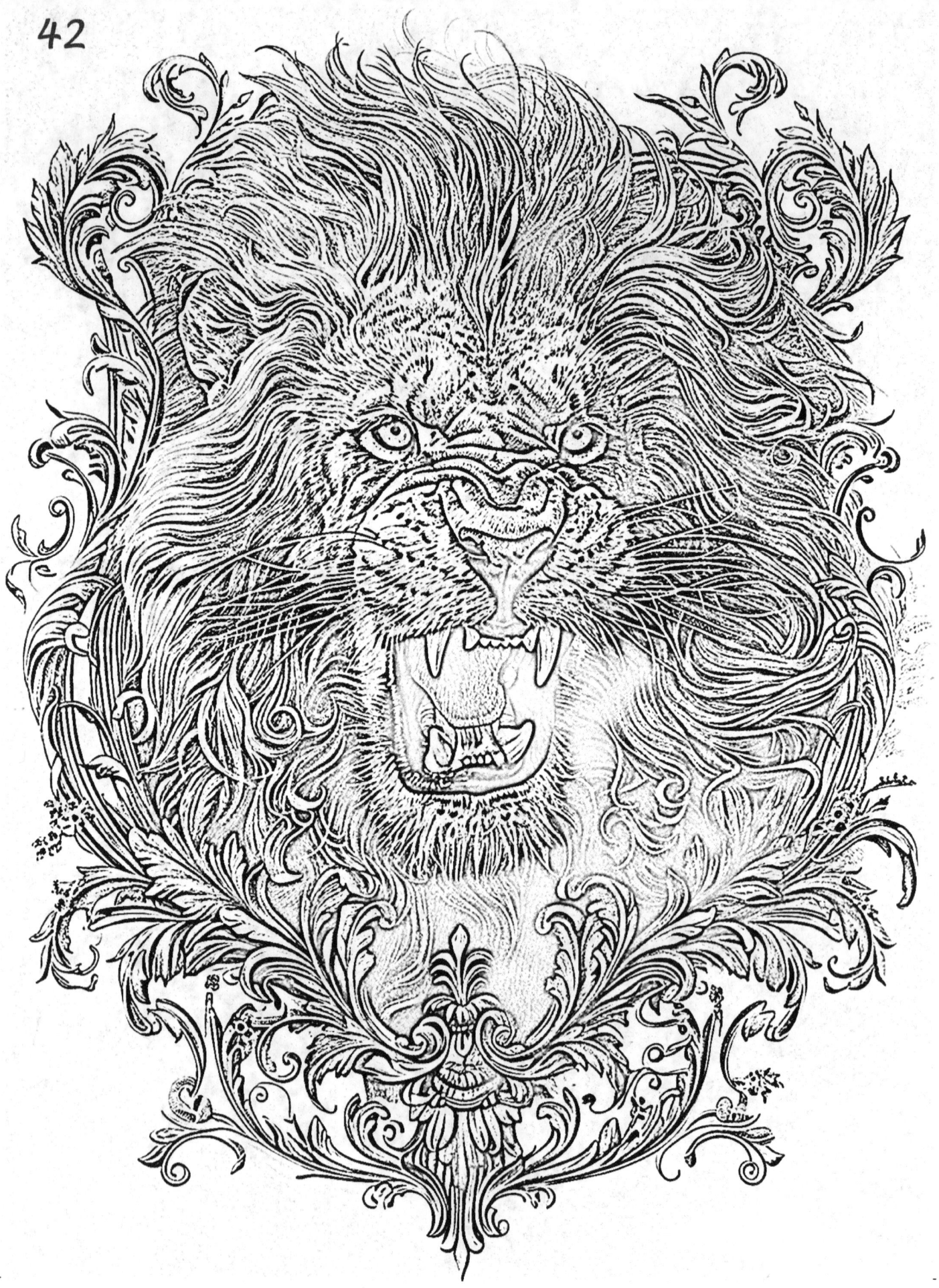

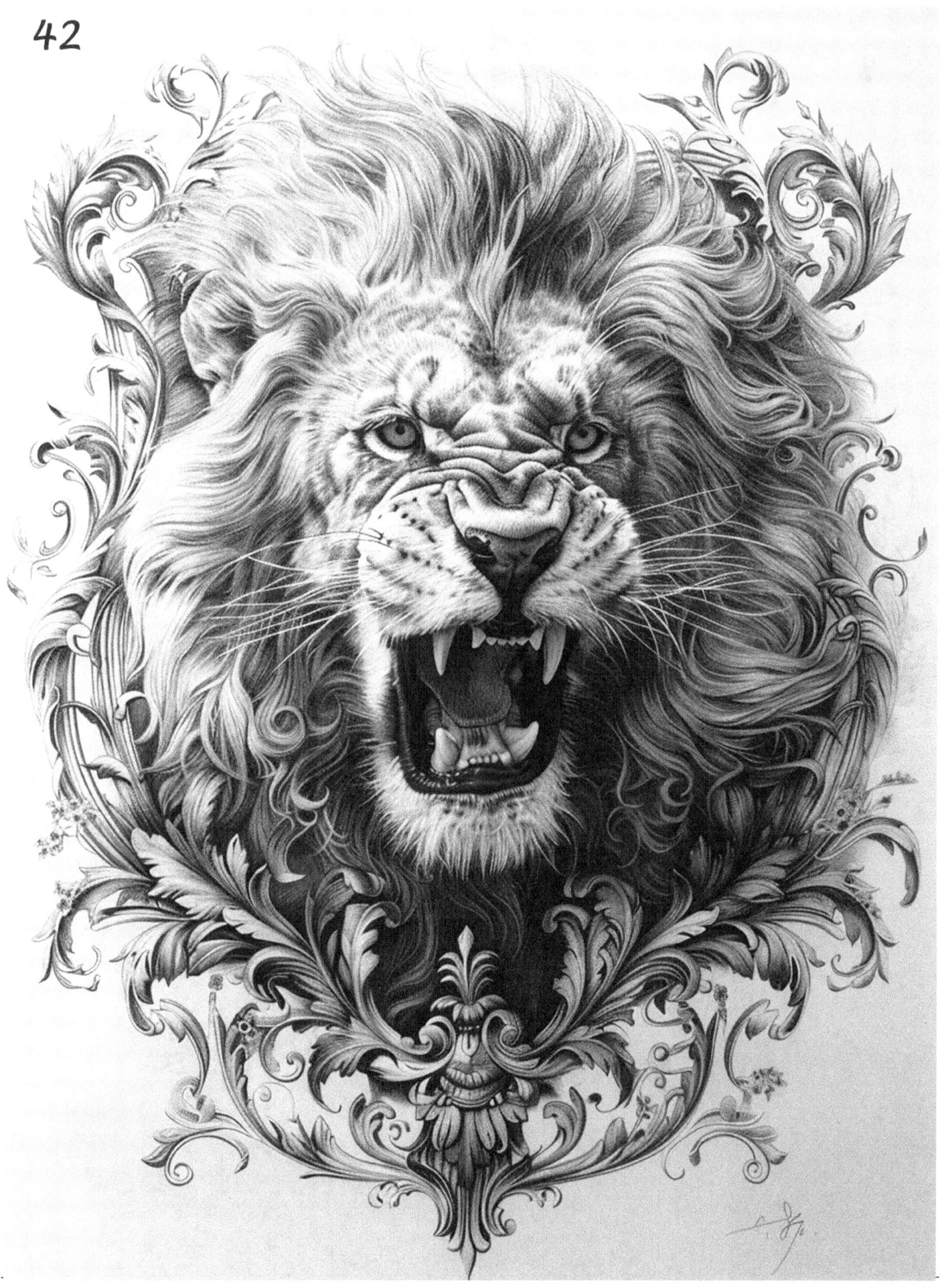

43

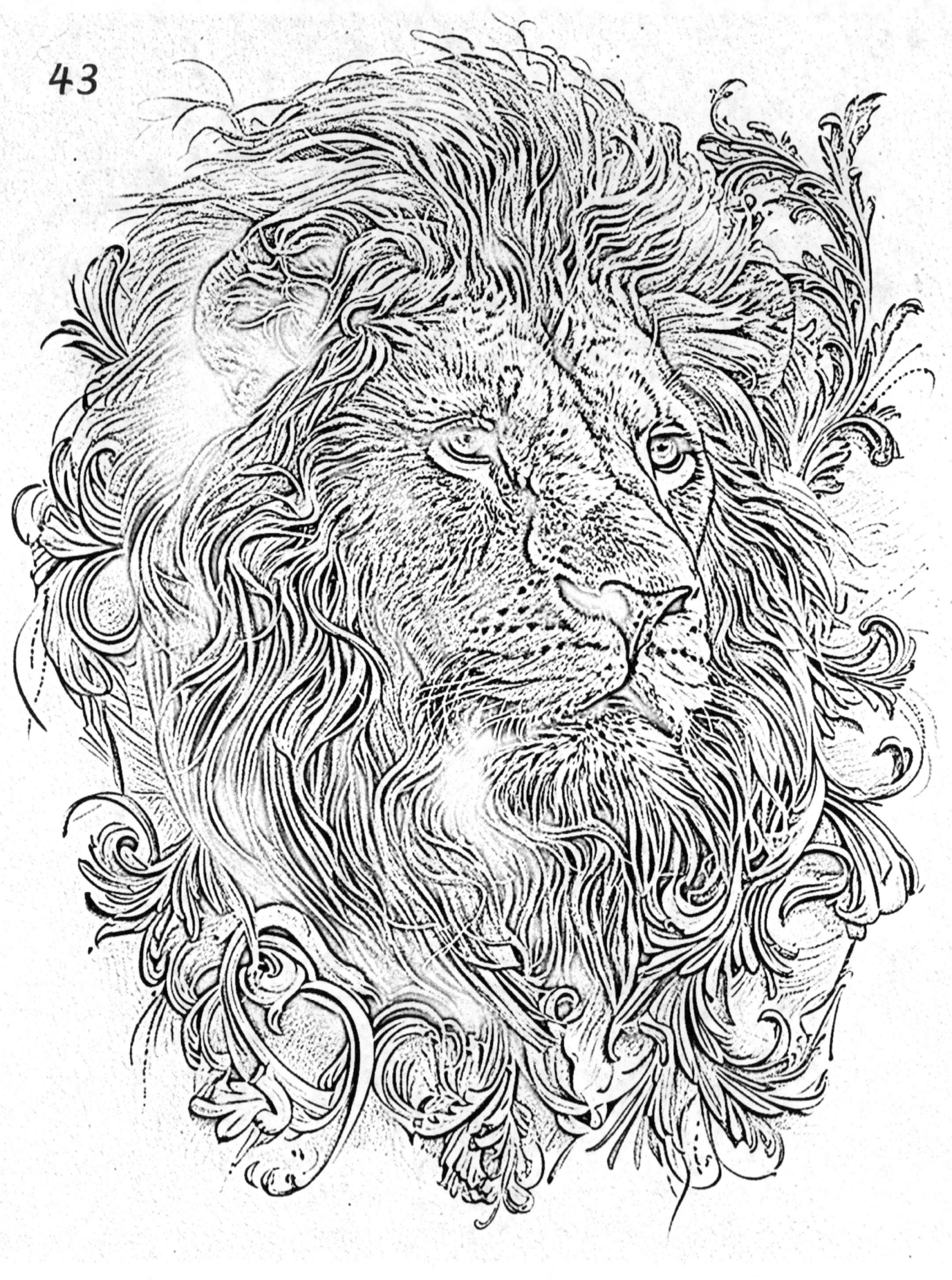

43

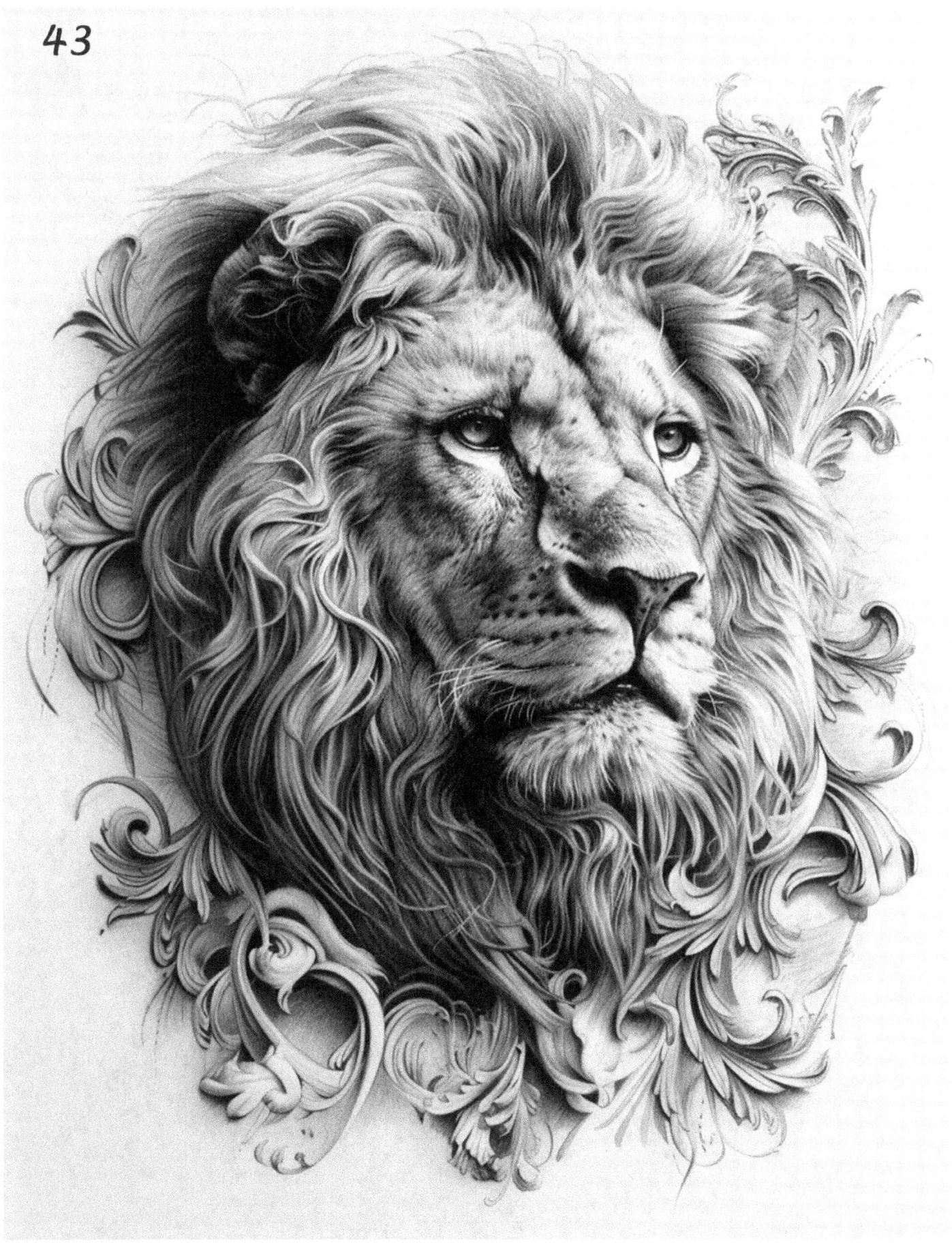

44

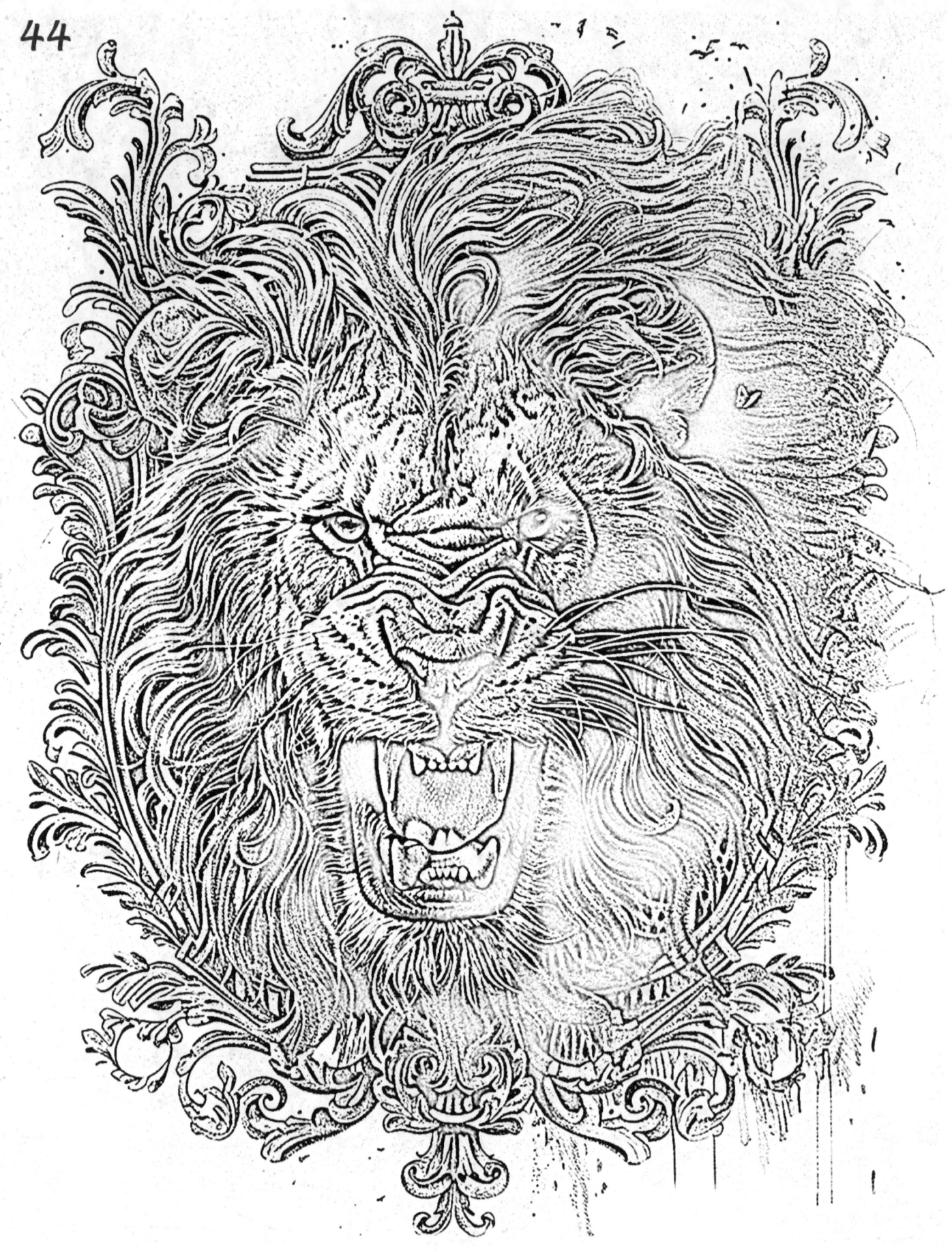

44

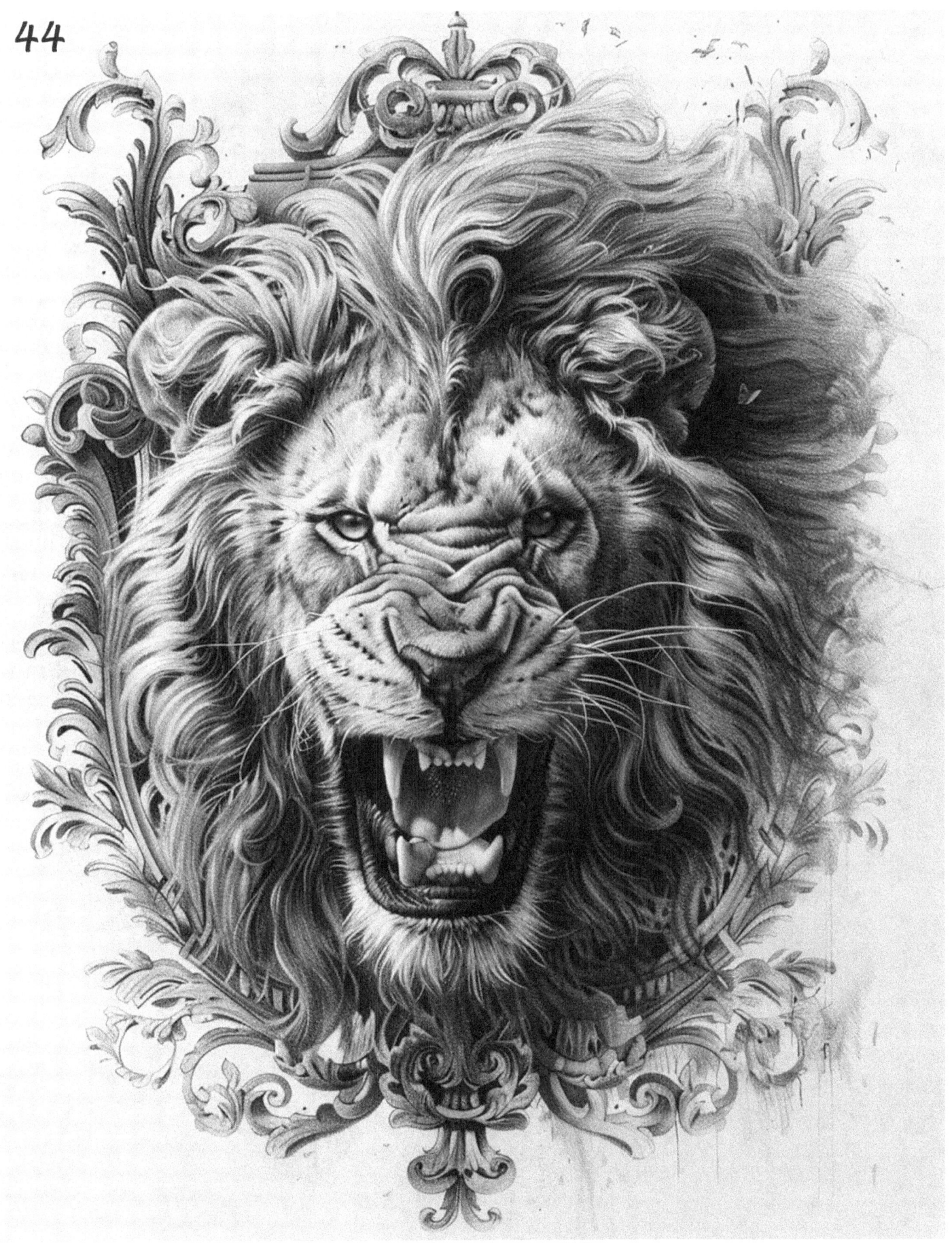

45

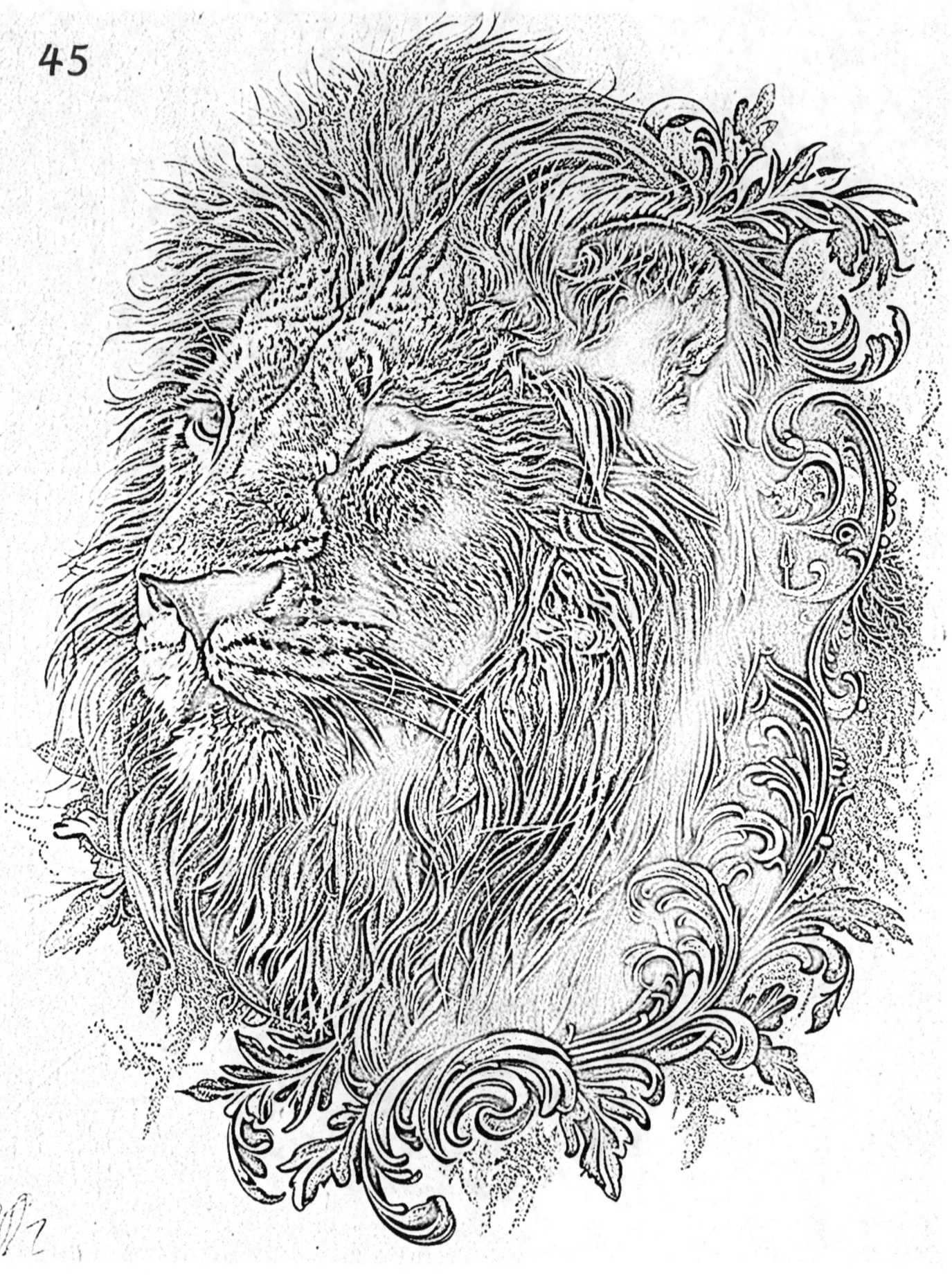

45

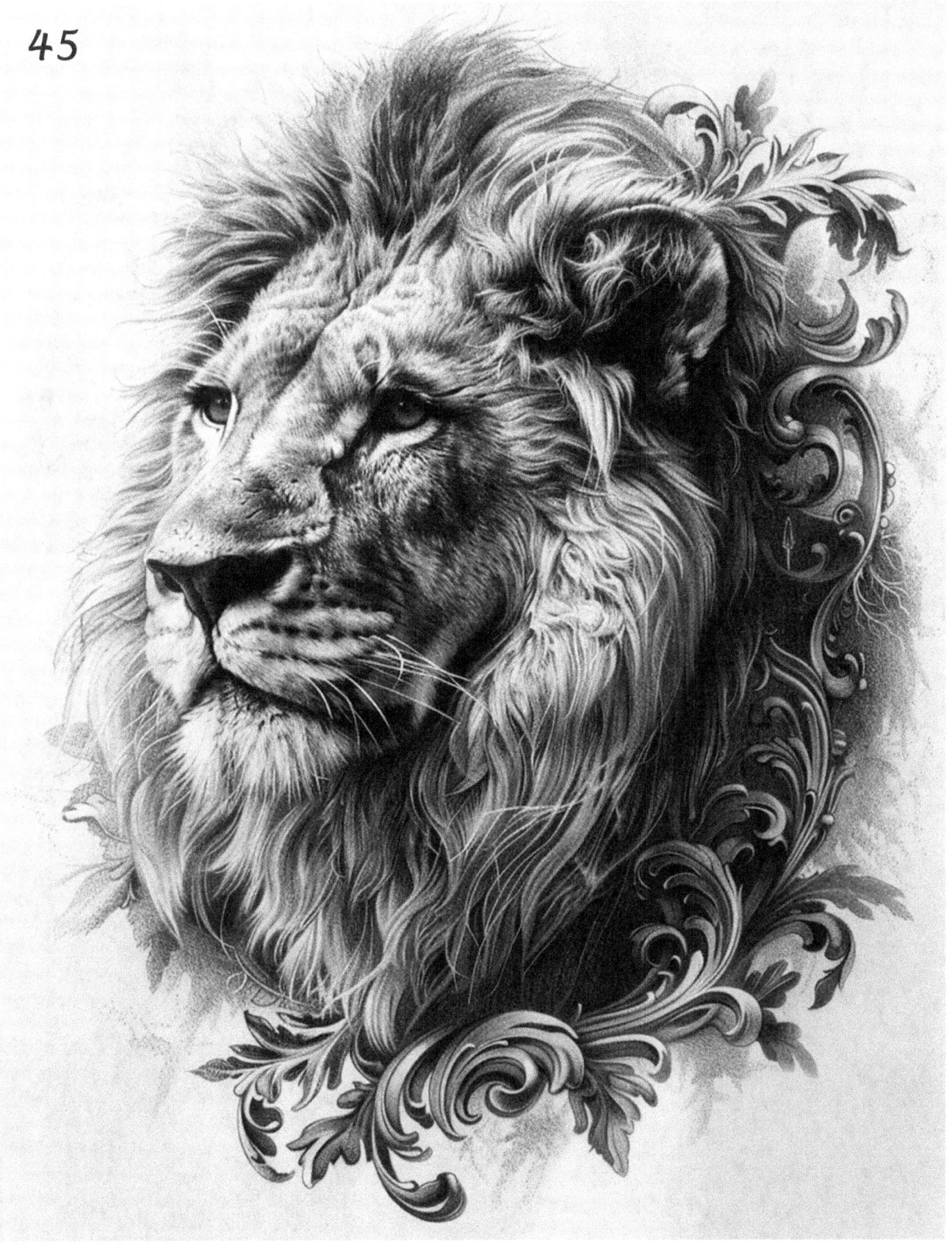

46

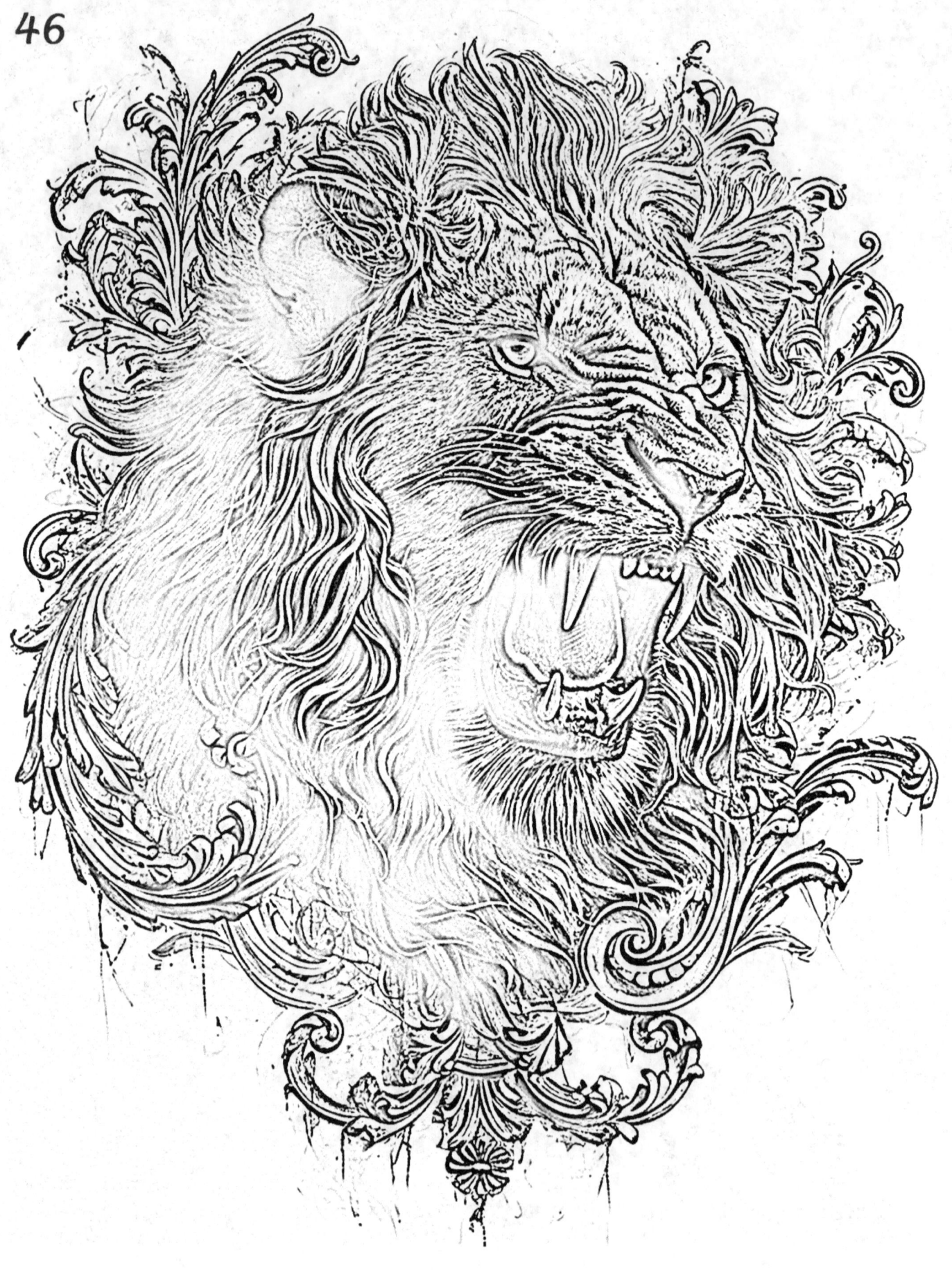

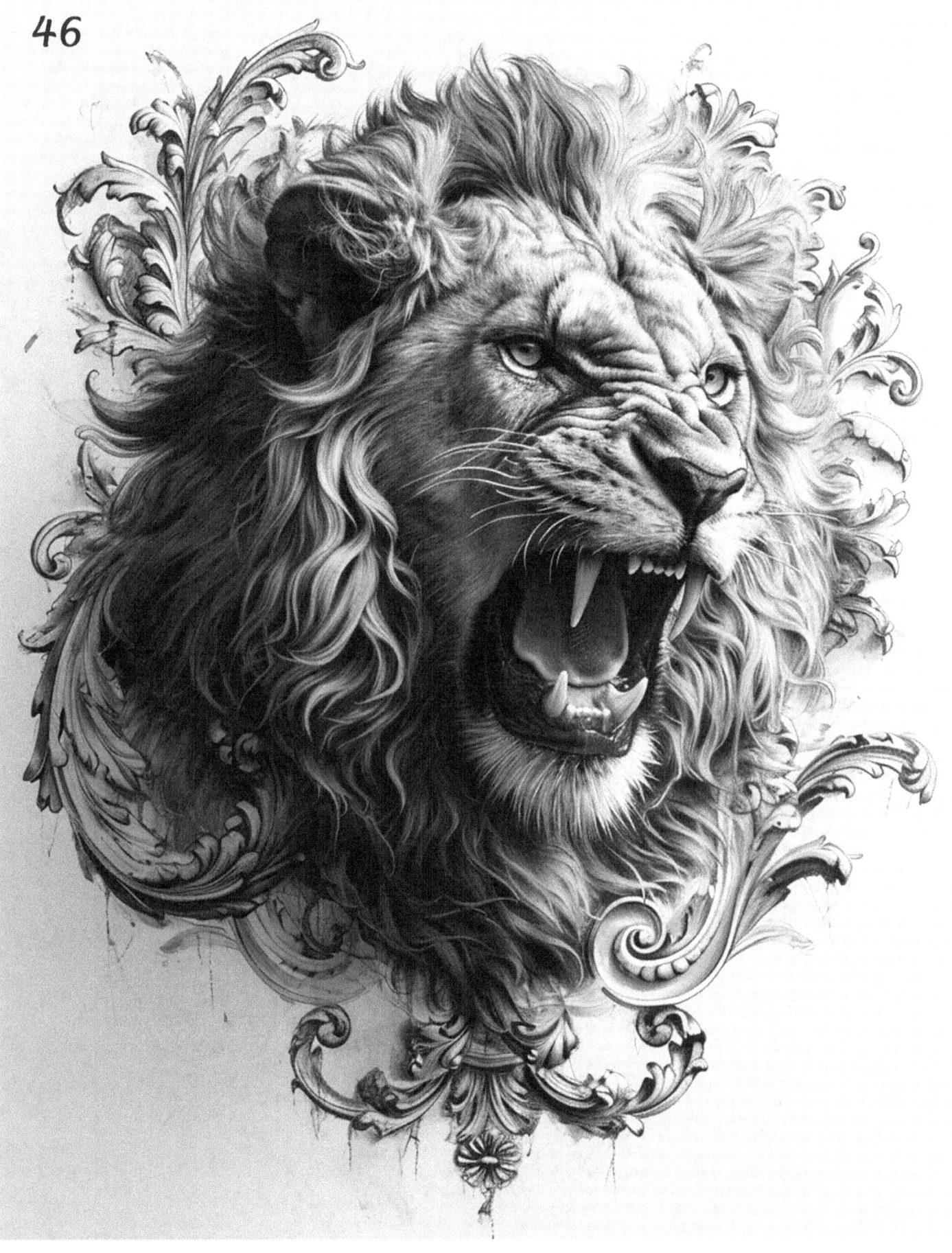

47

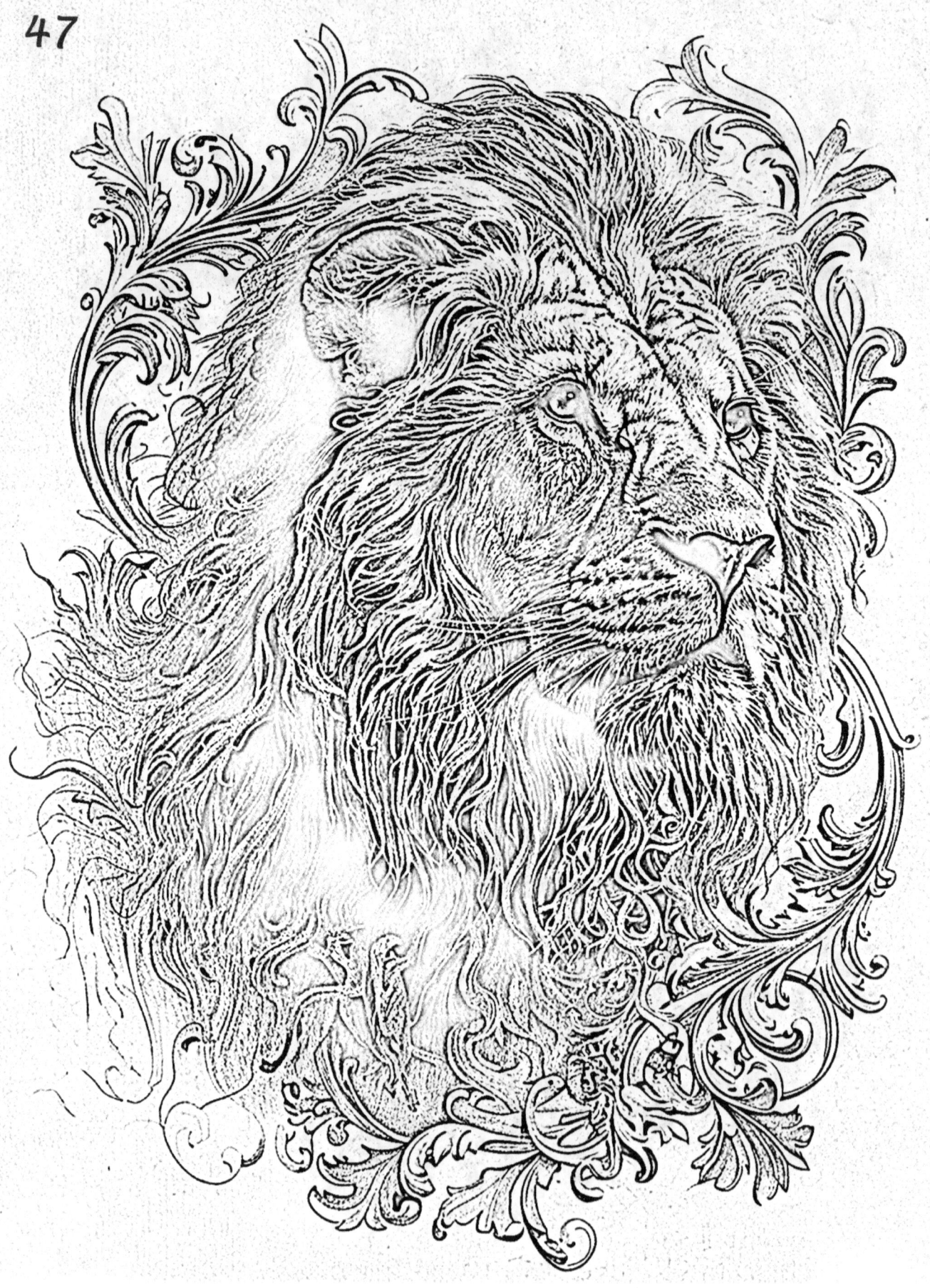

47

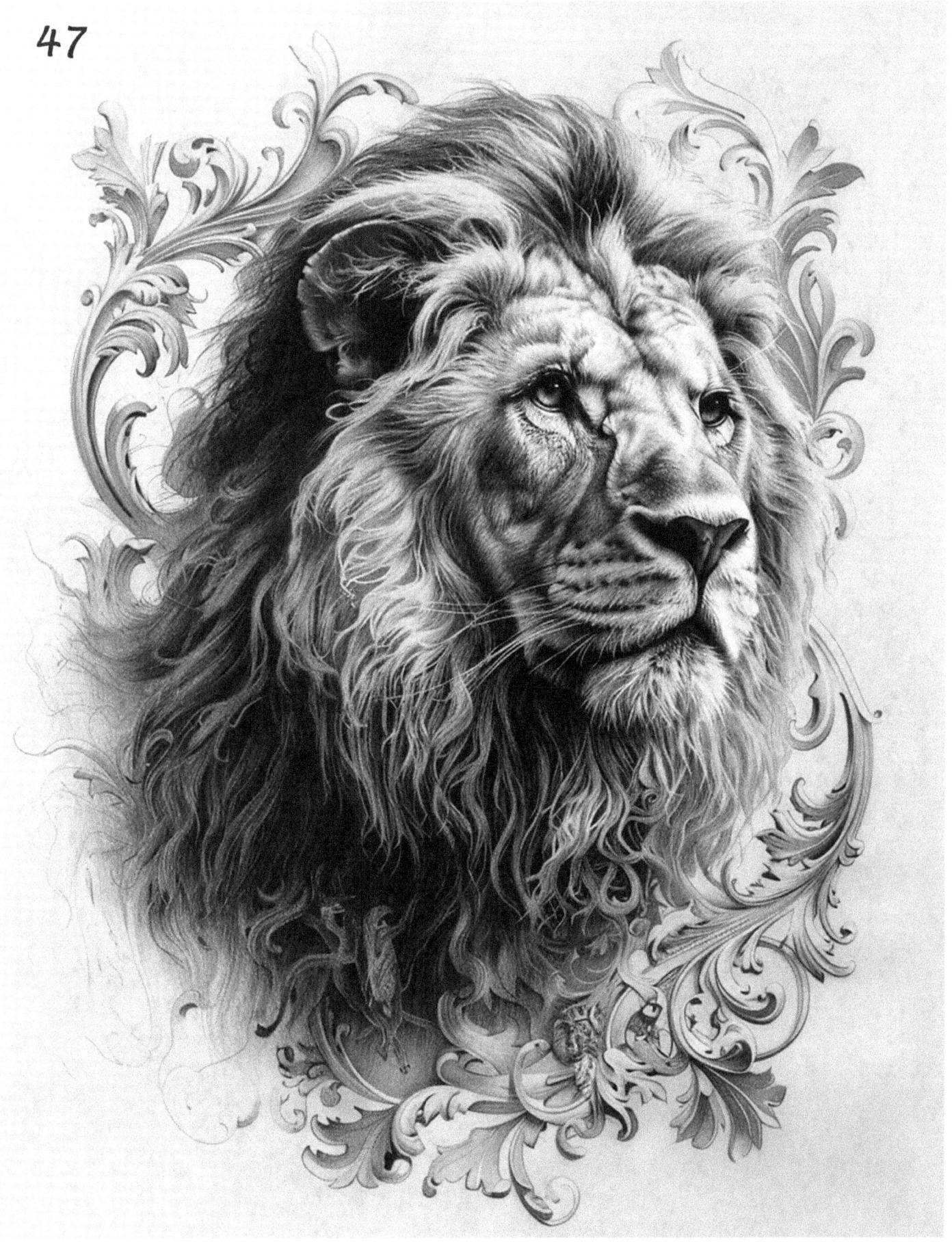

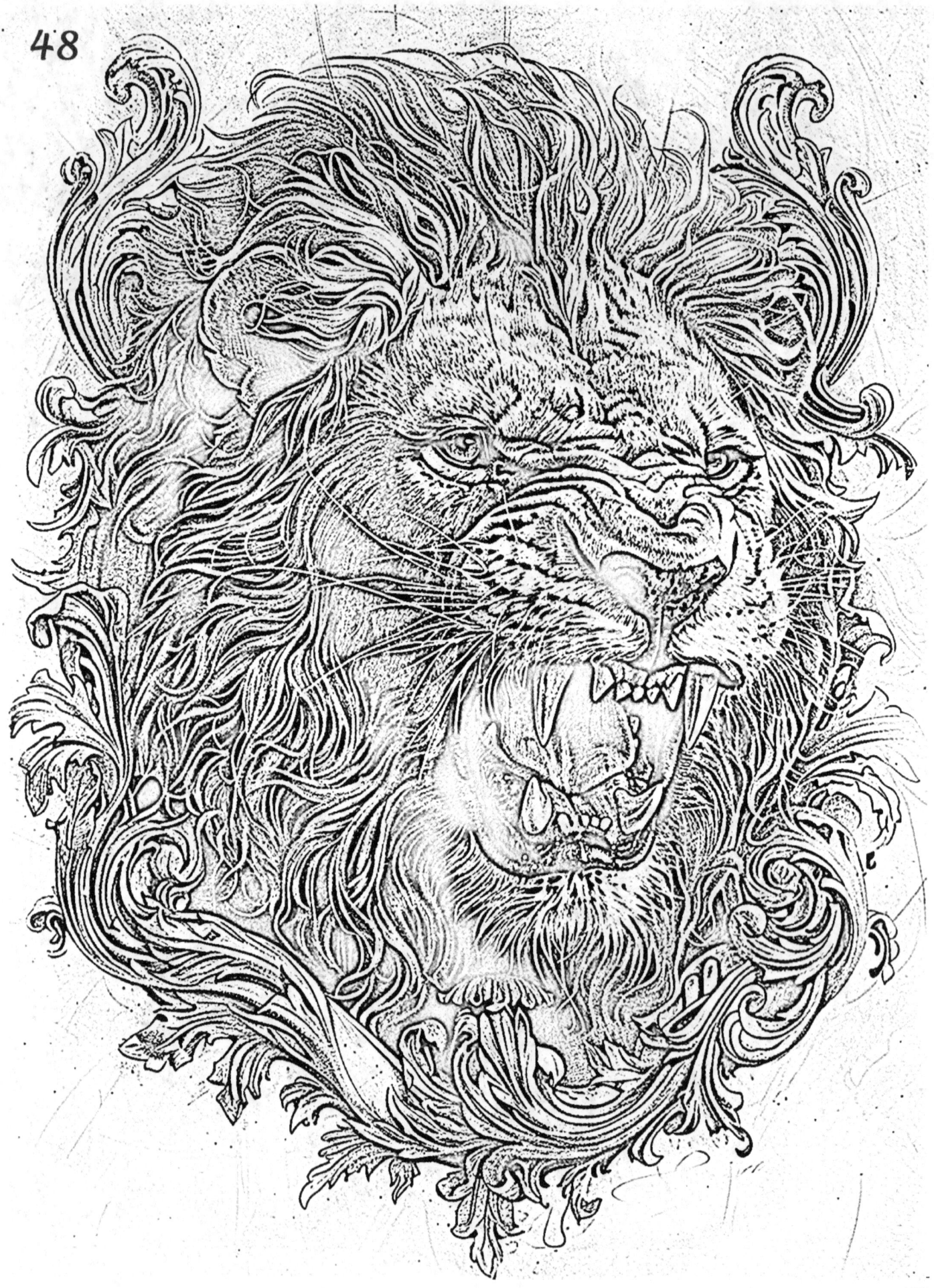

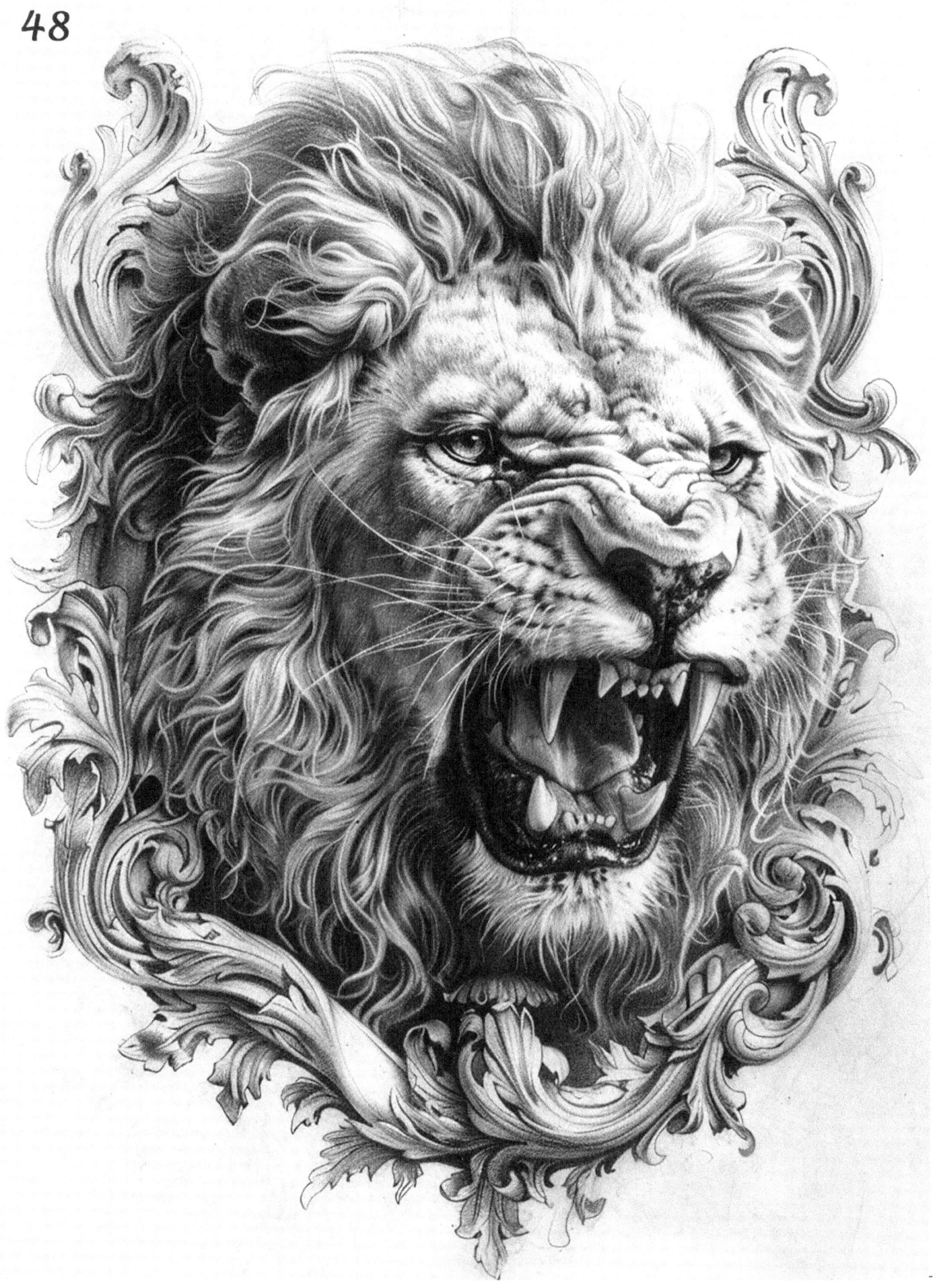

49

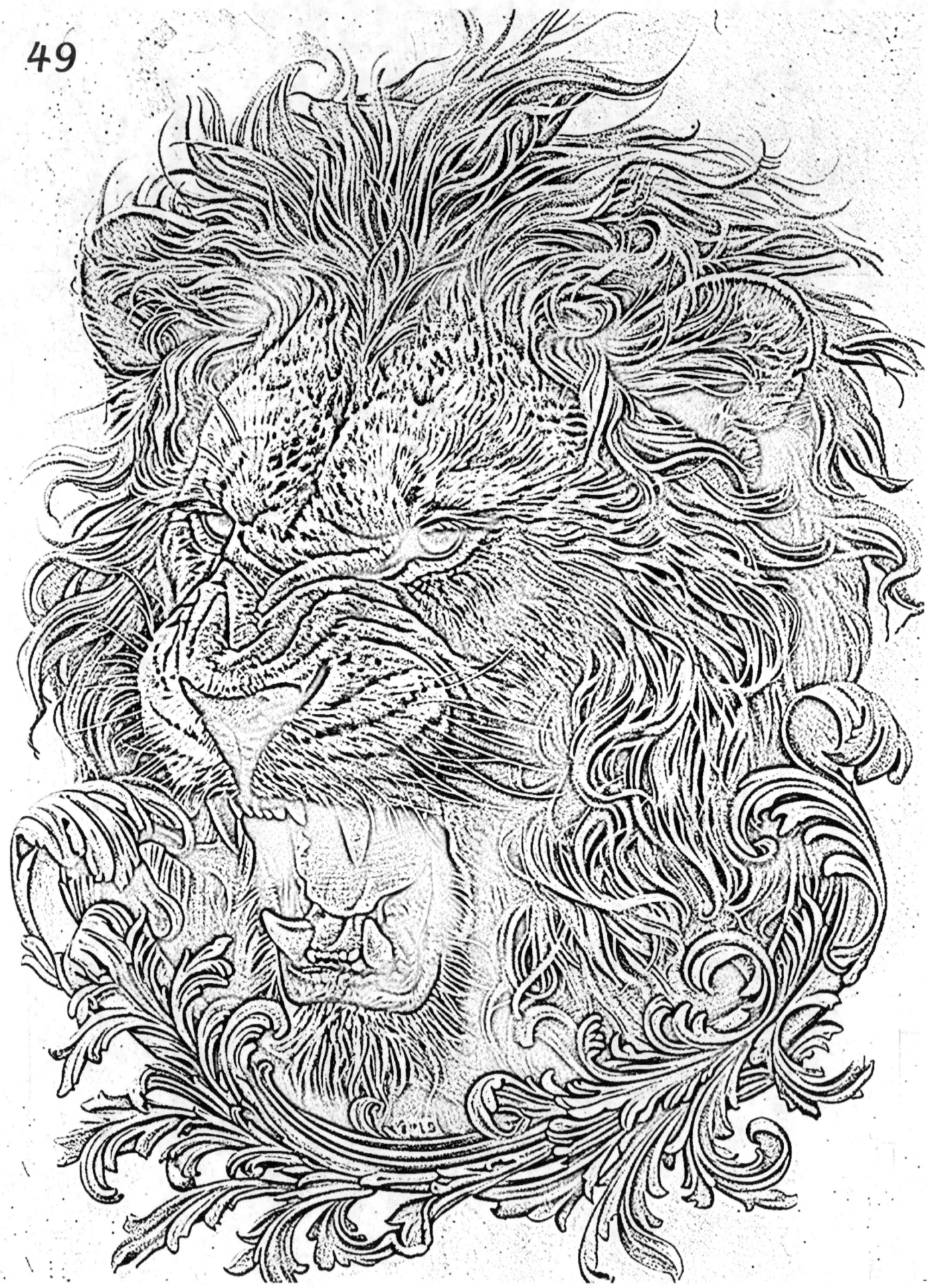

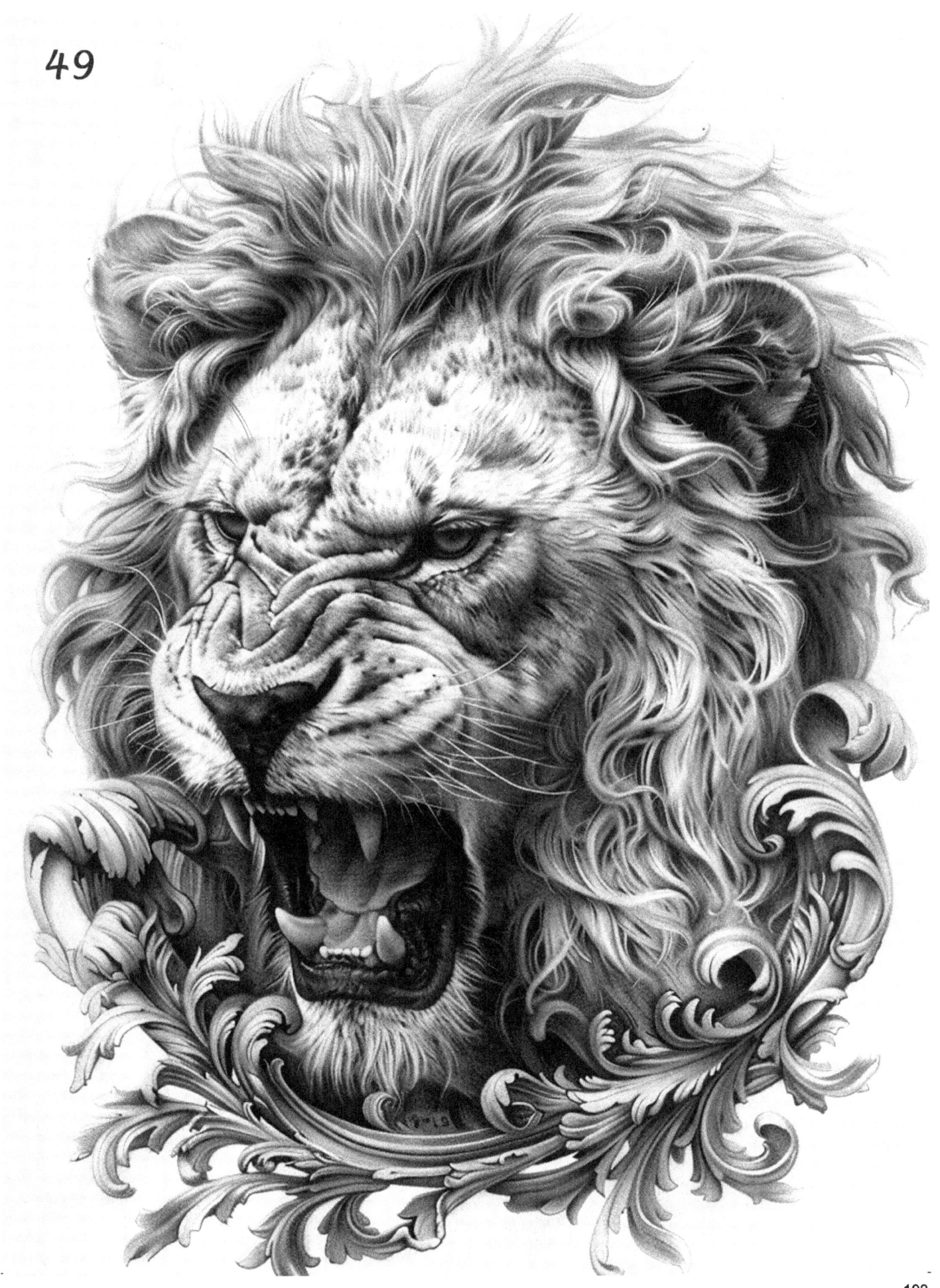

50

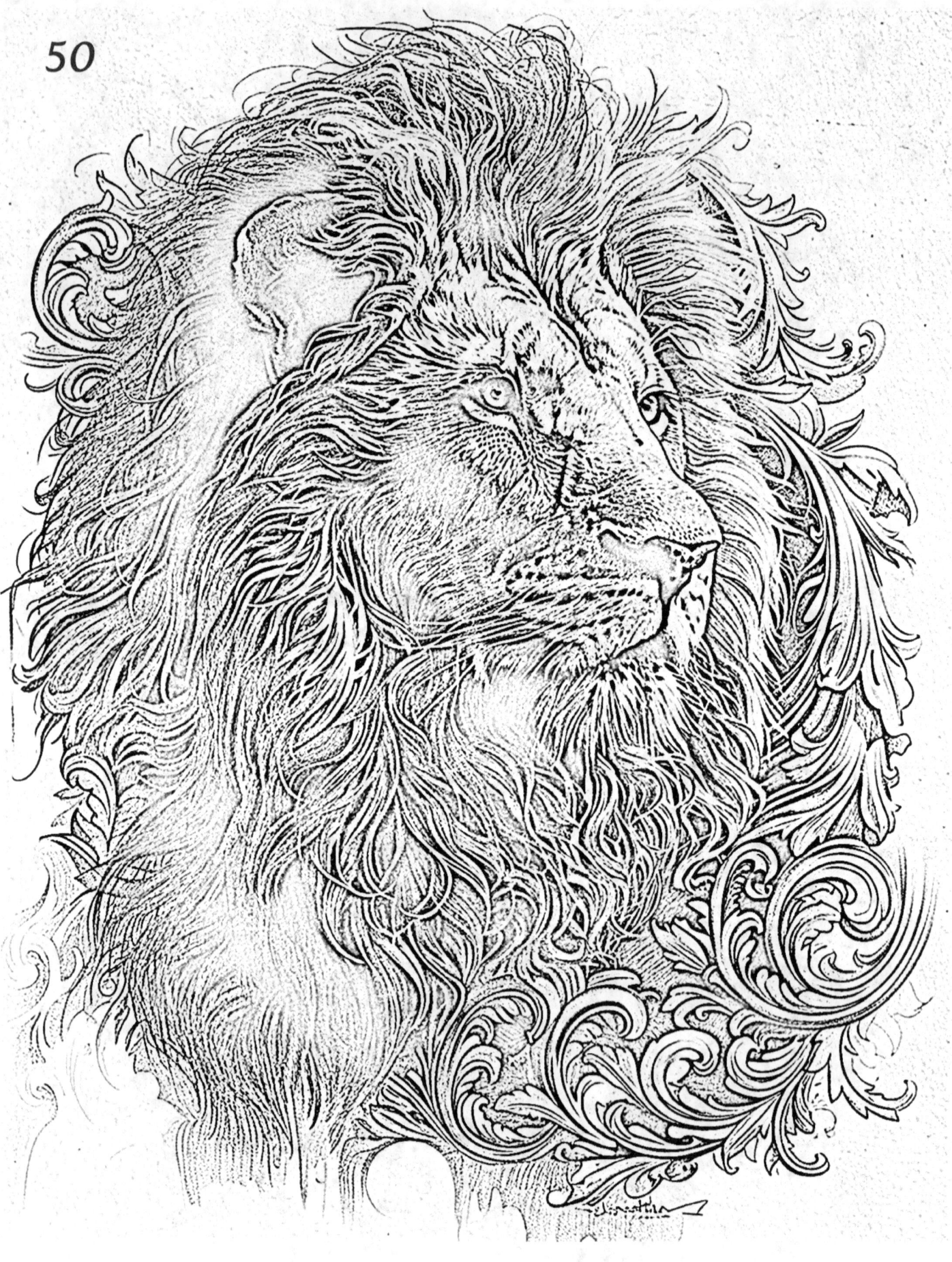

50

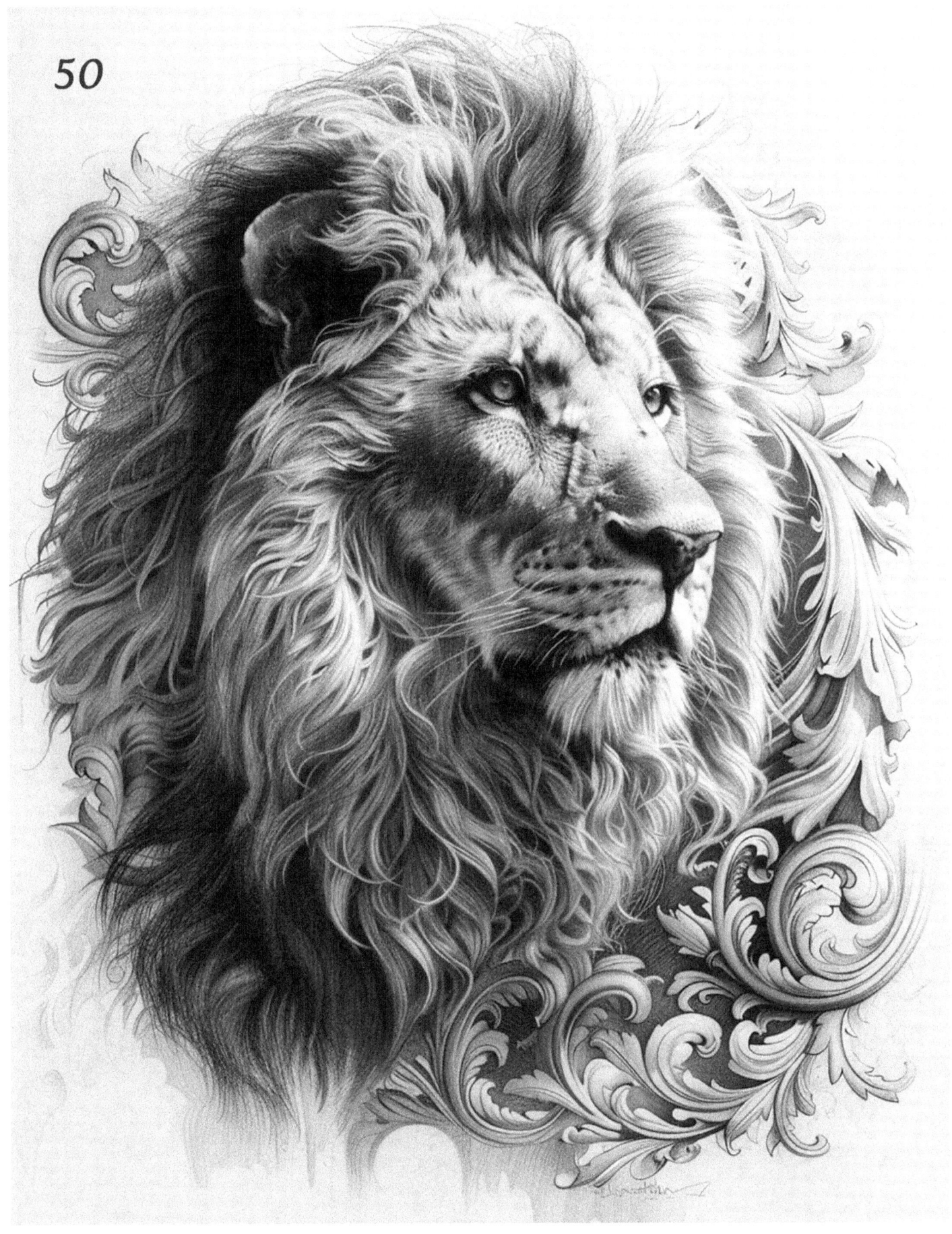

51

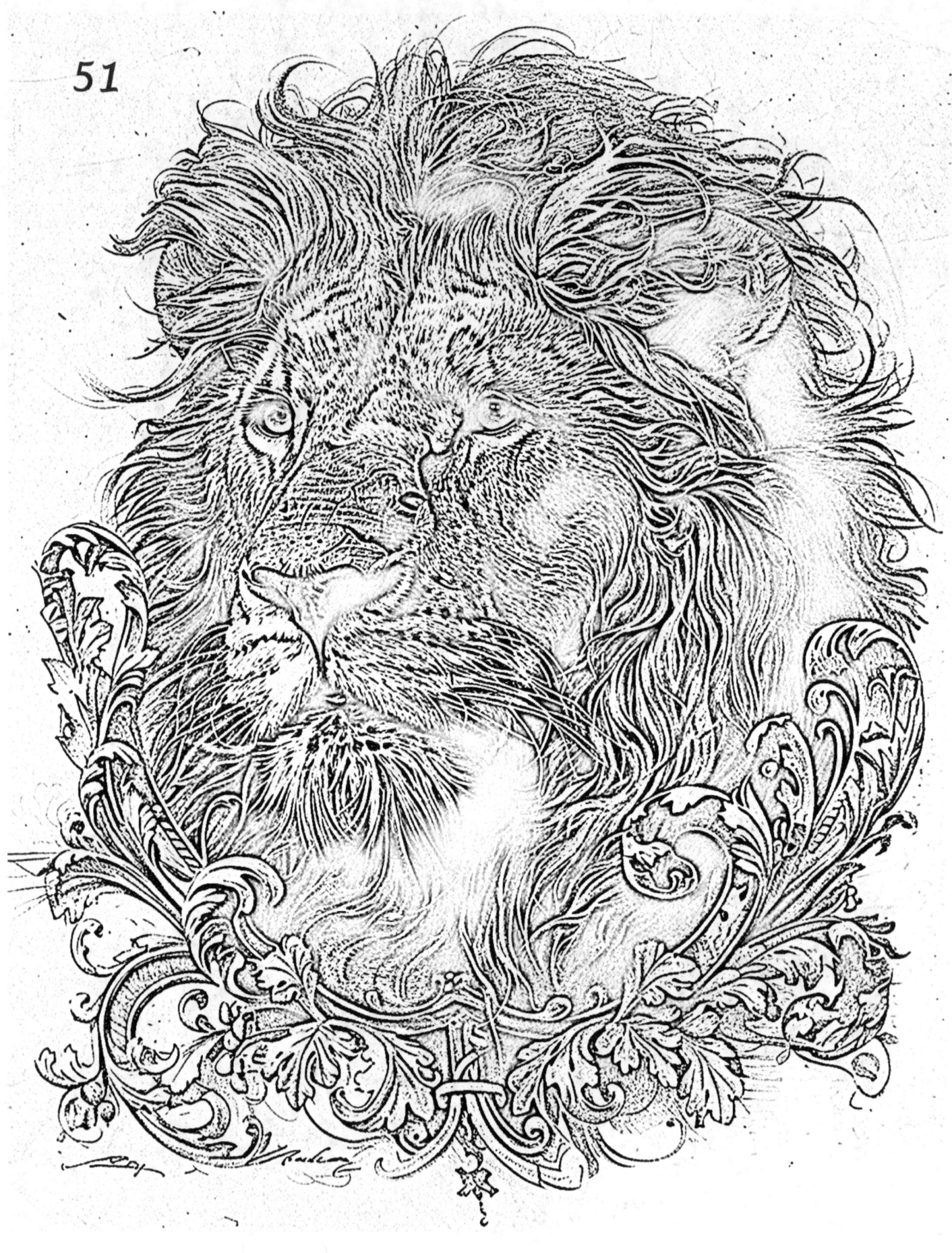

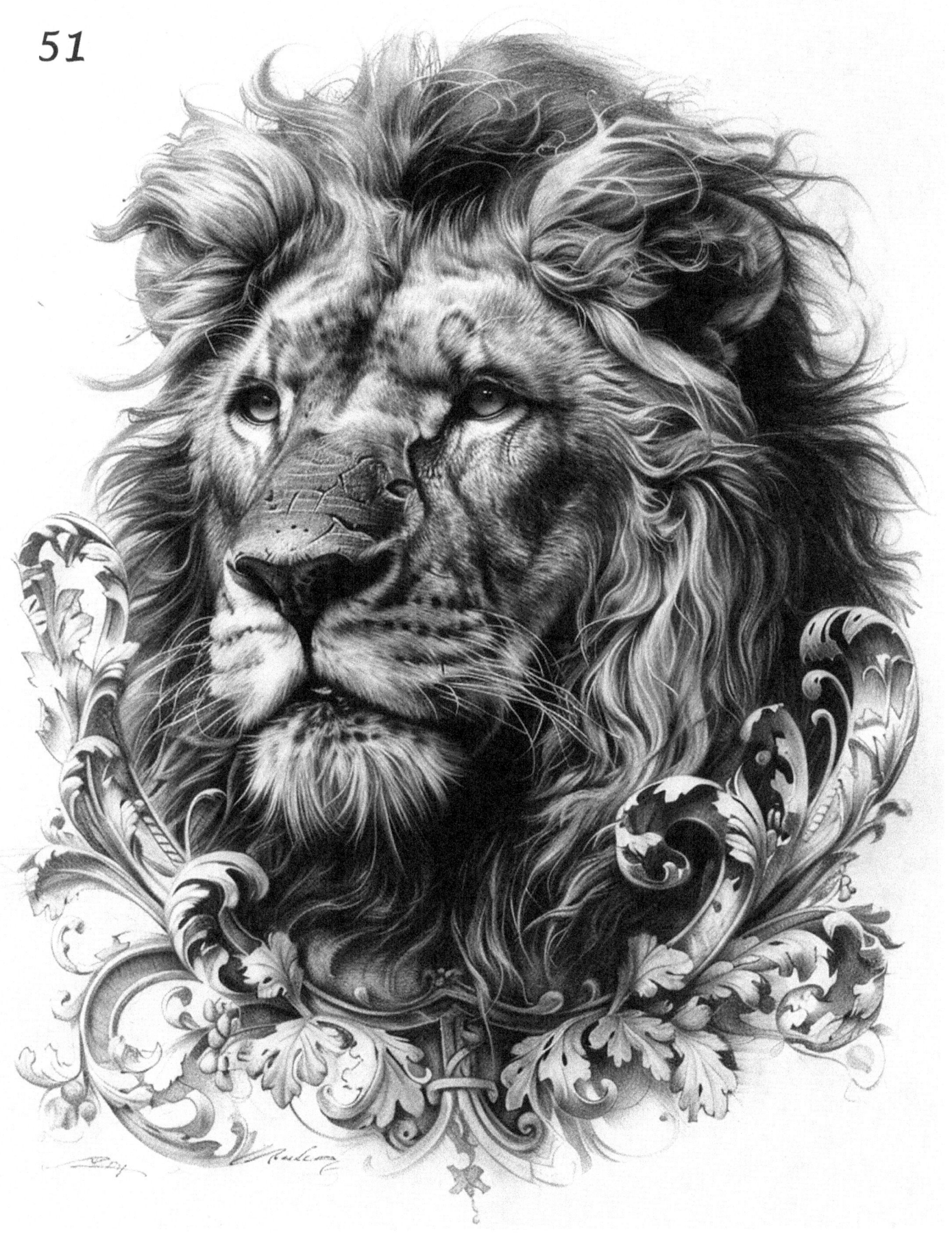

52

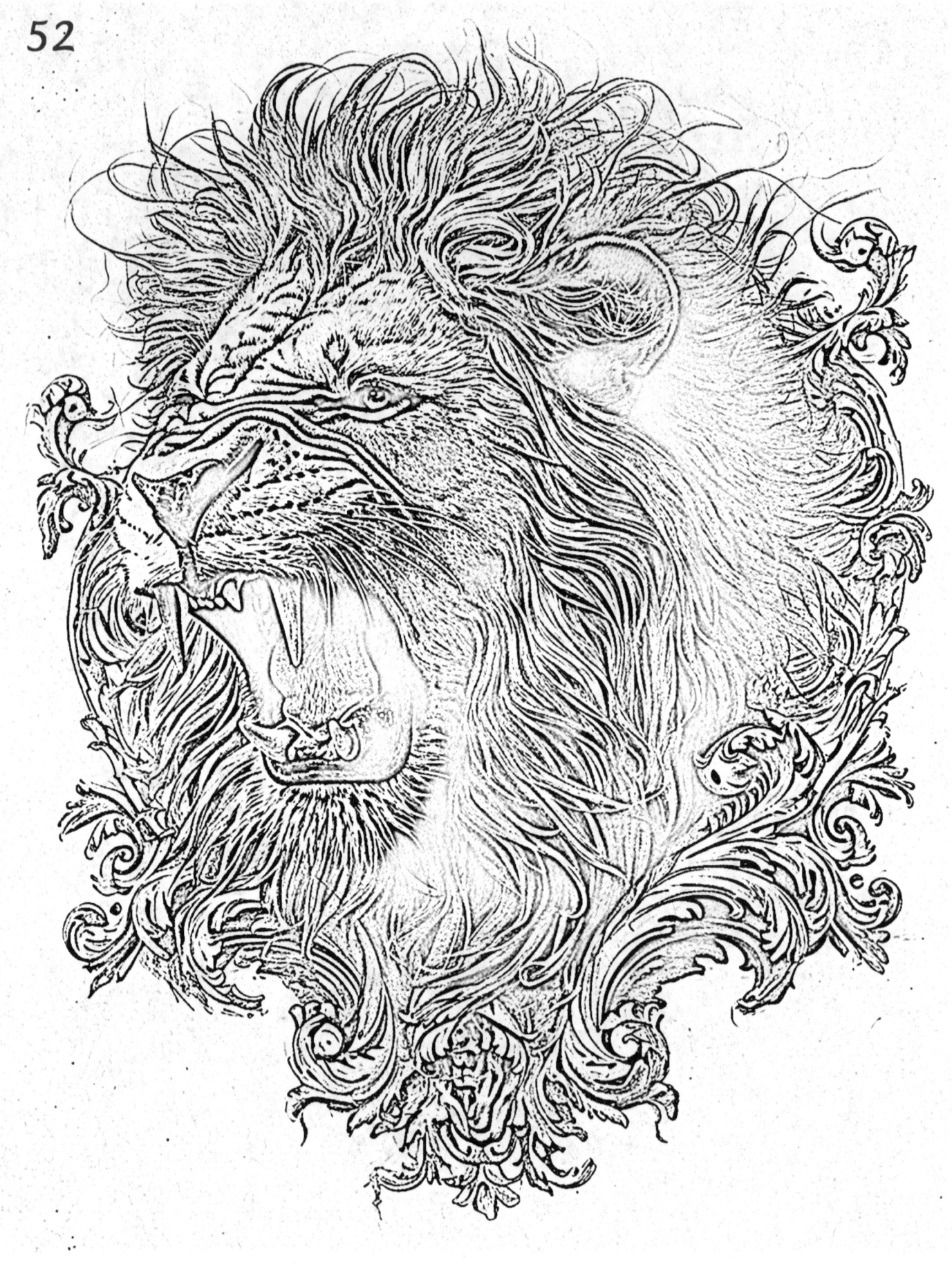

52

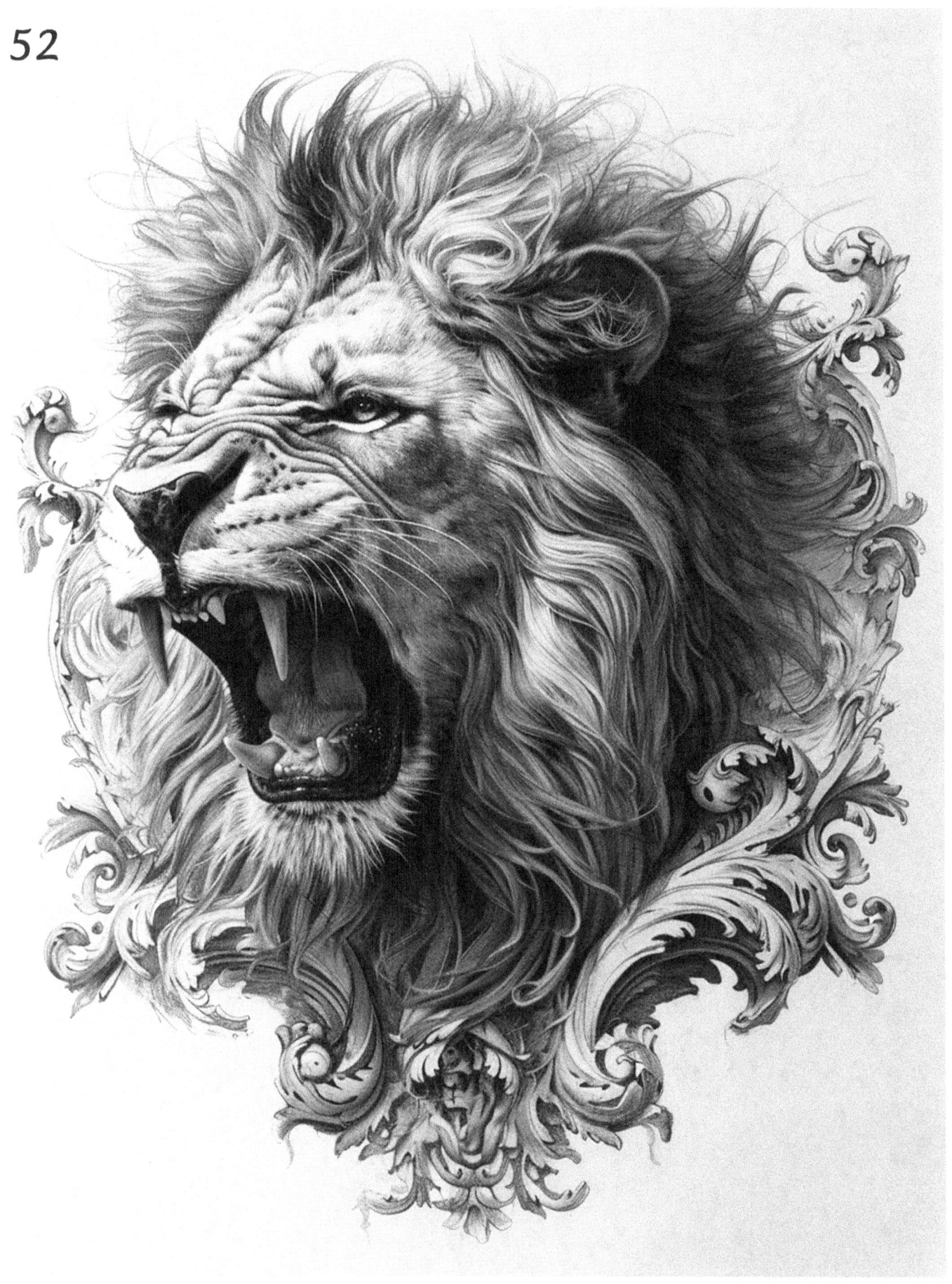

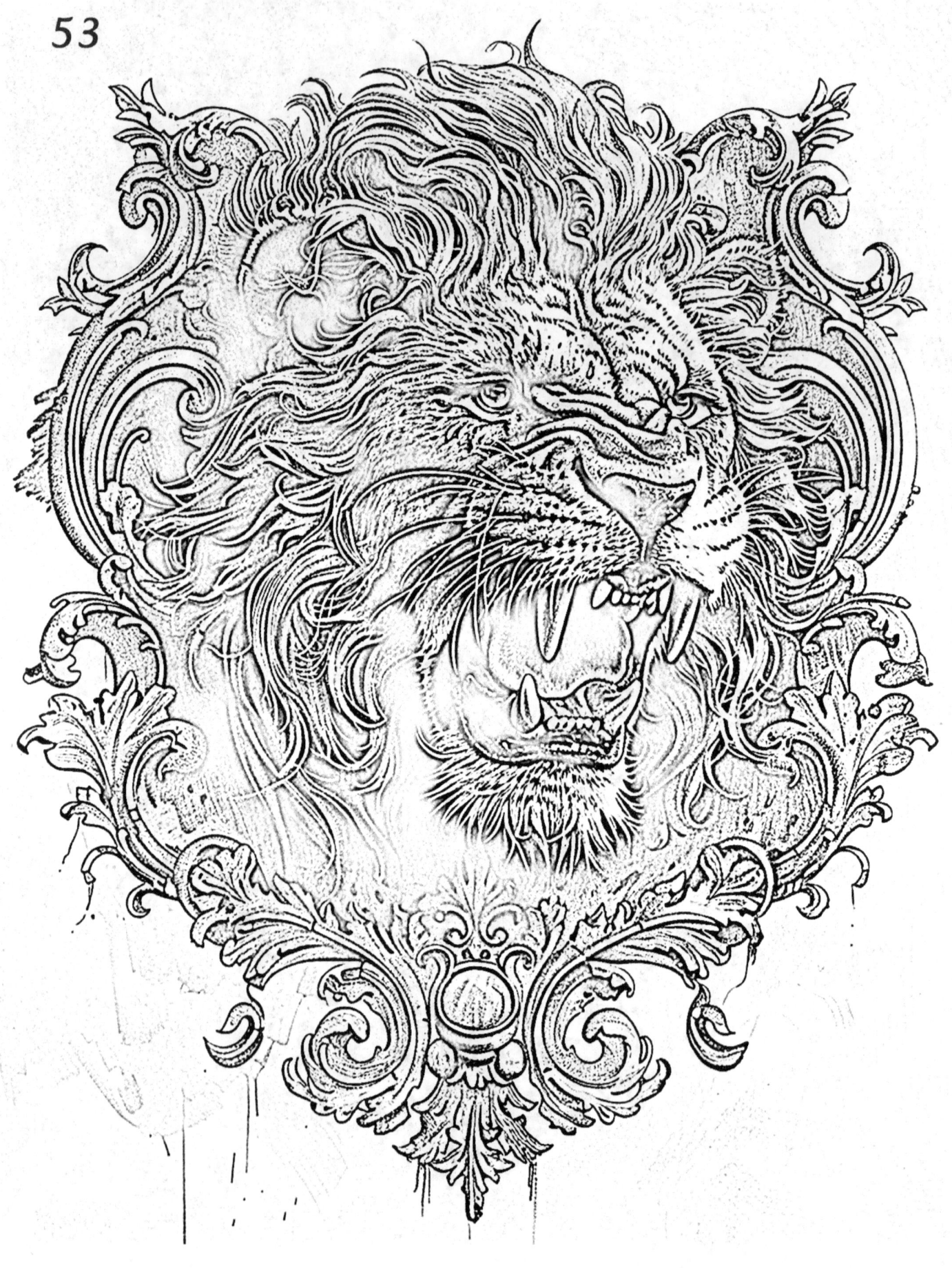

53

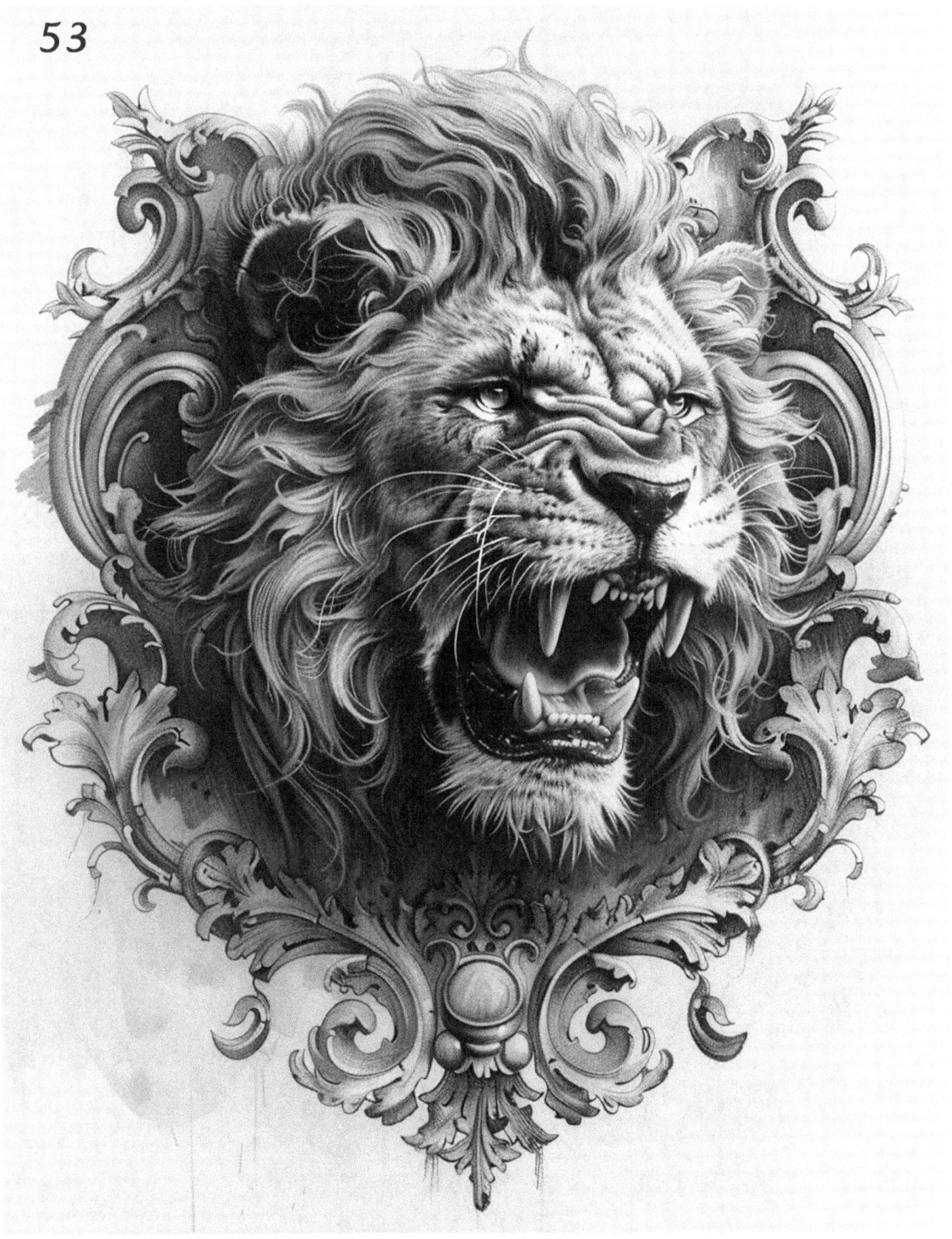

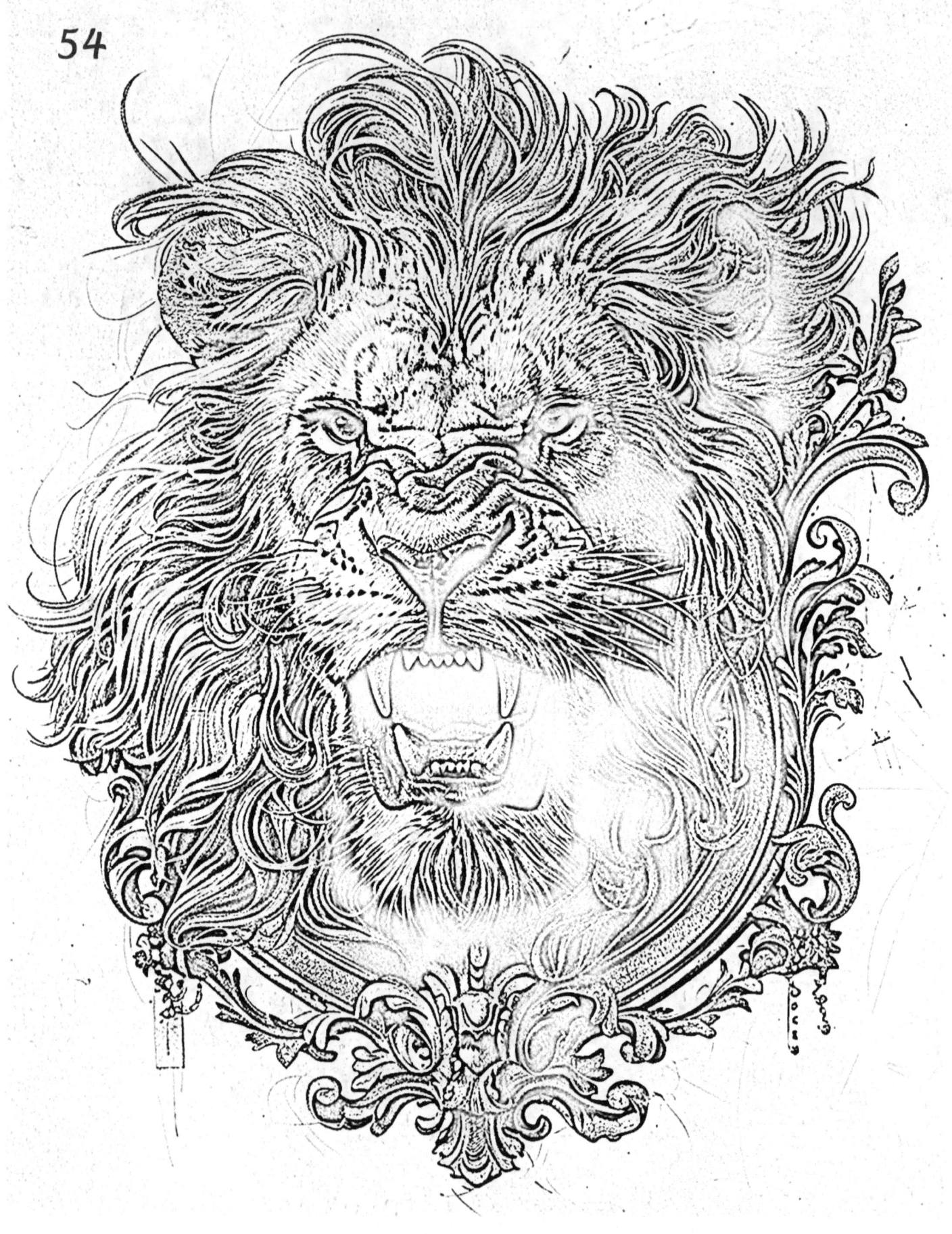

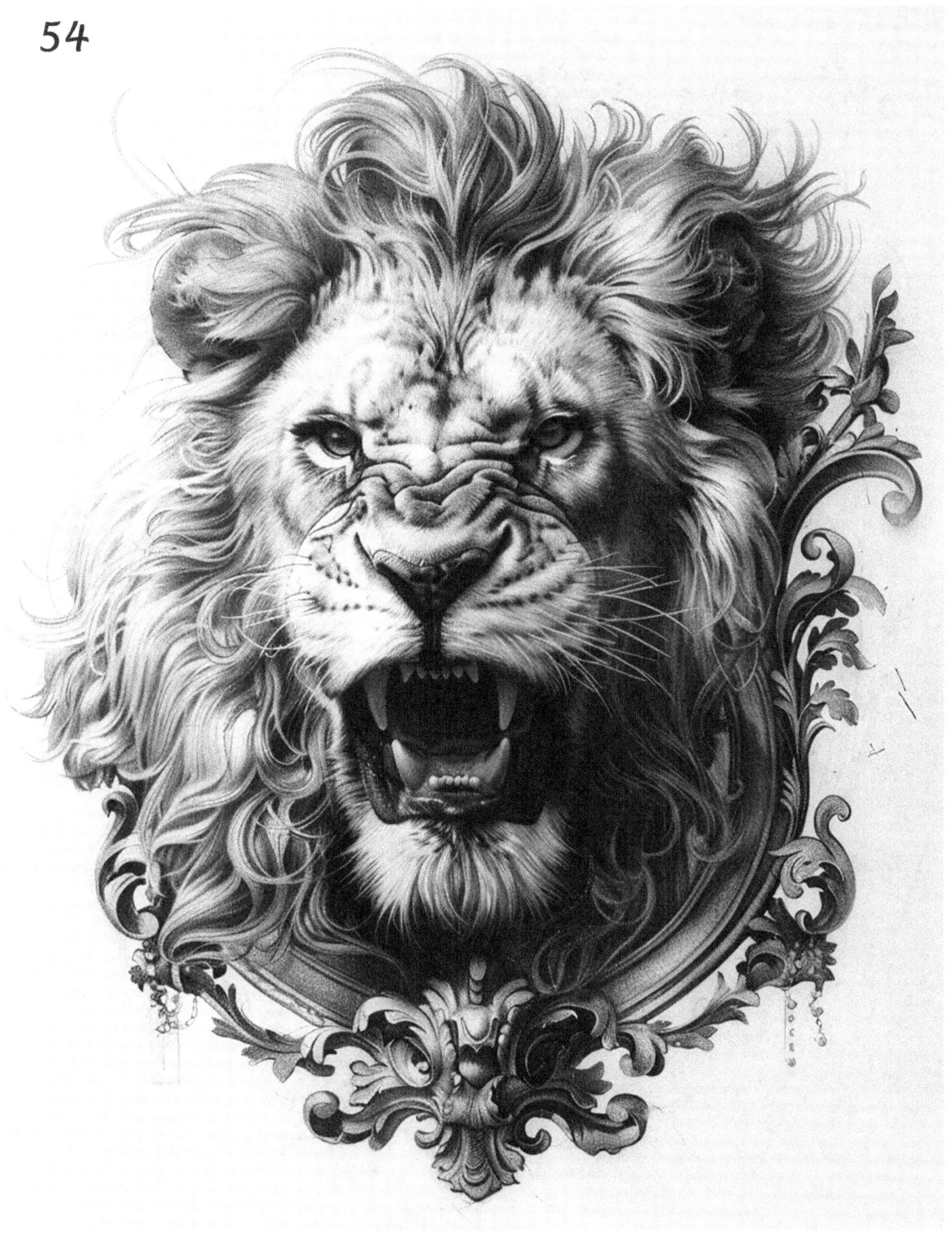

55

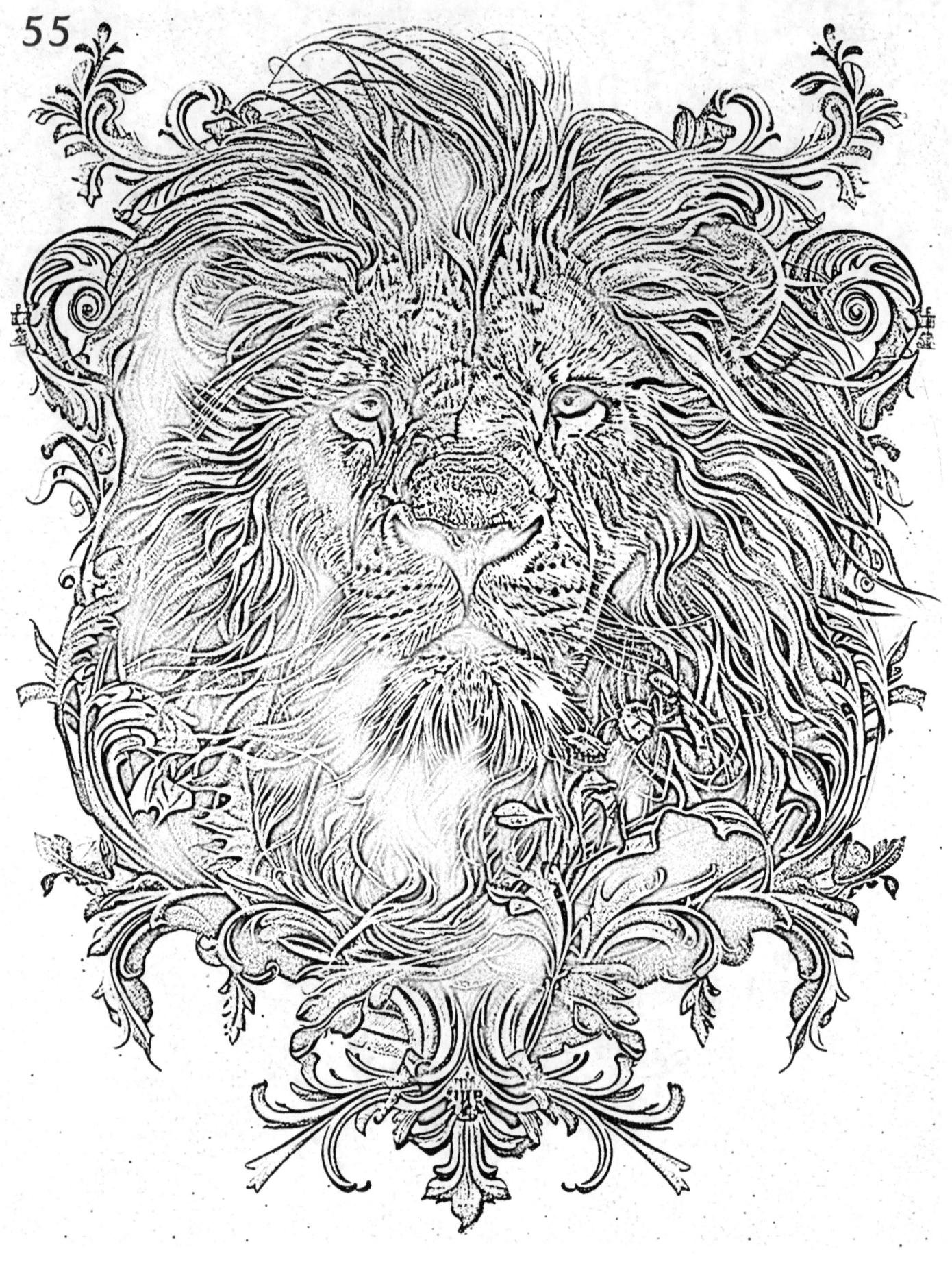

55

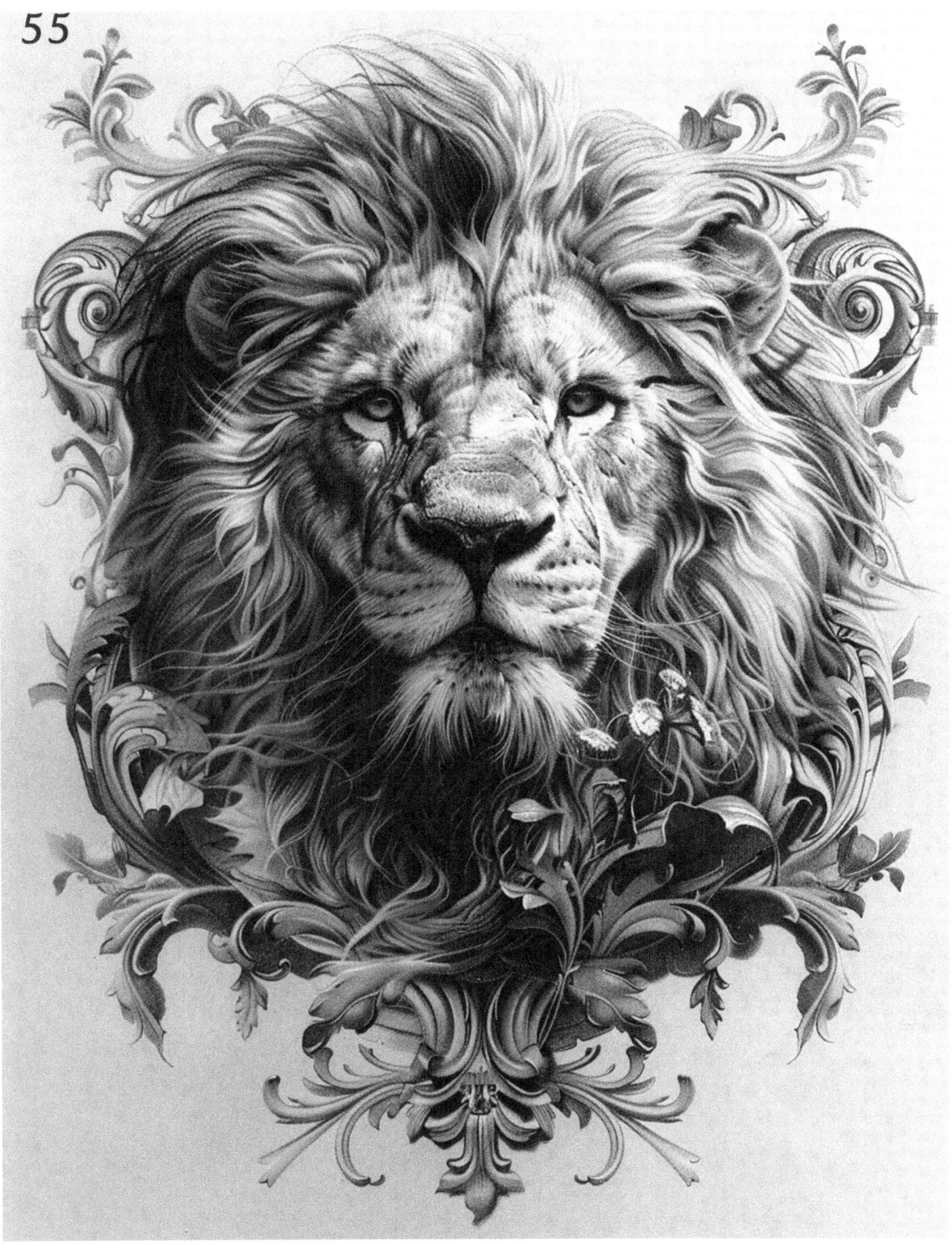

56

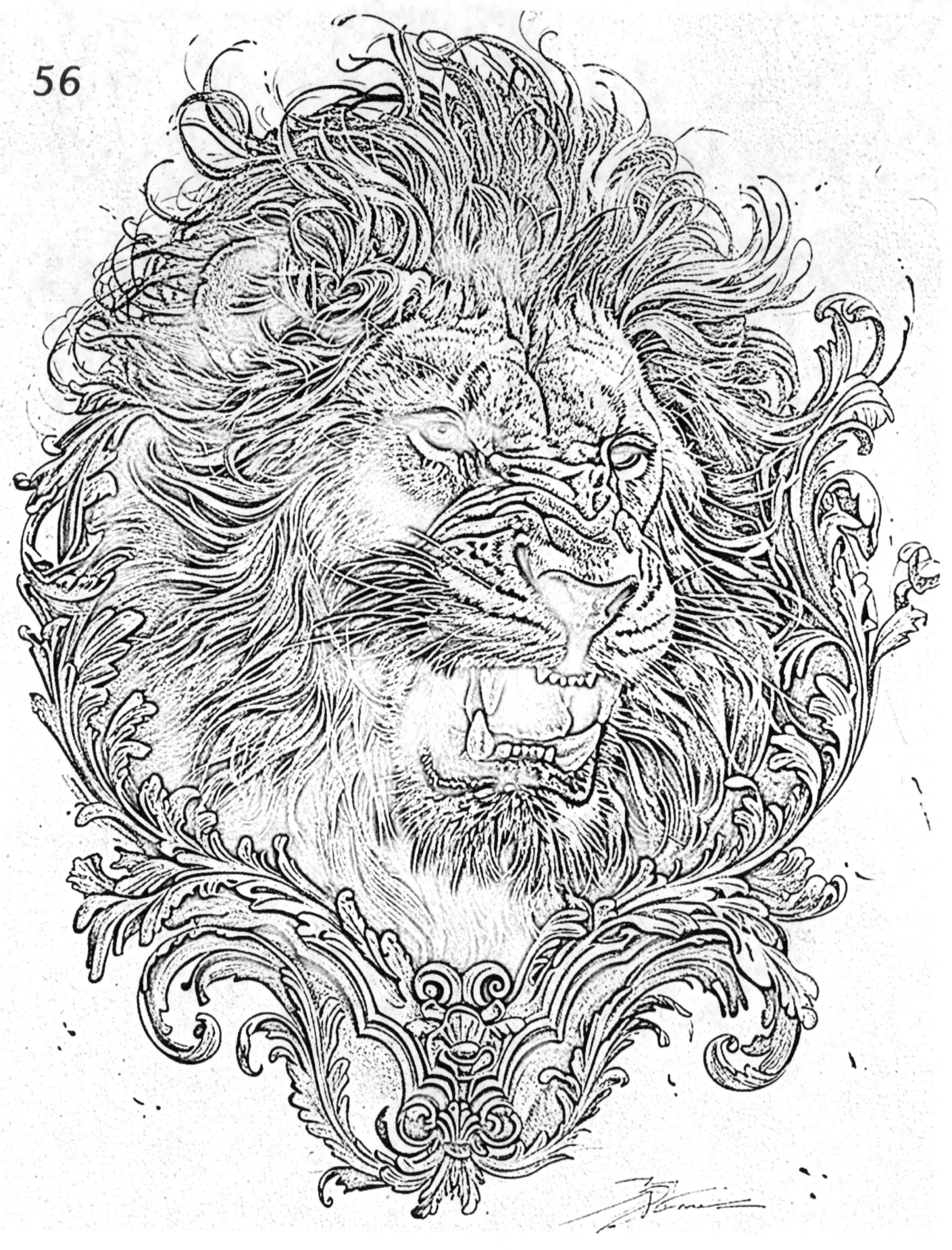

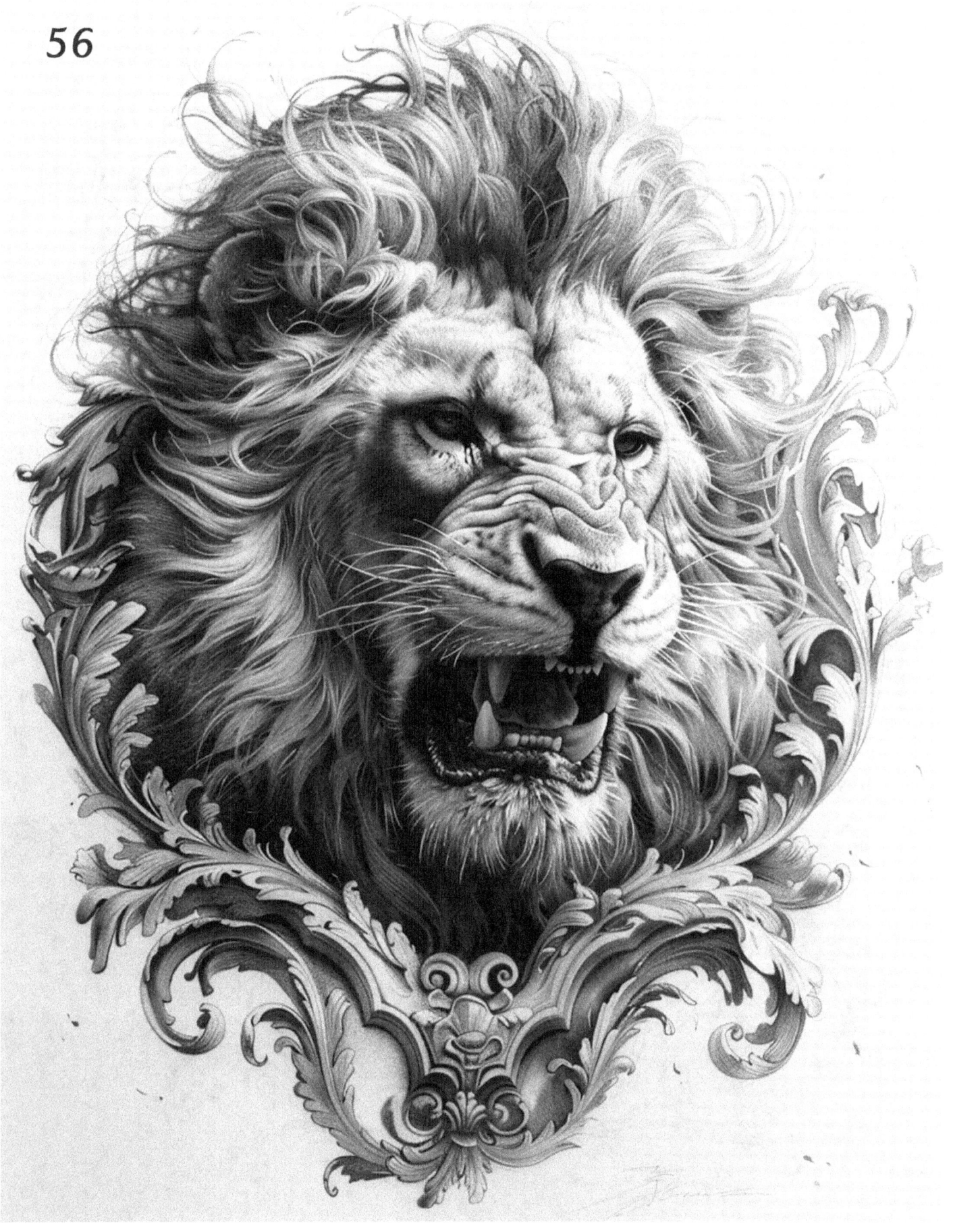

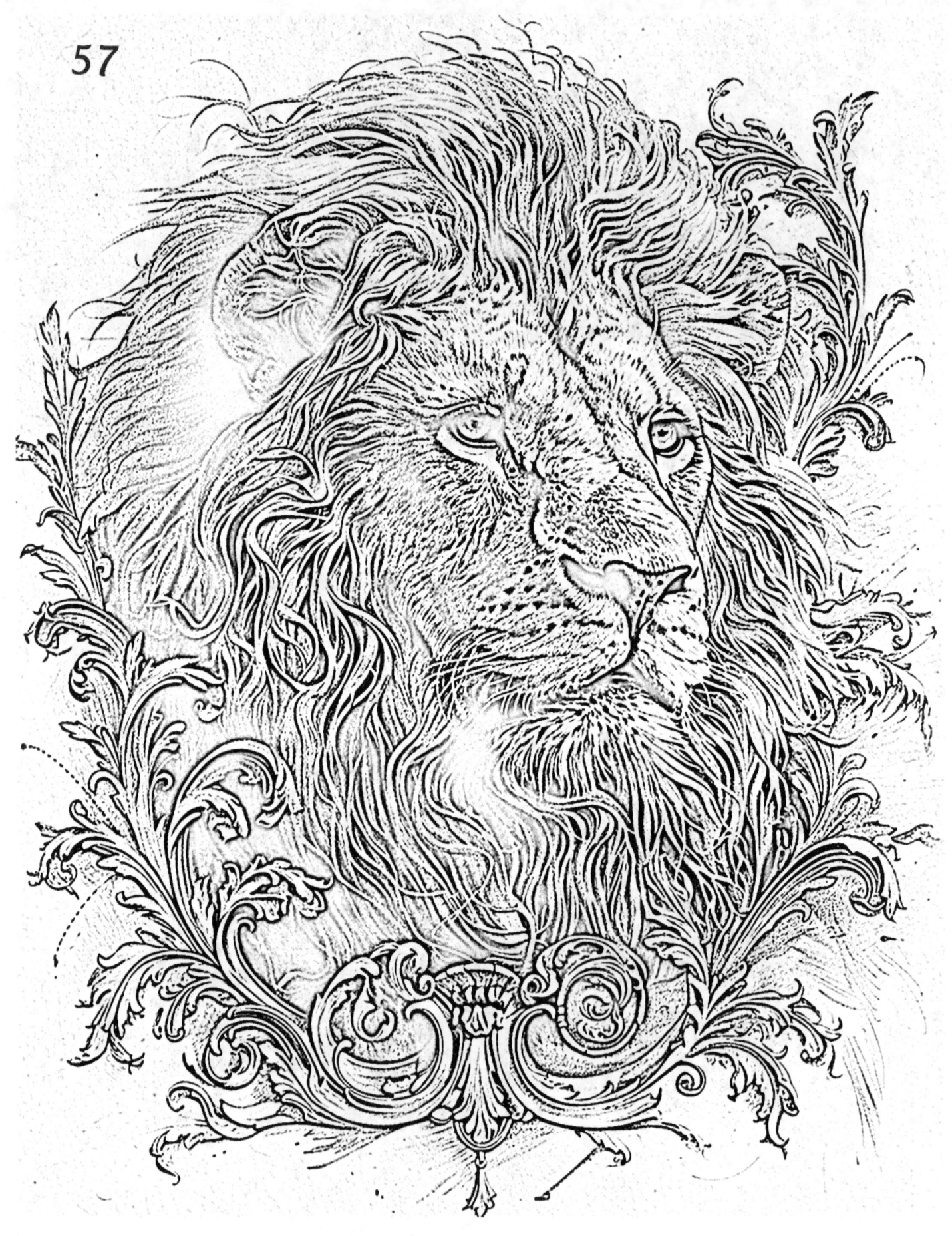

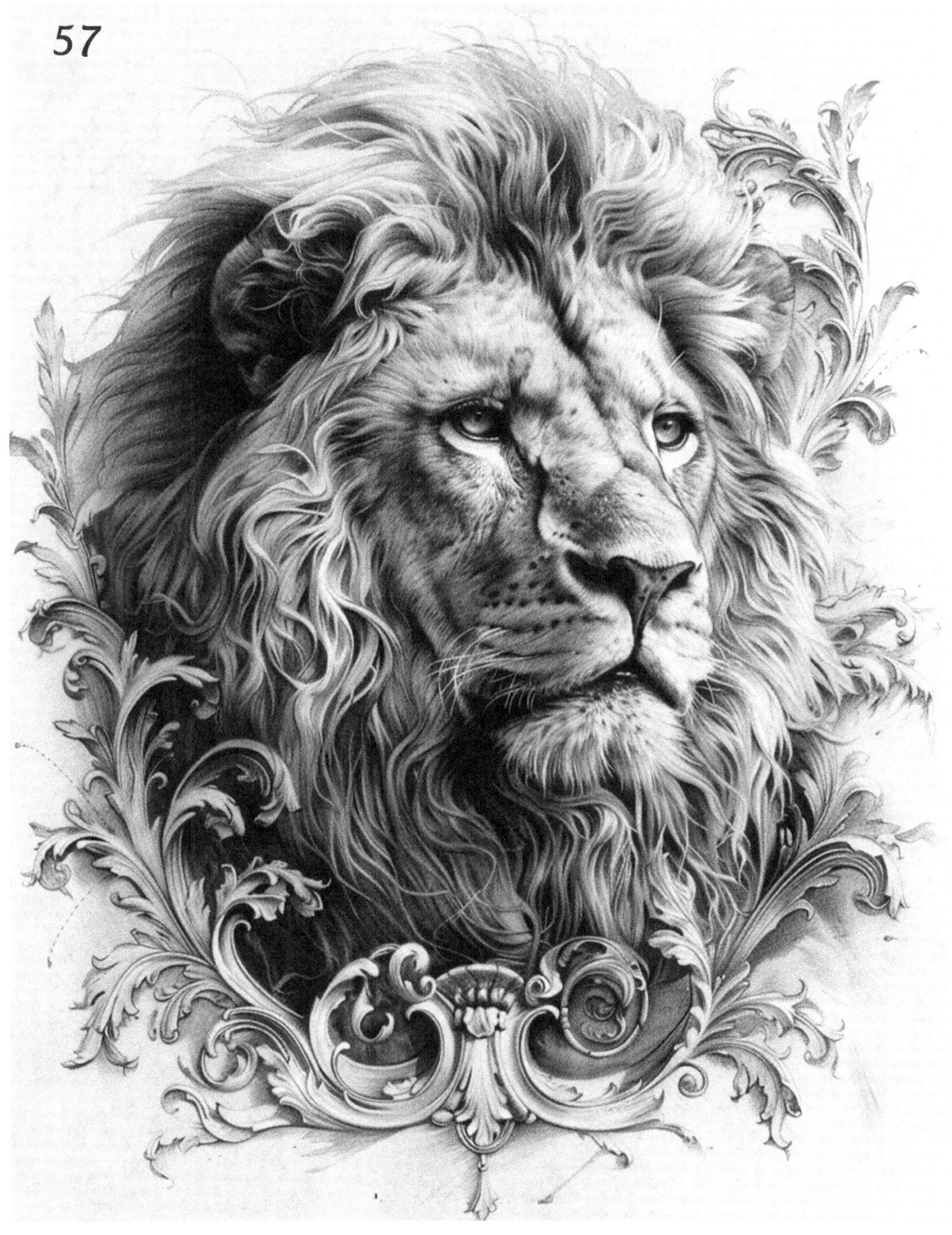

58

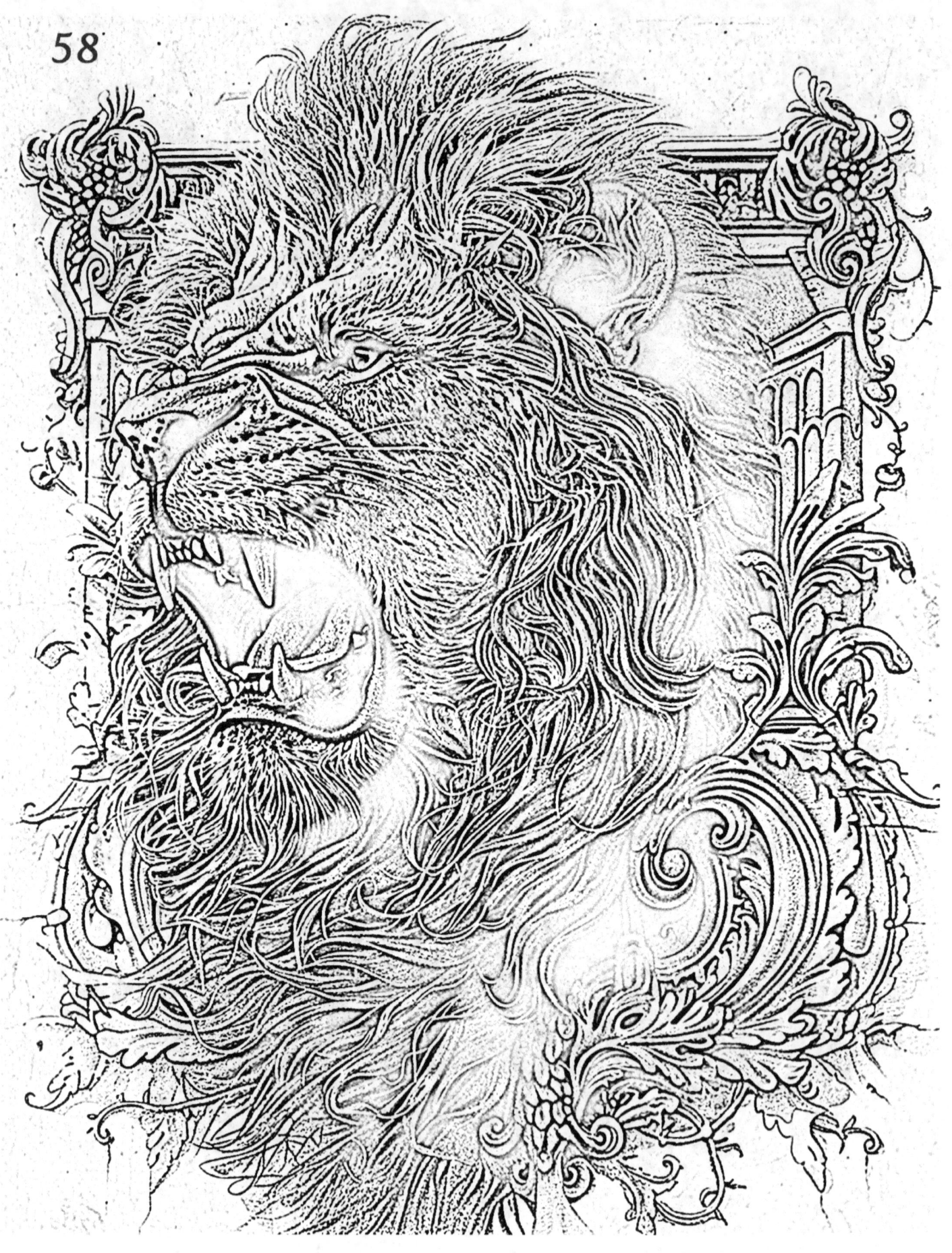

58

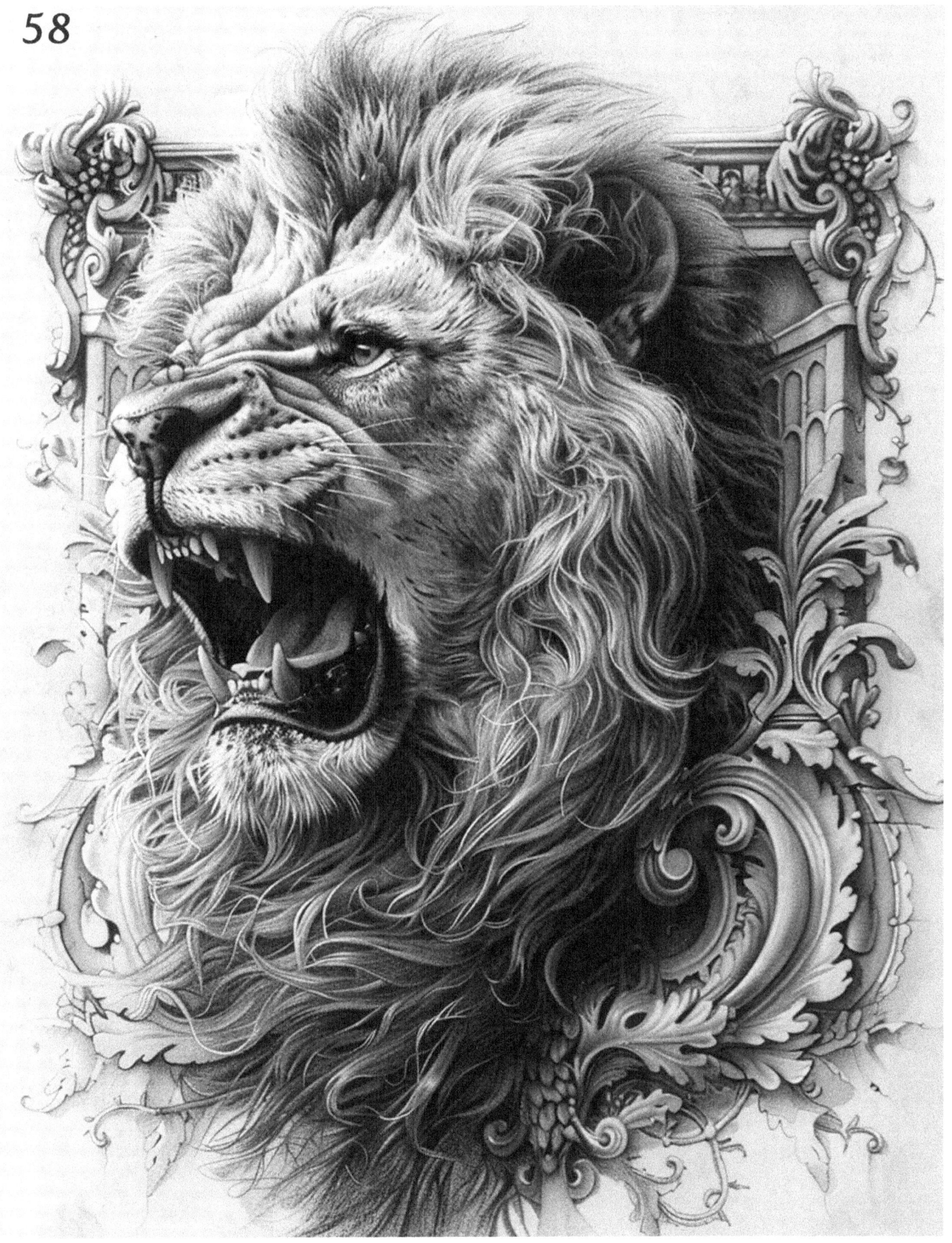

59

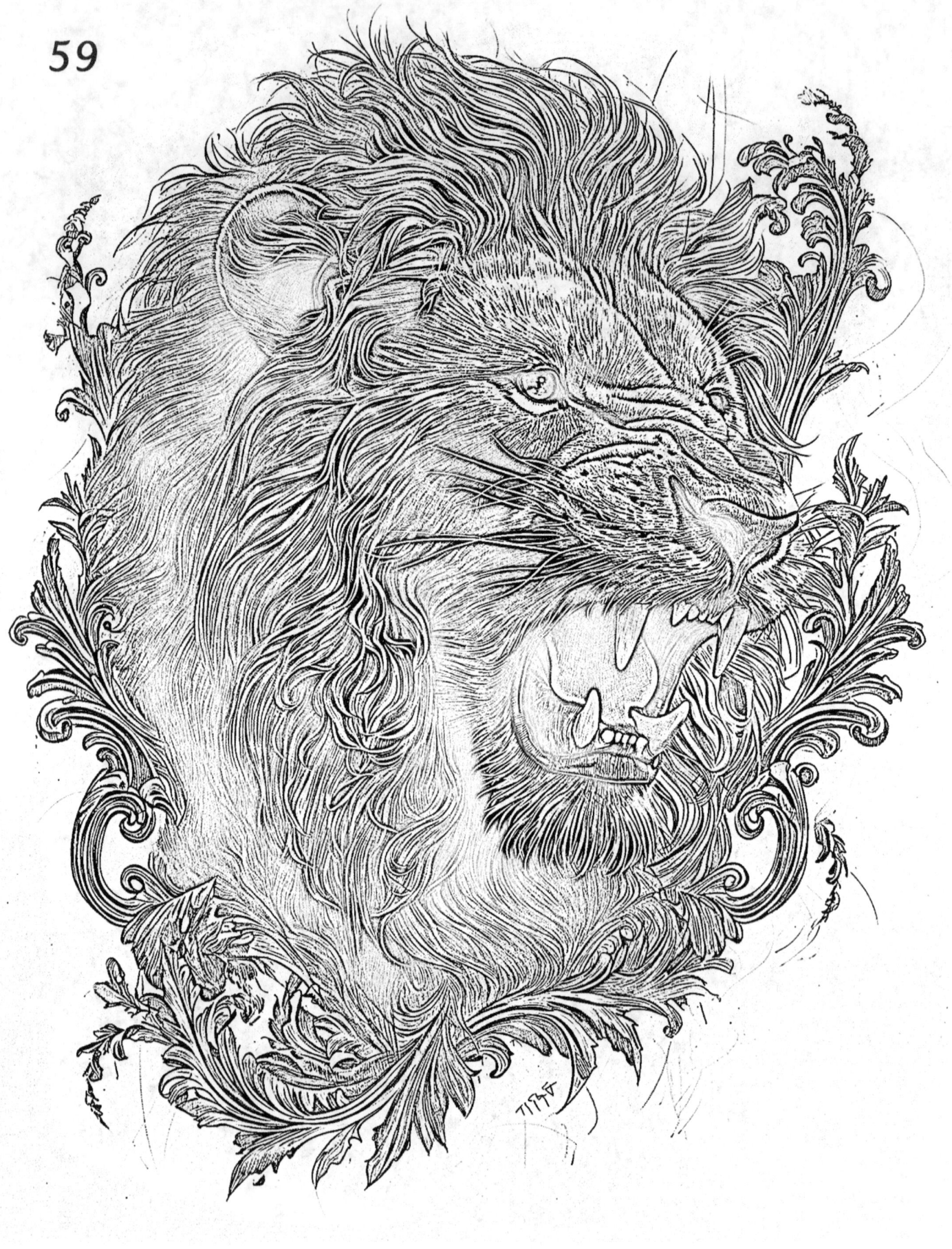

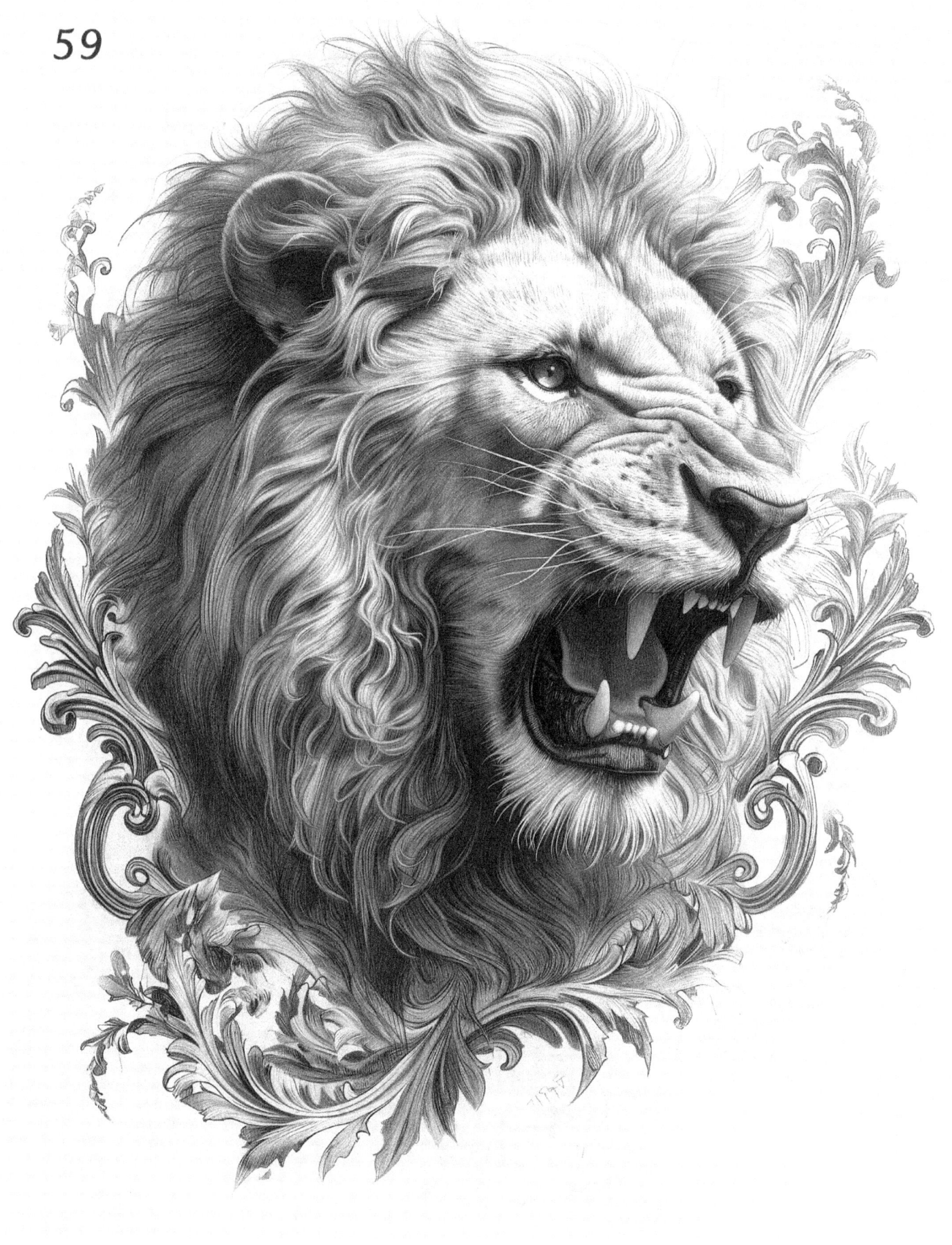

60

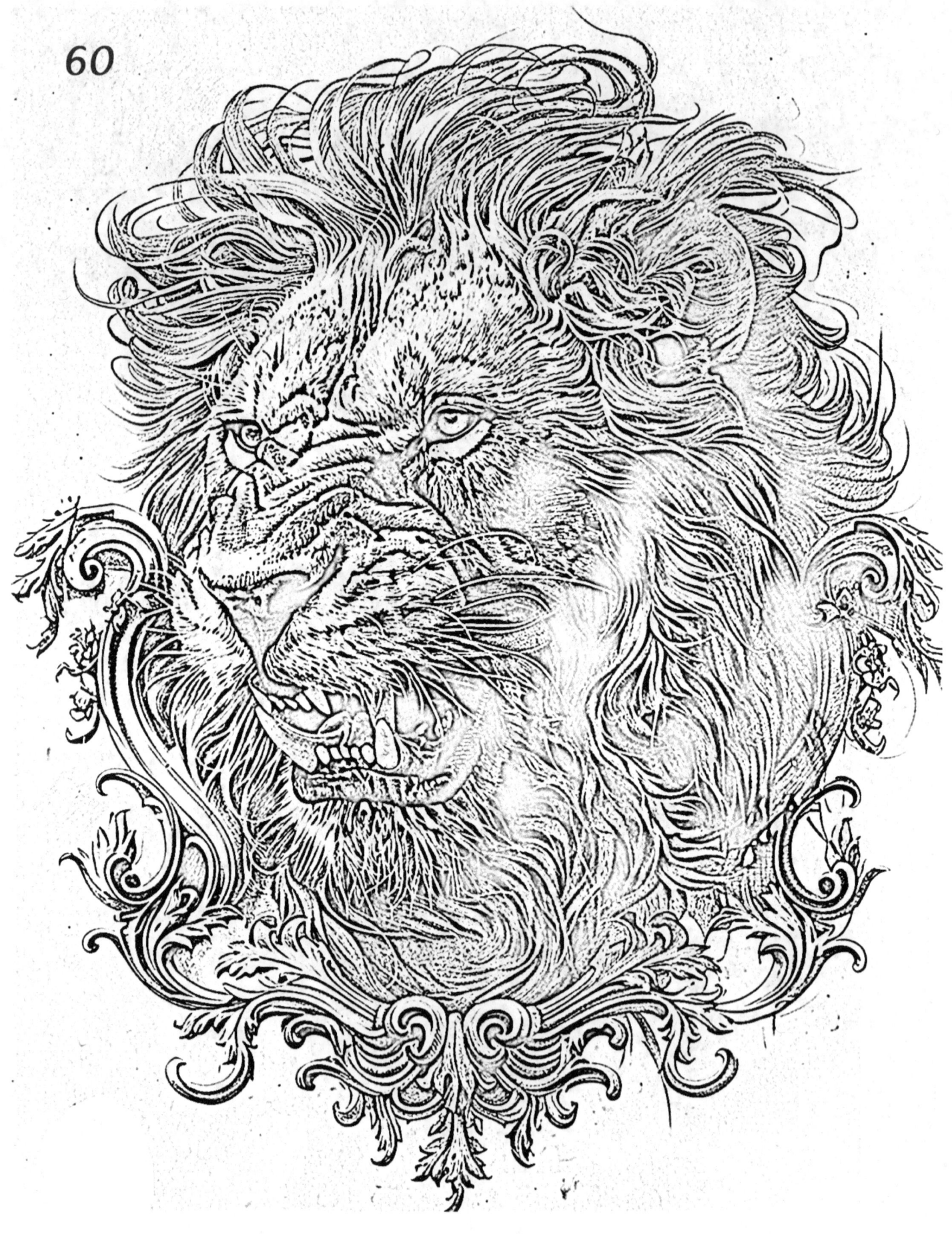

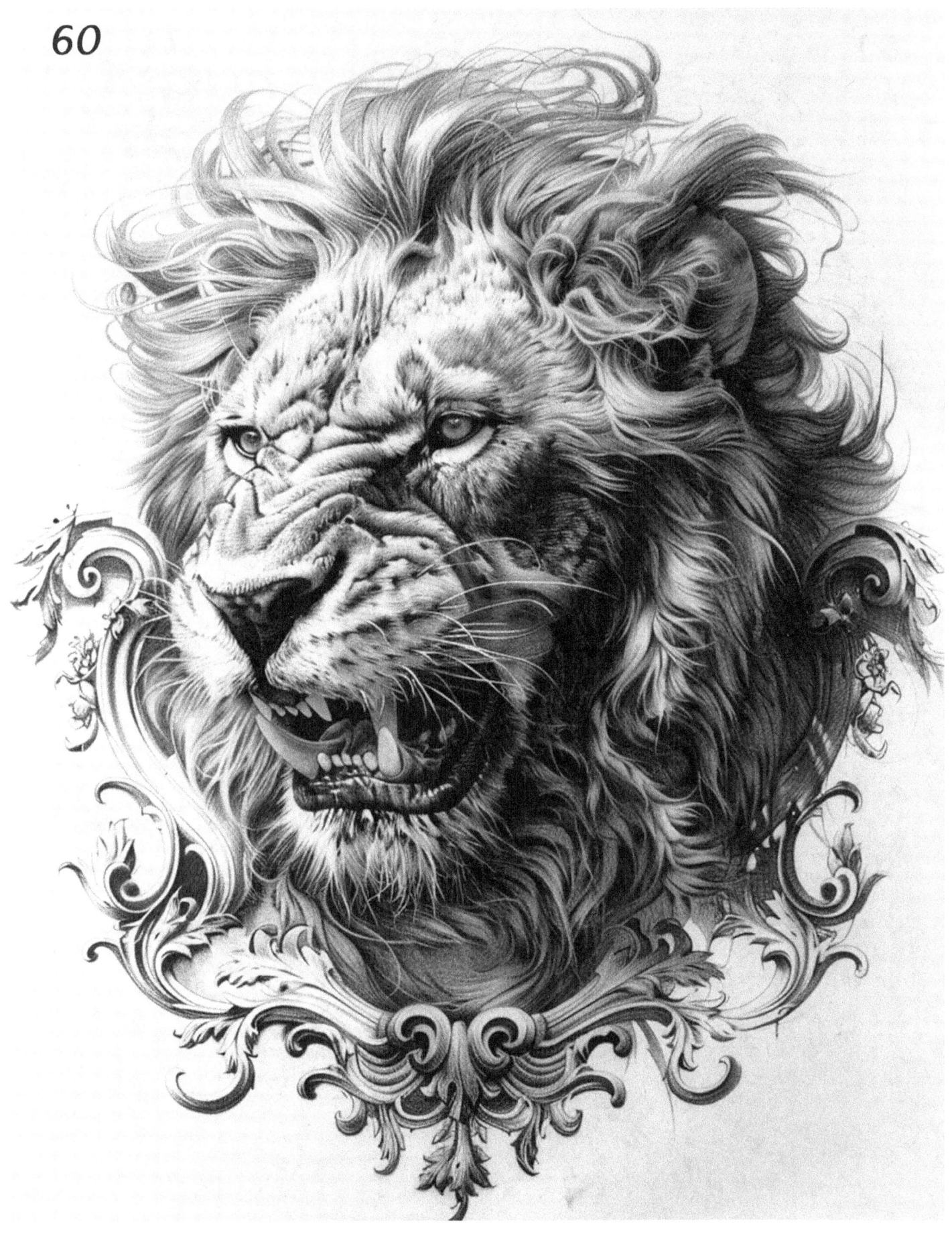

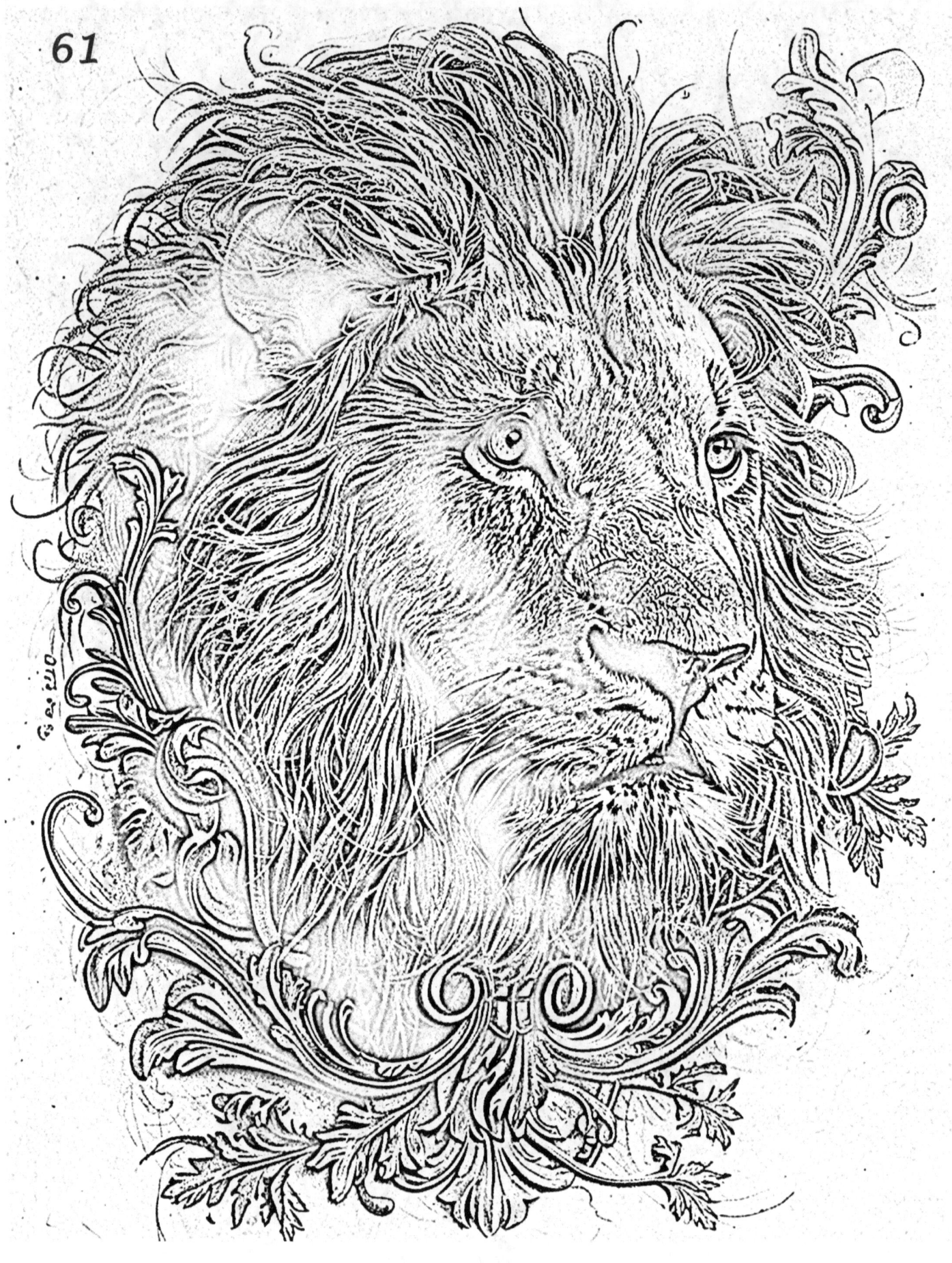

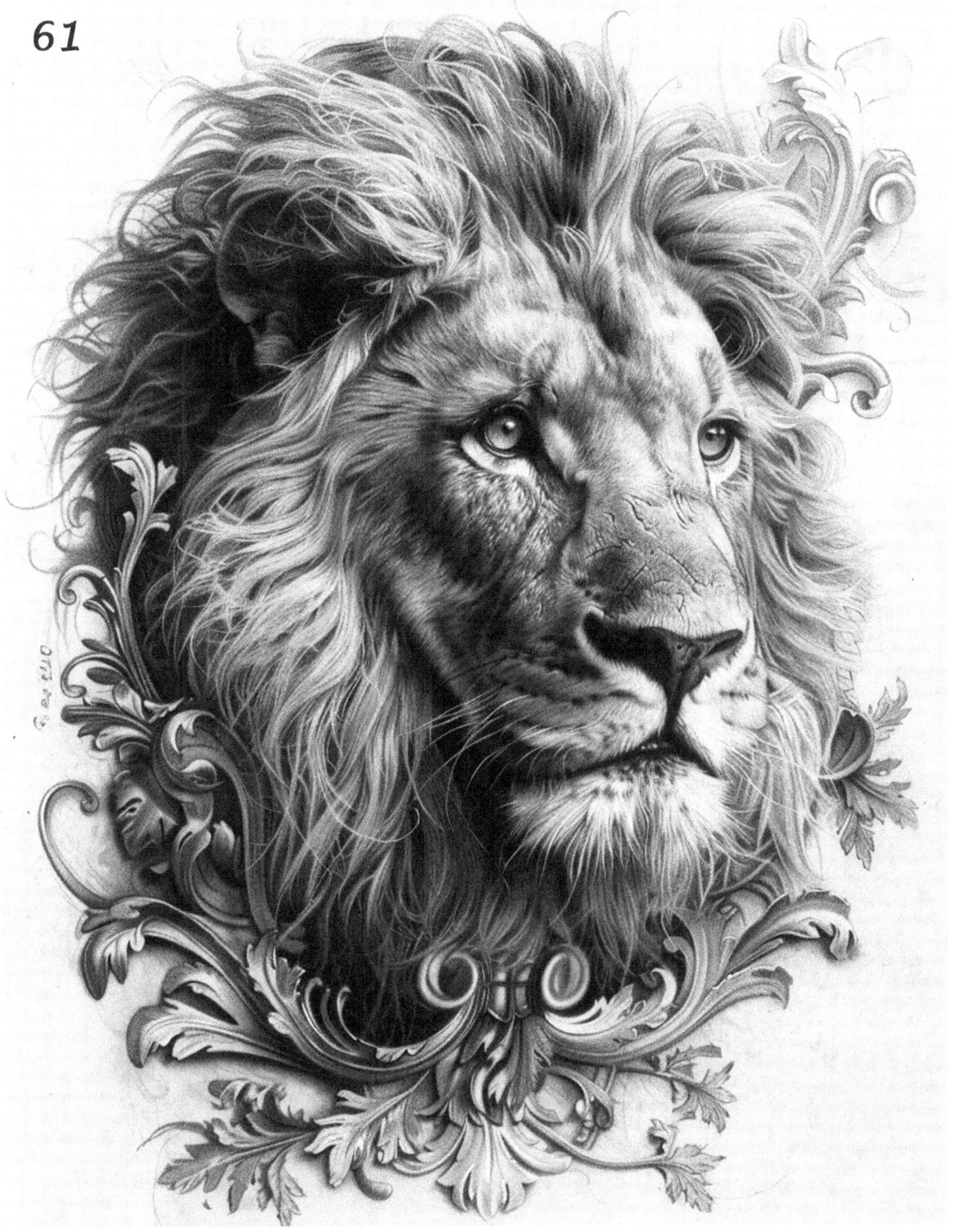

62

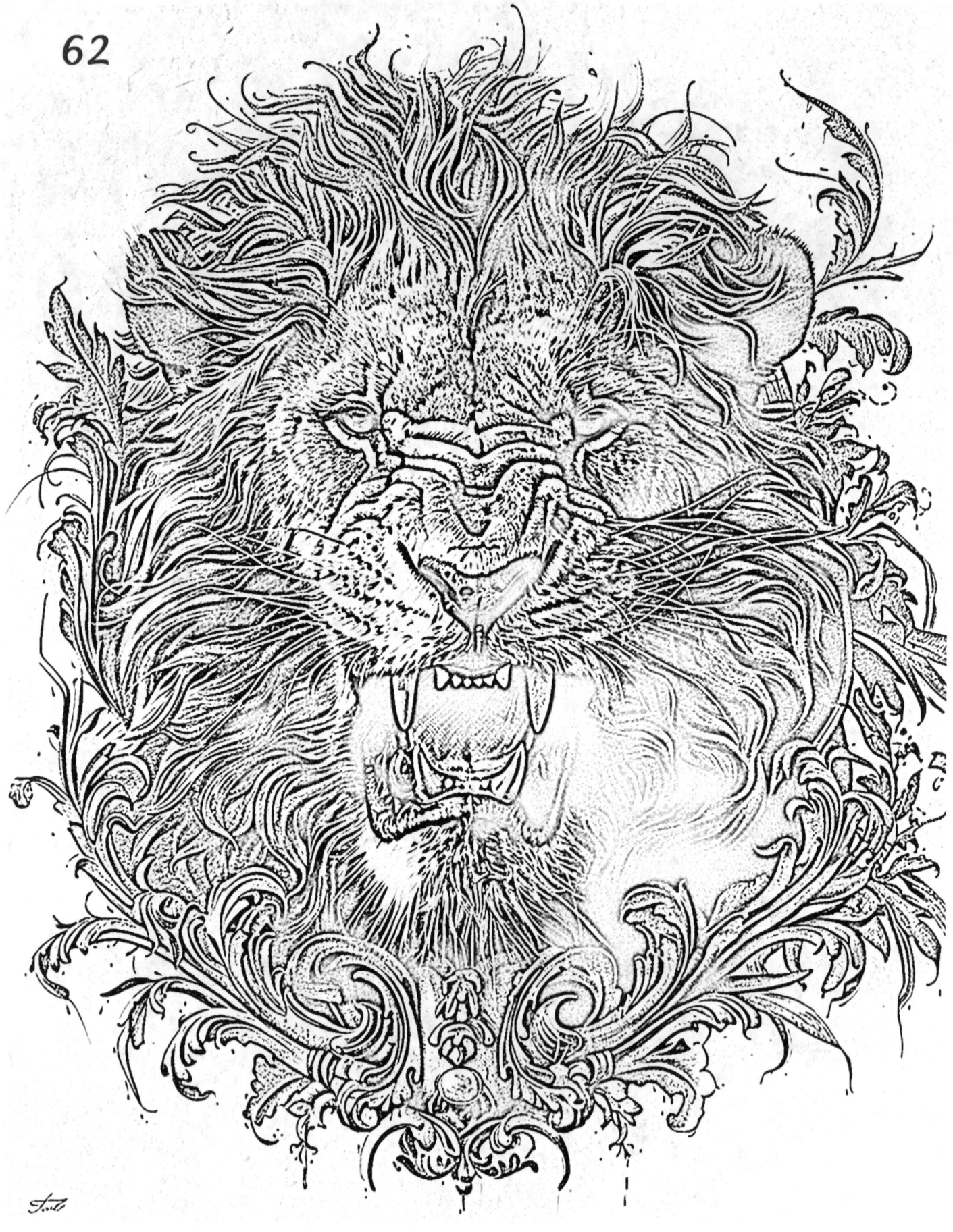

62

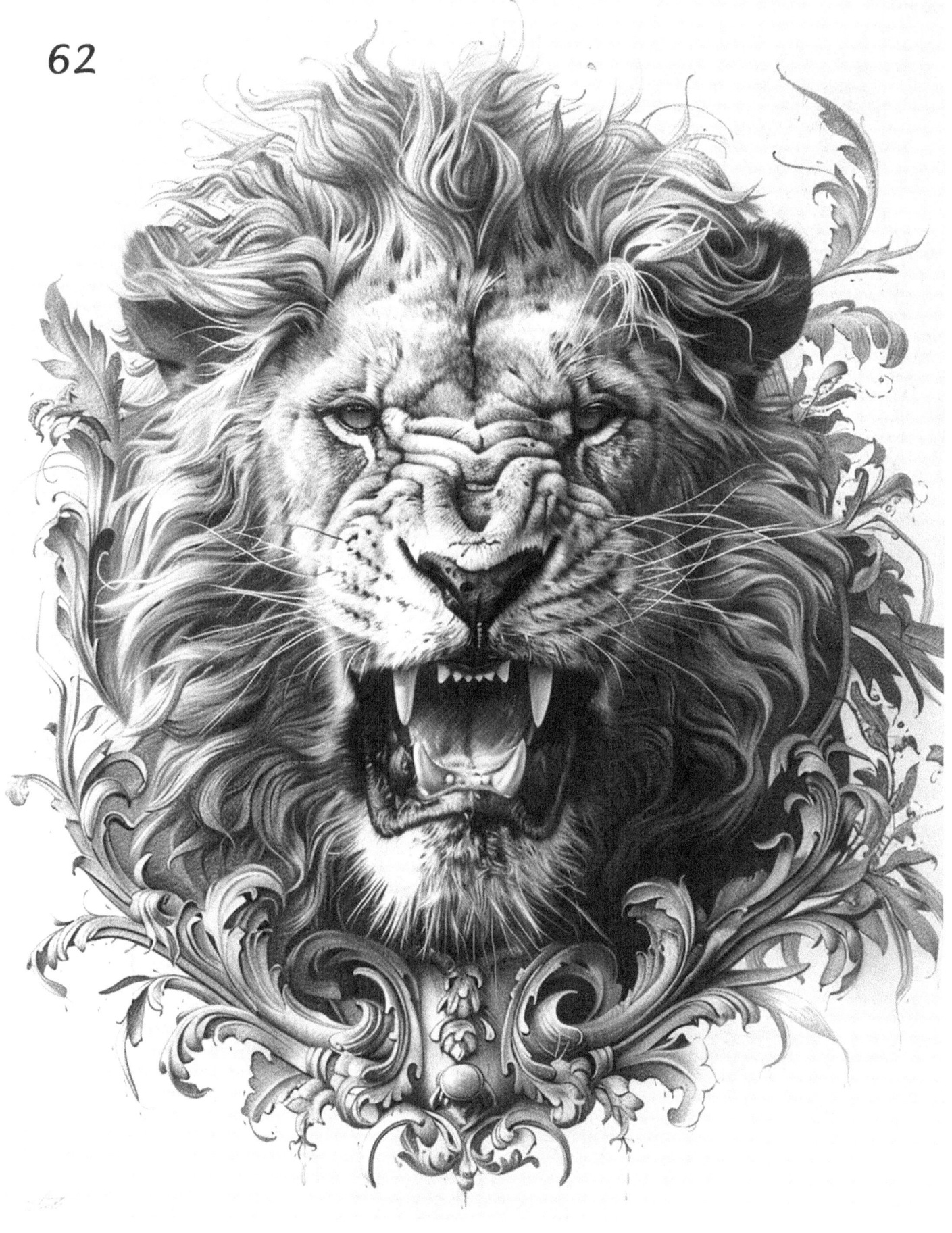

63

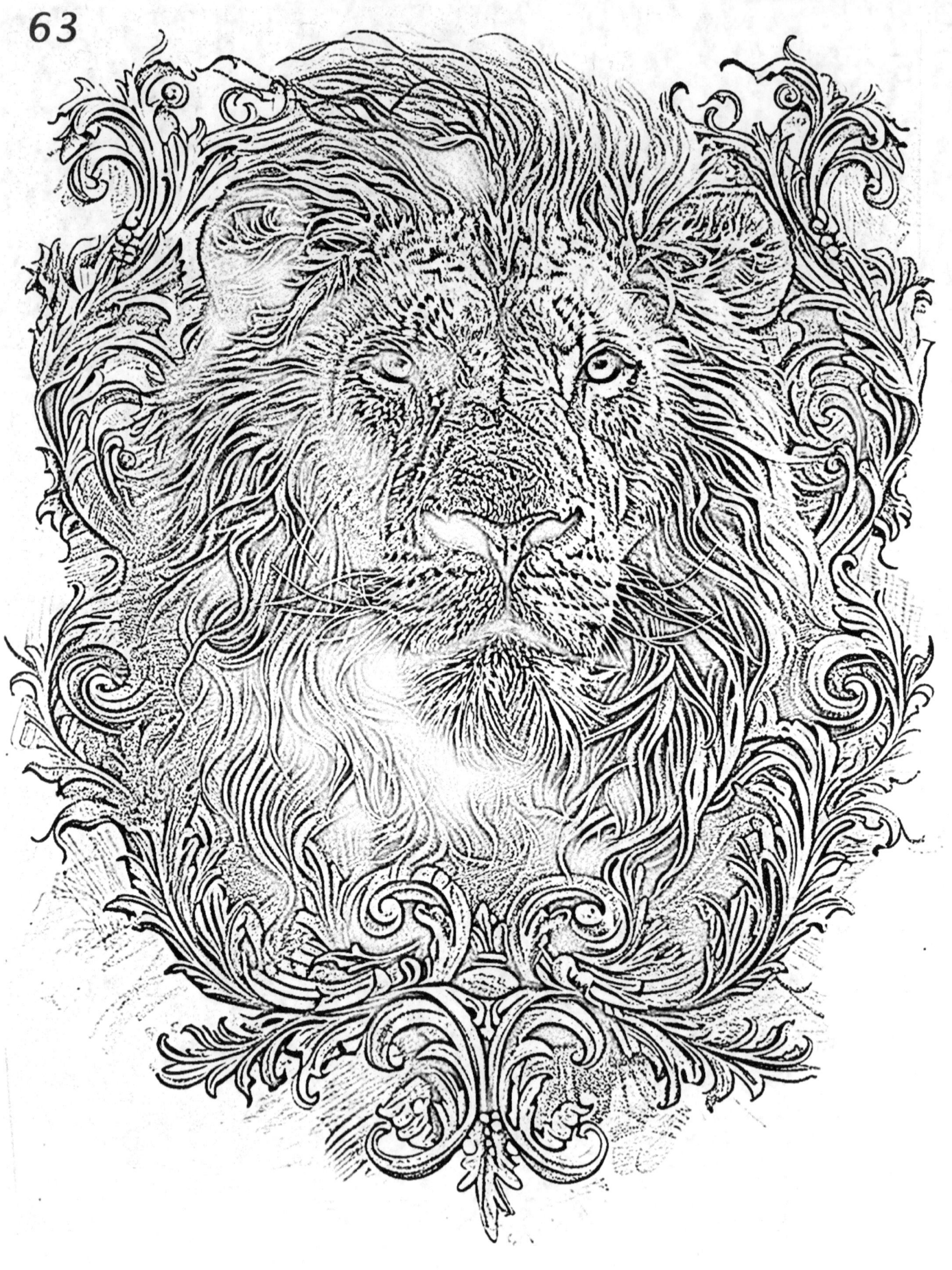

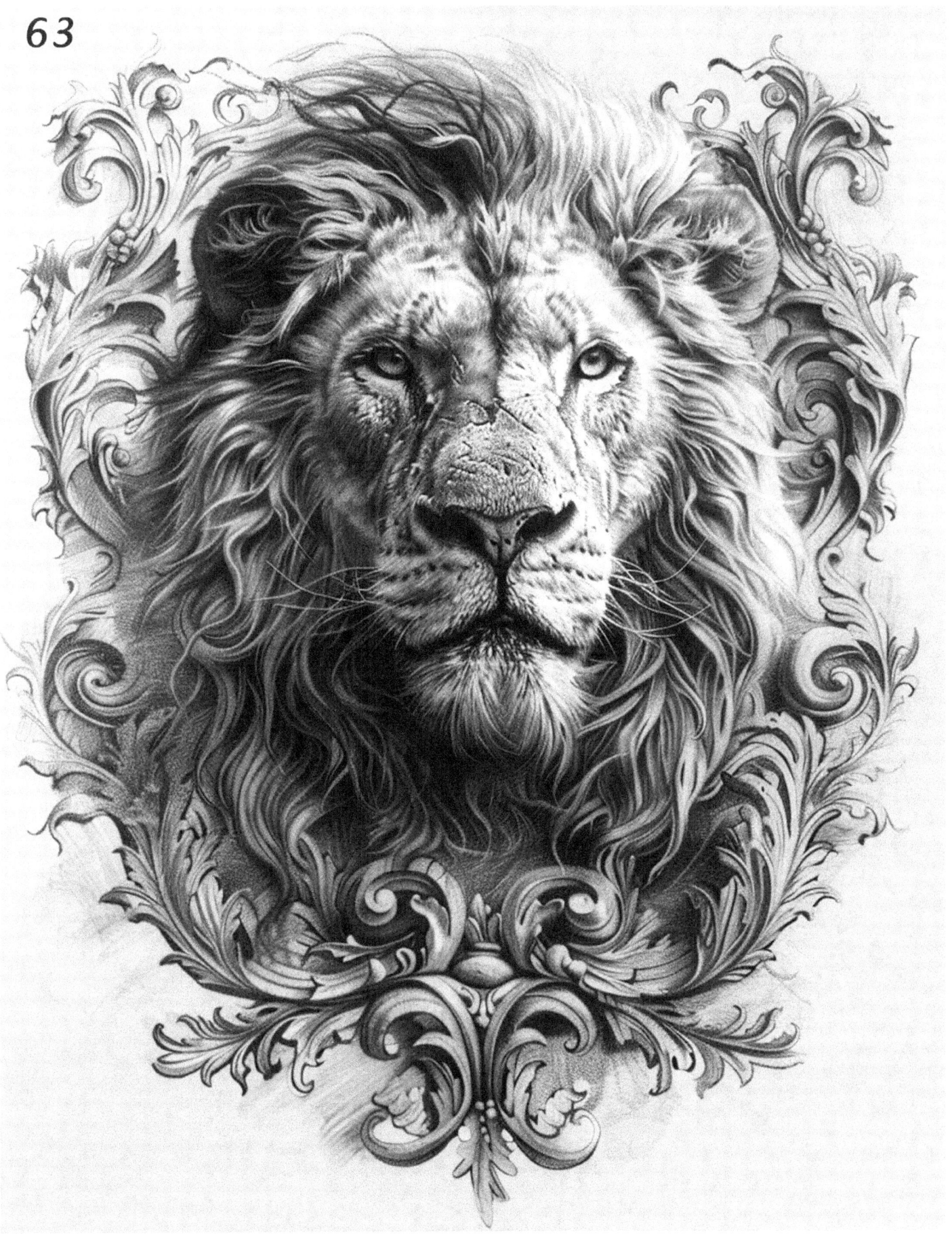

64

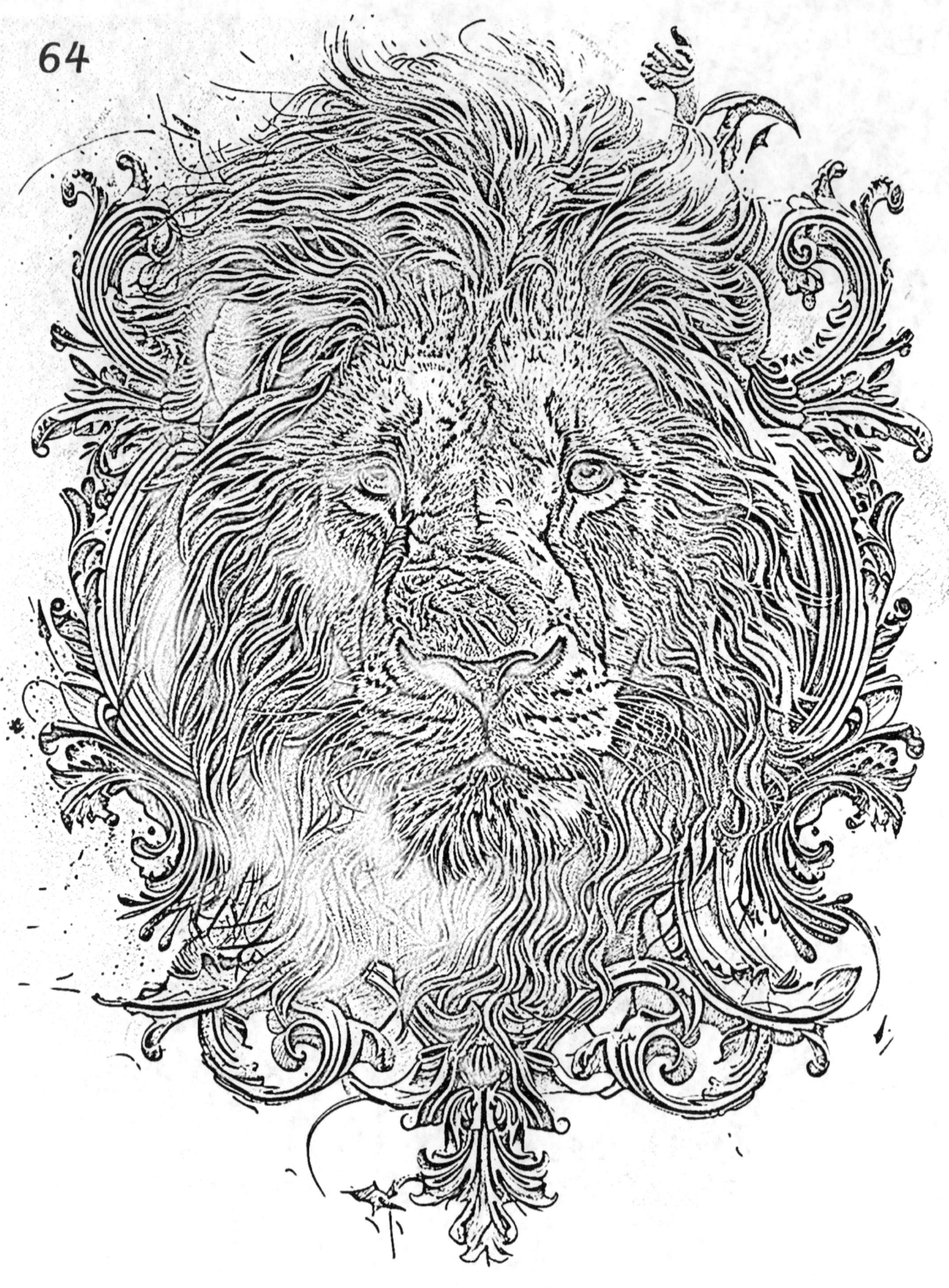

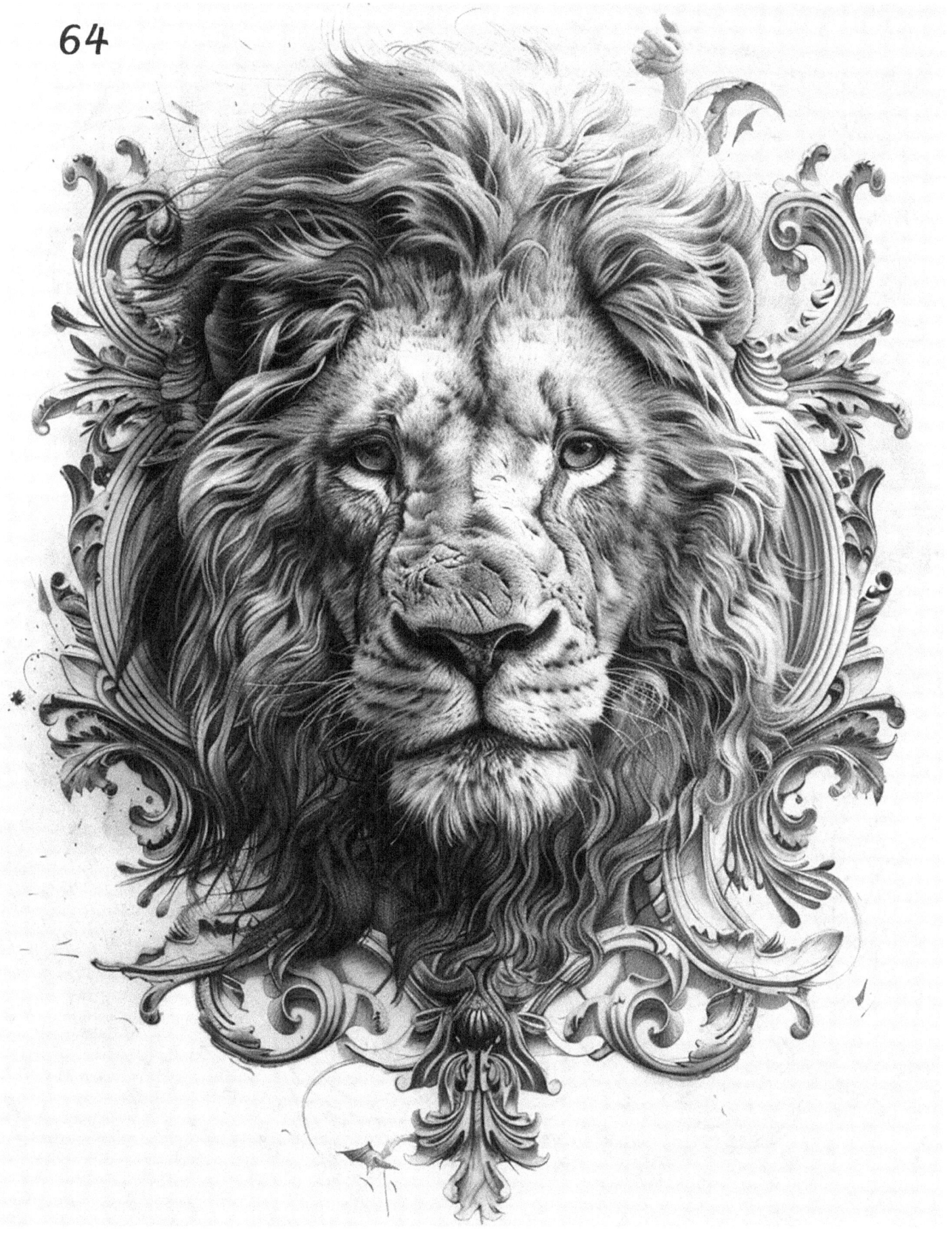

65

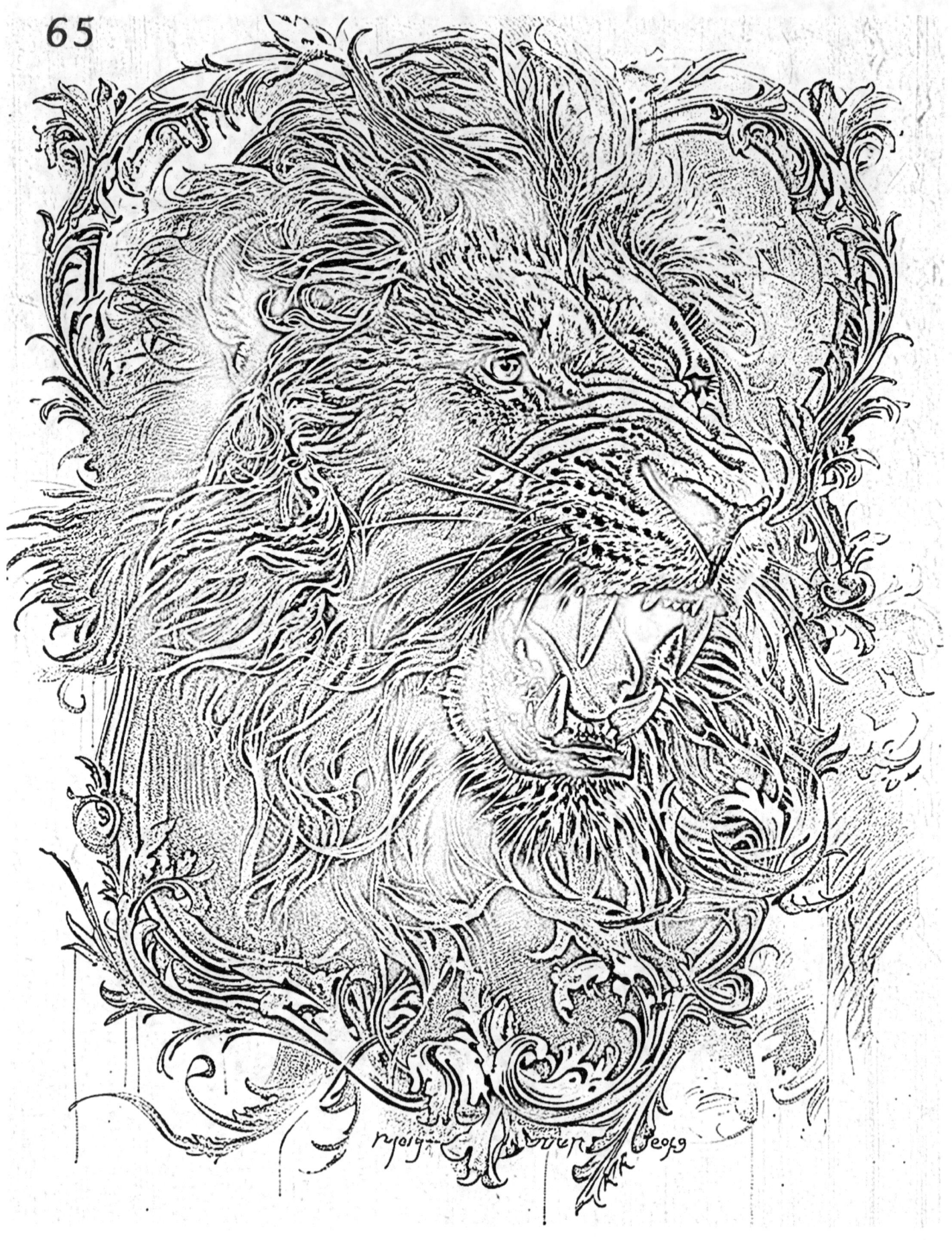

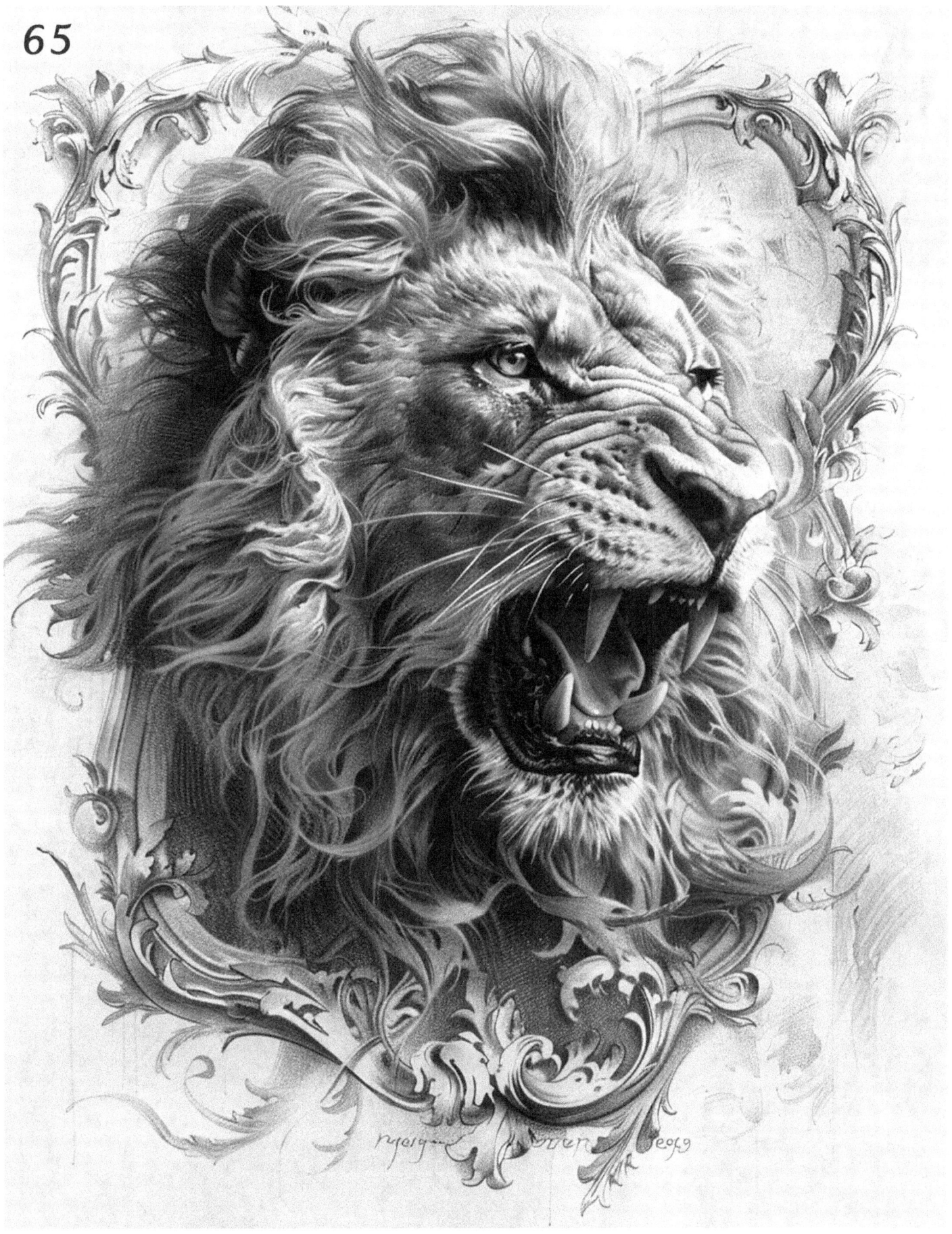

66

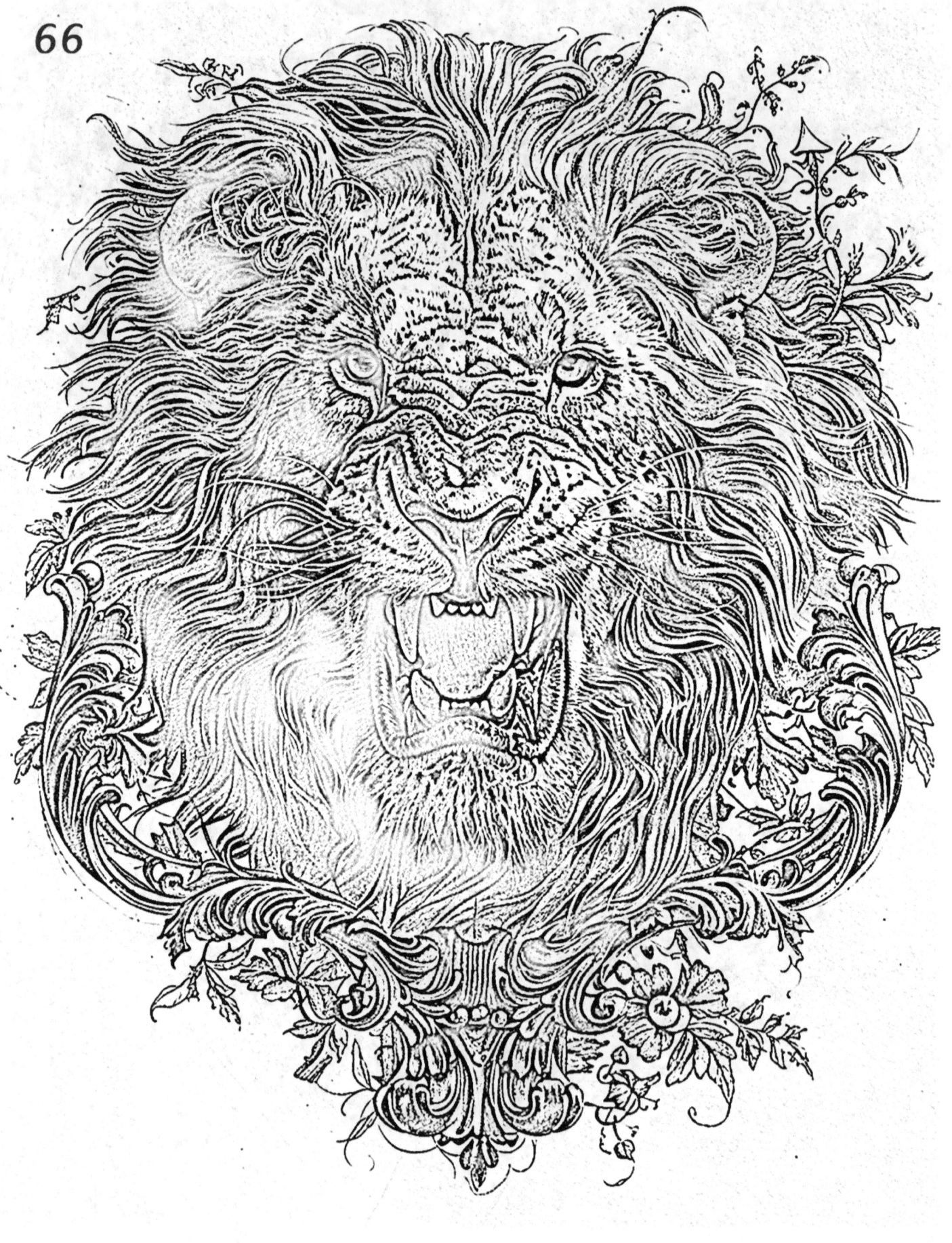

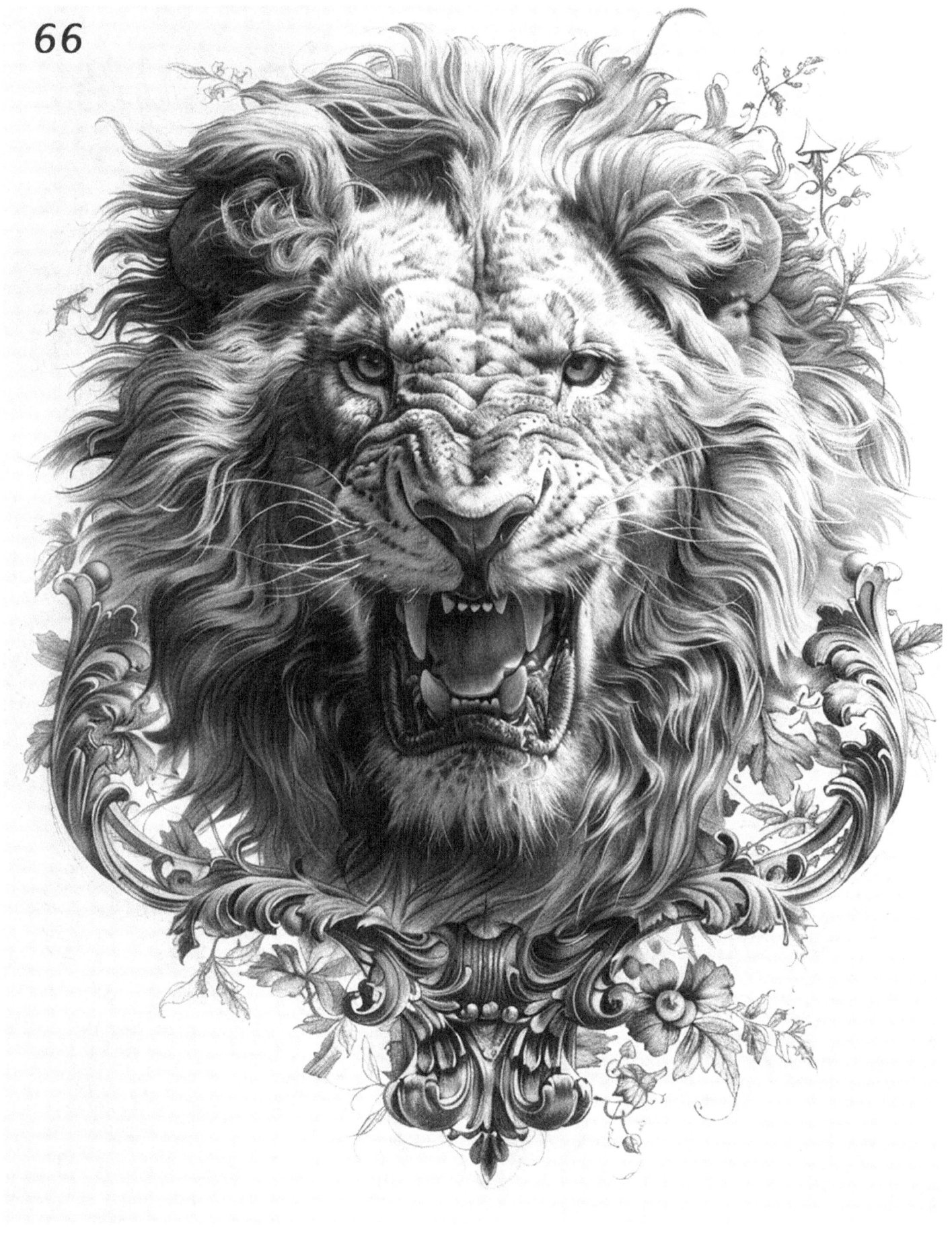

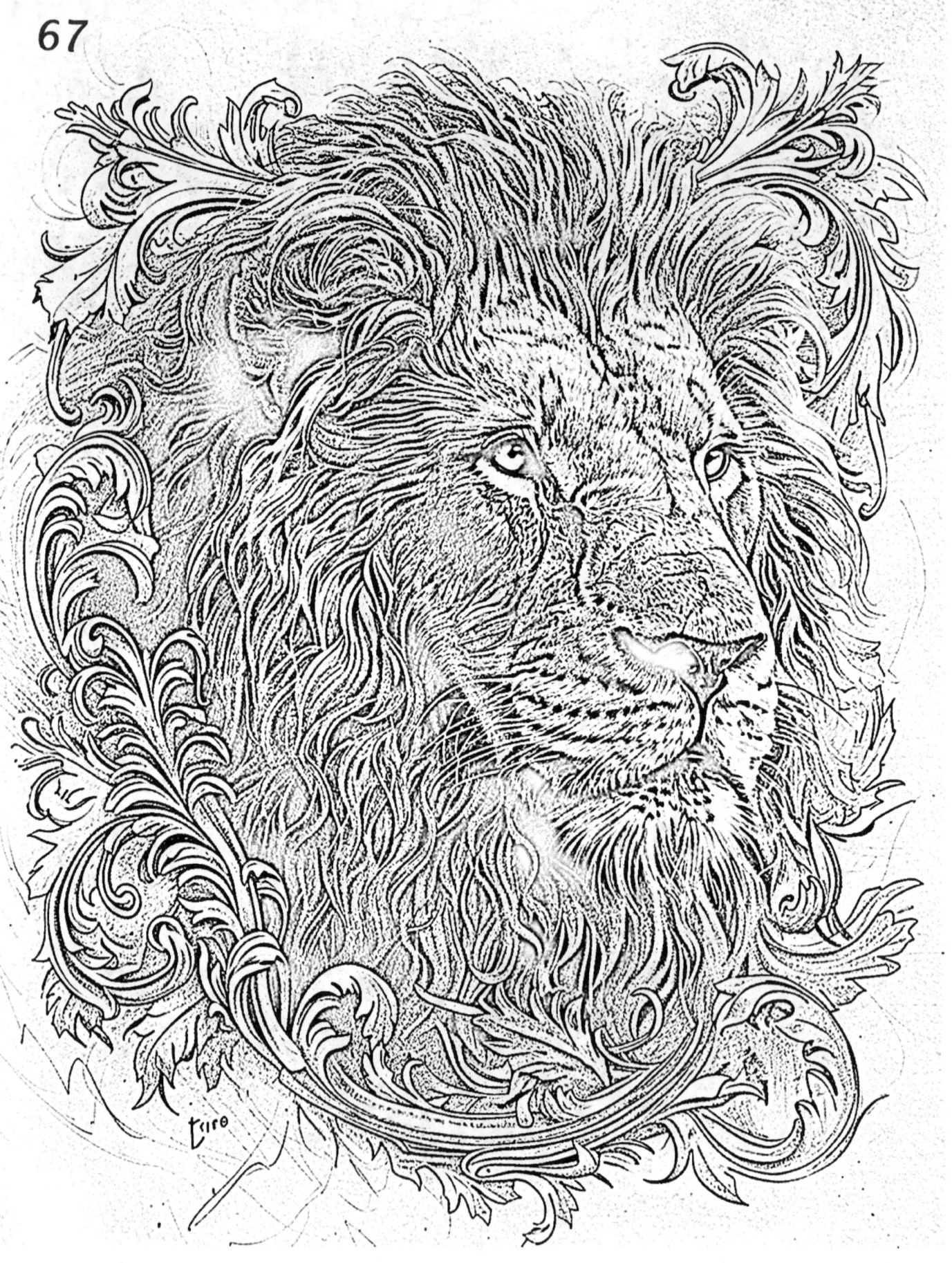

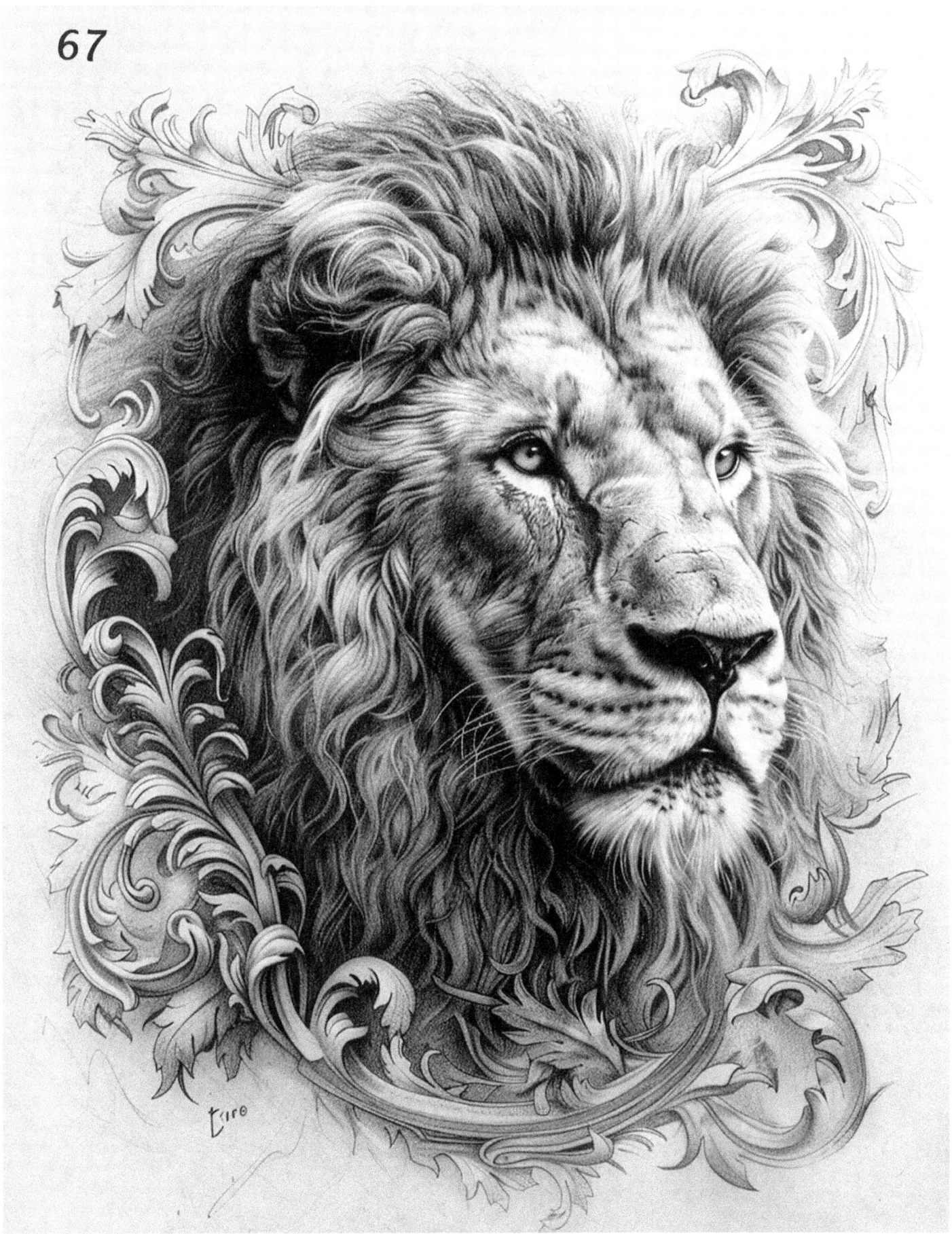

68

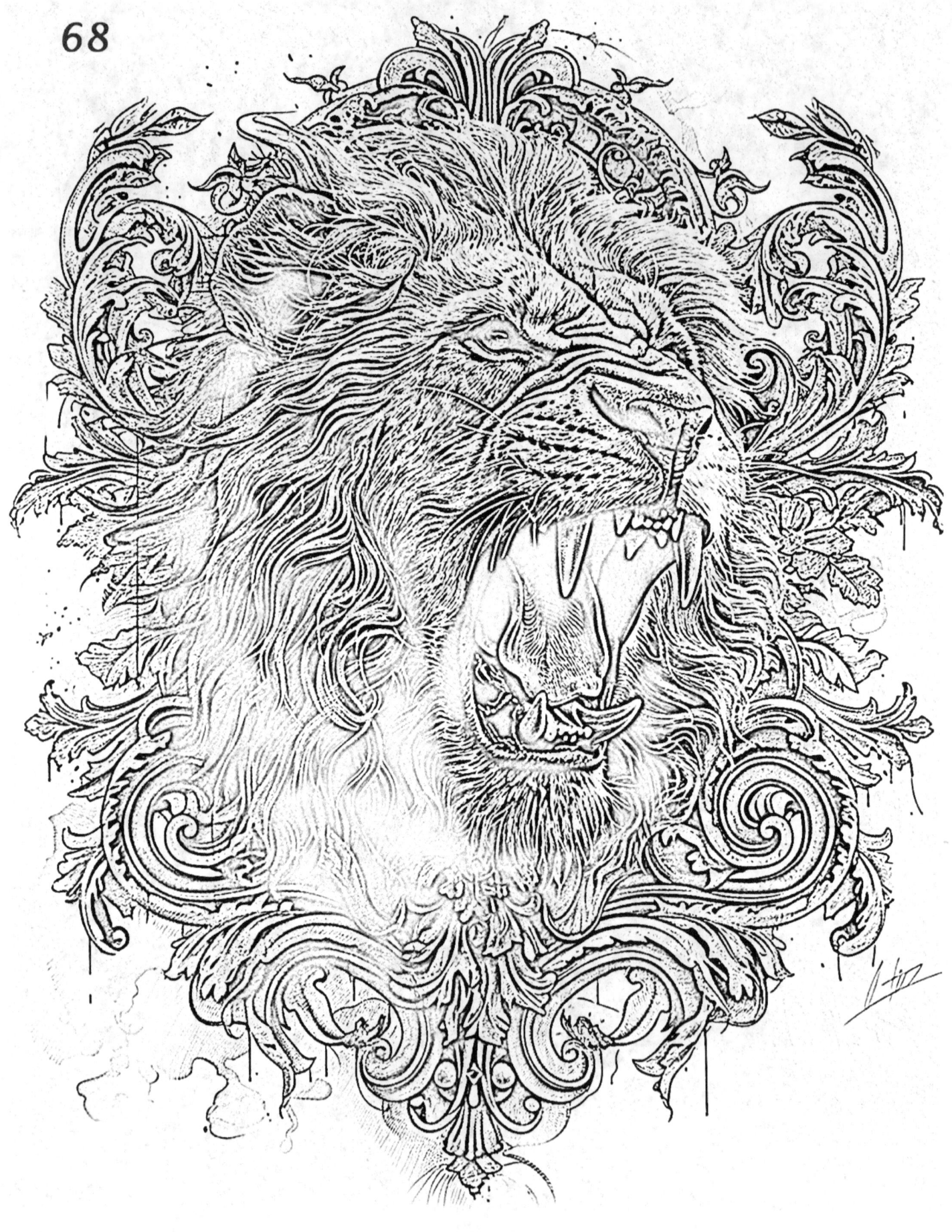

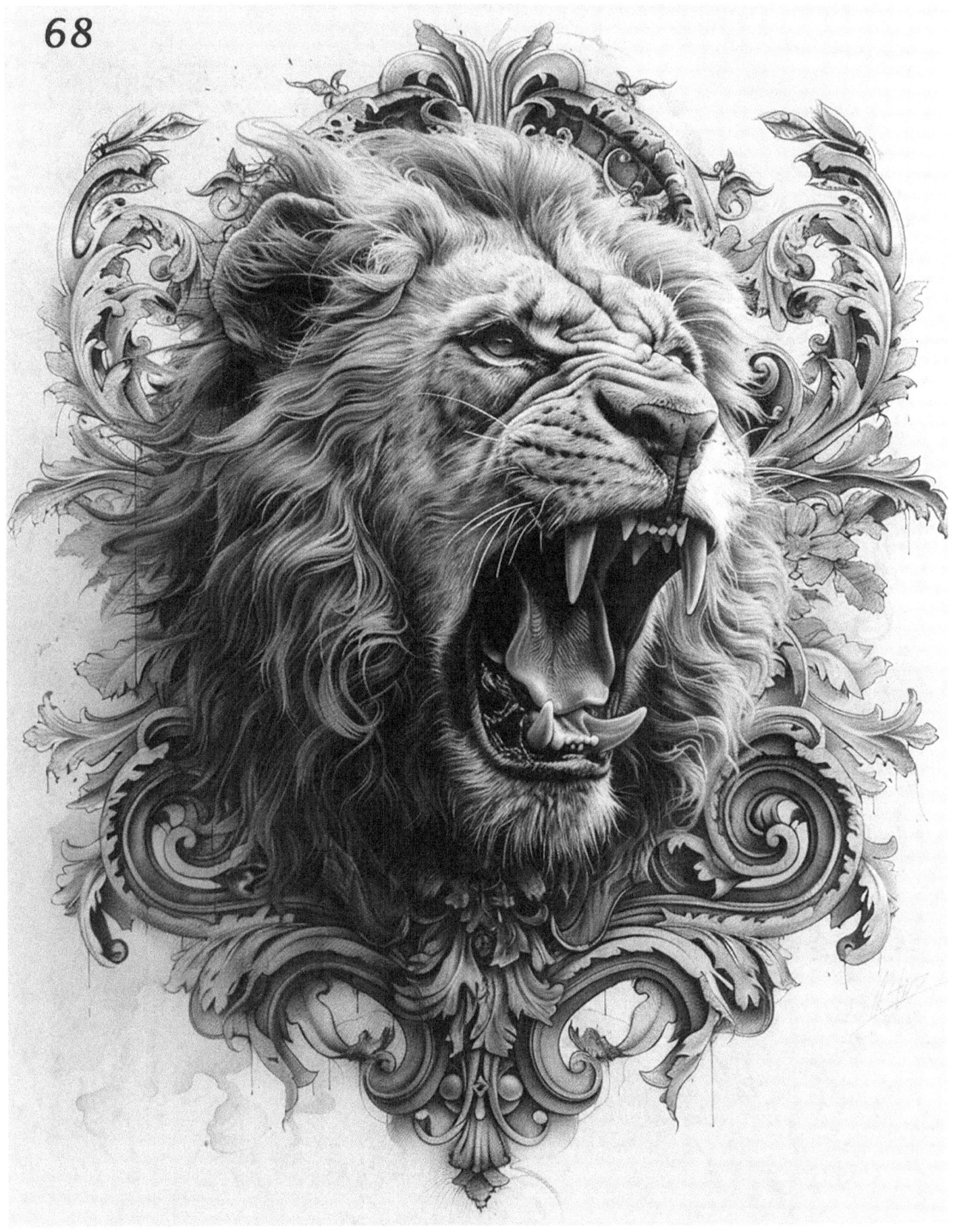

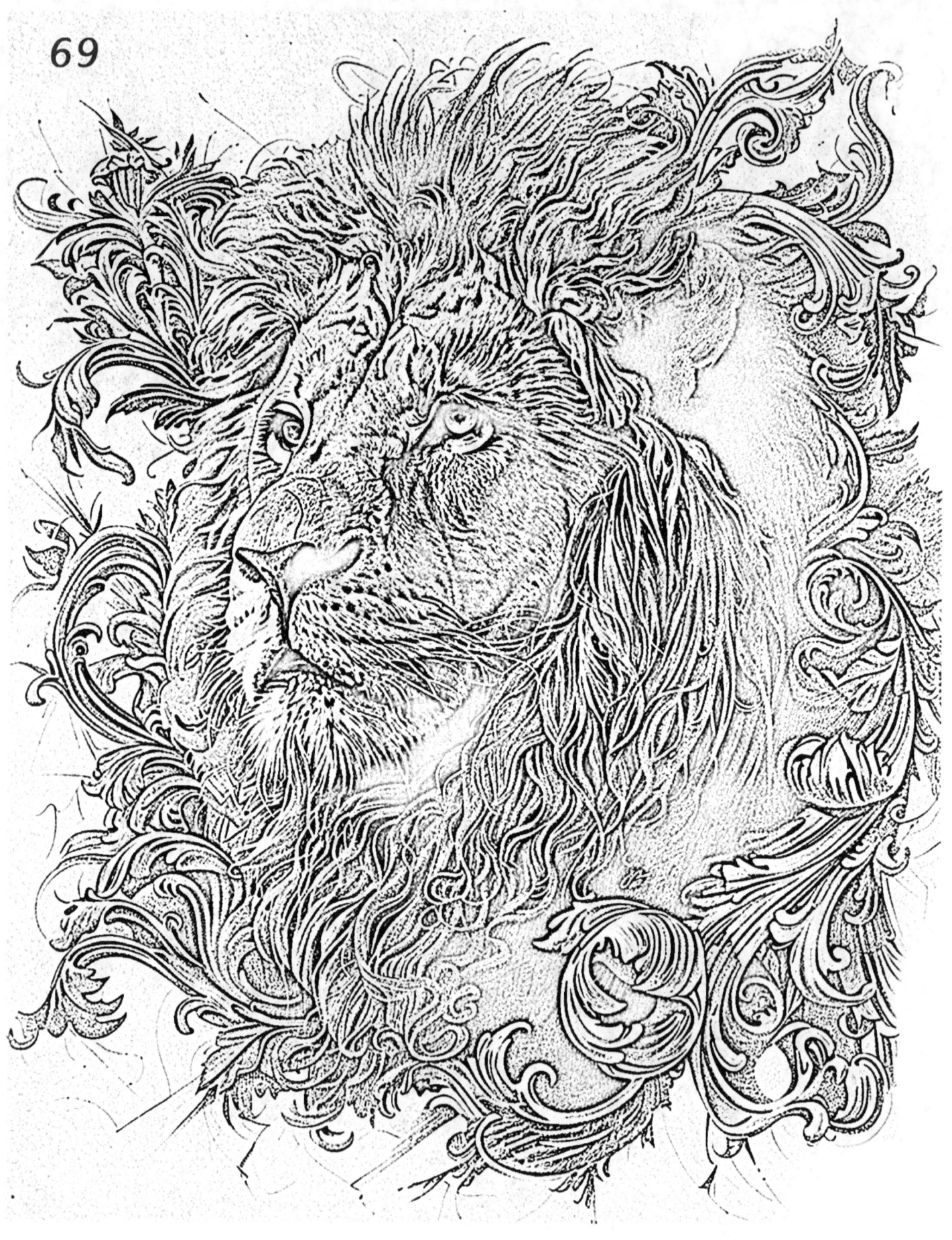

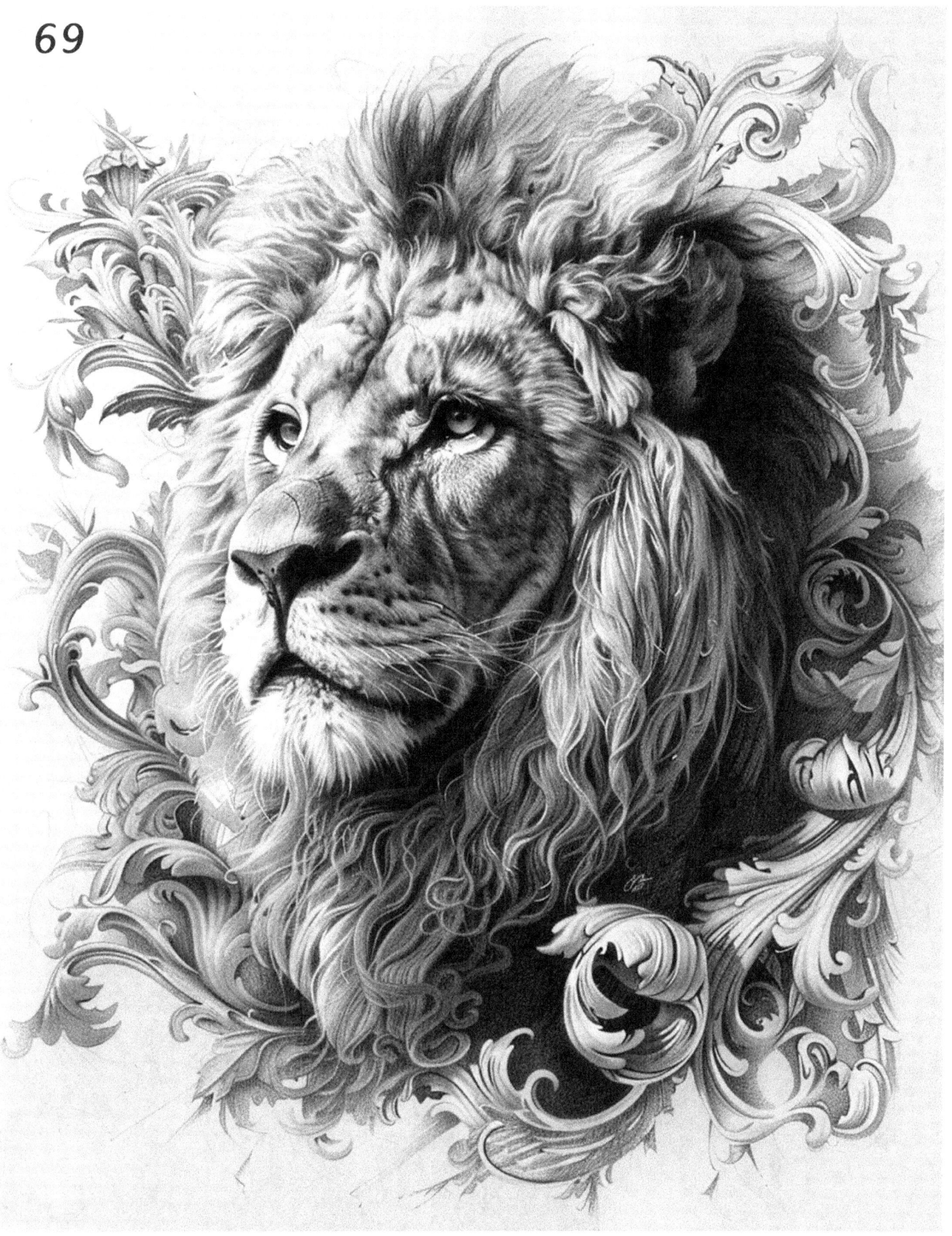

70.

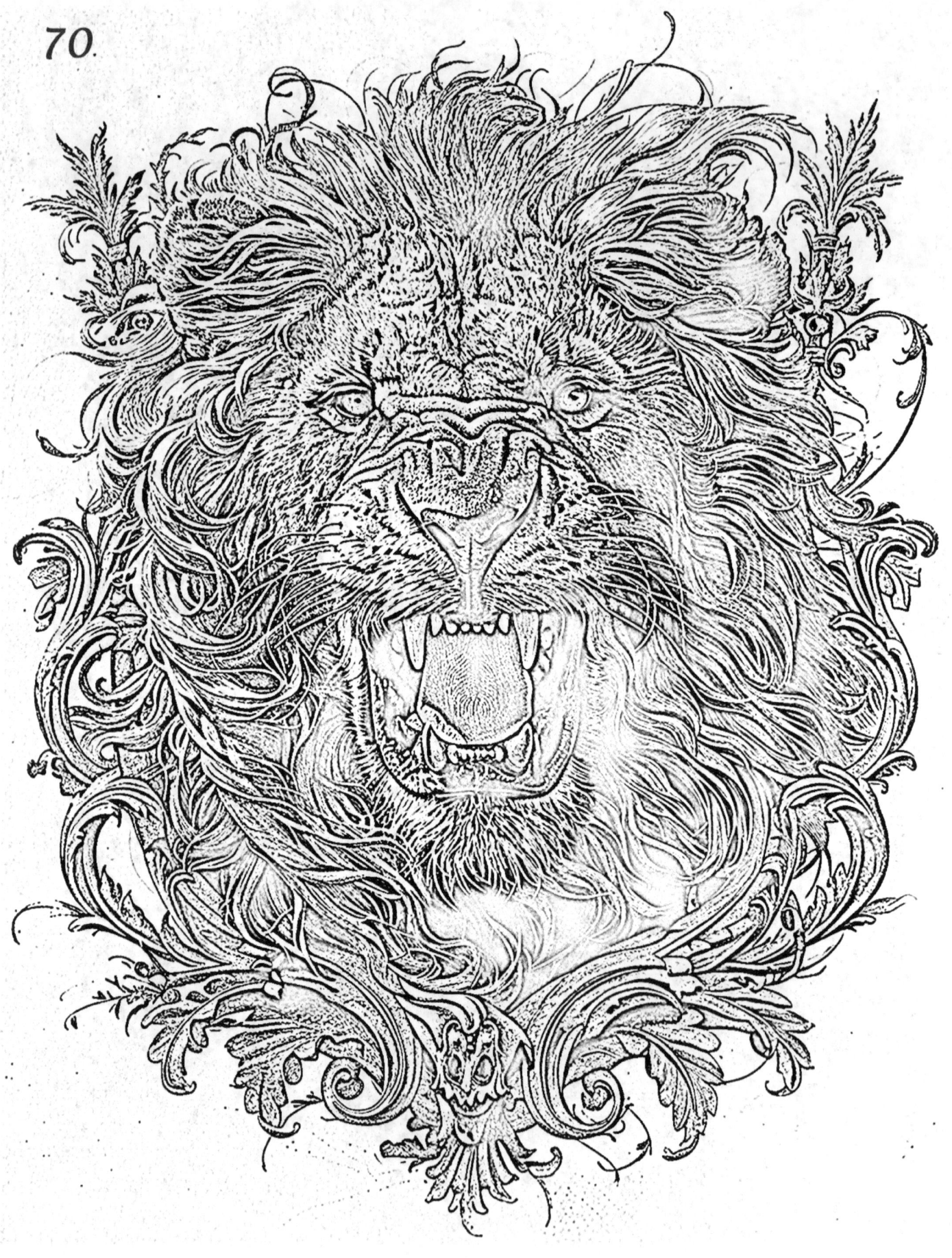

70

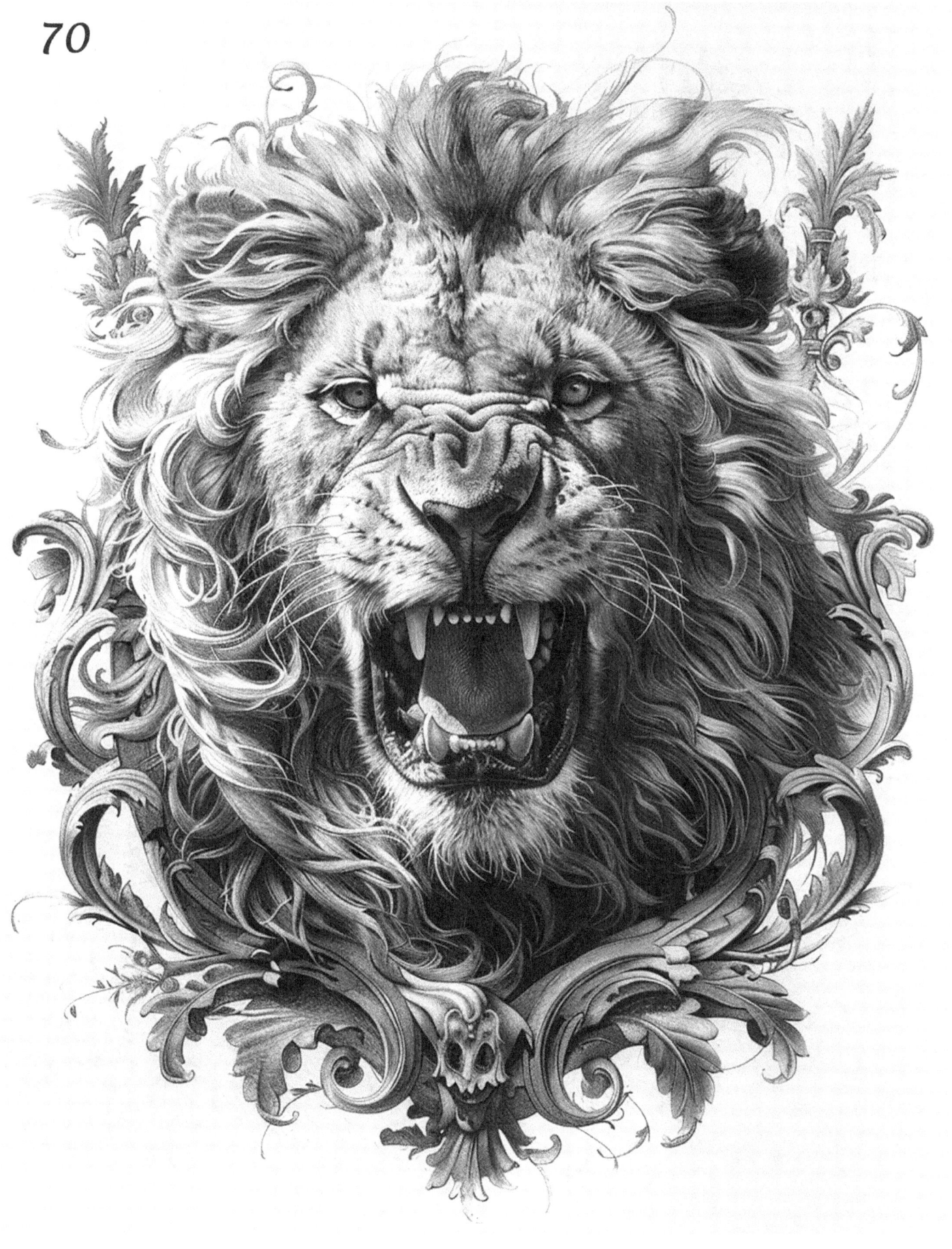

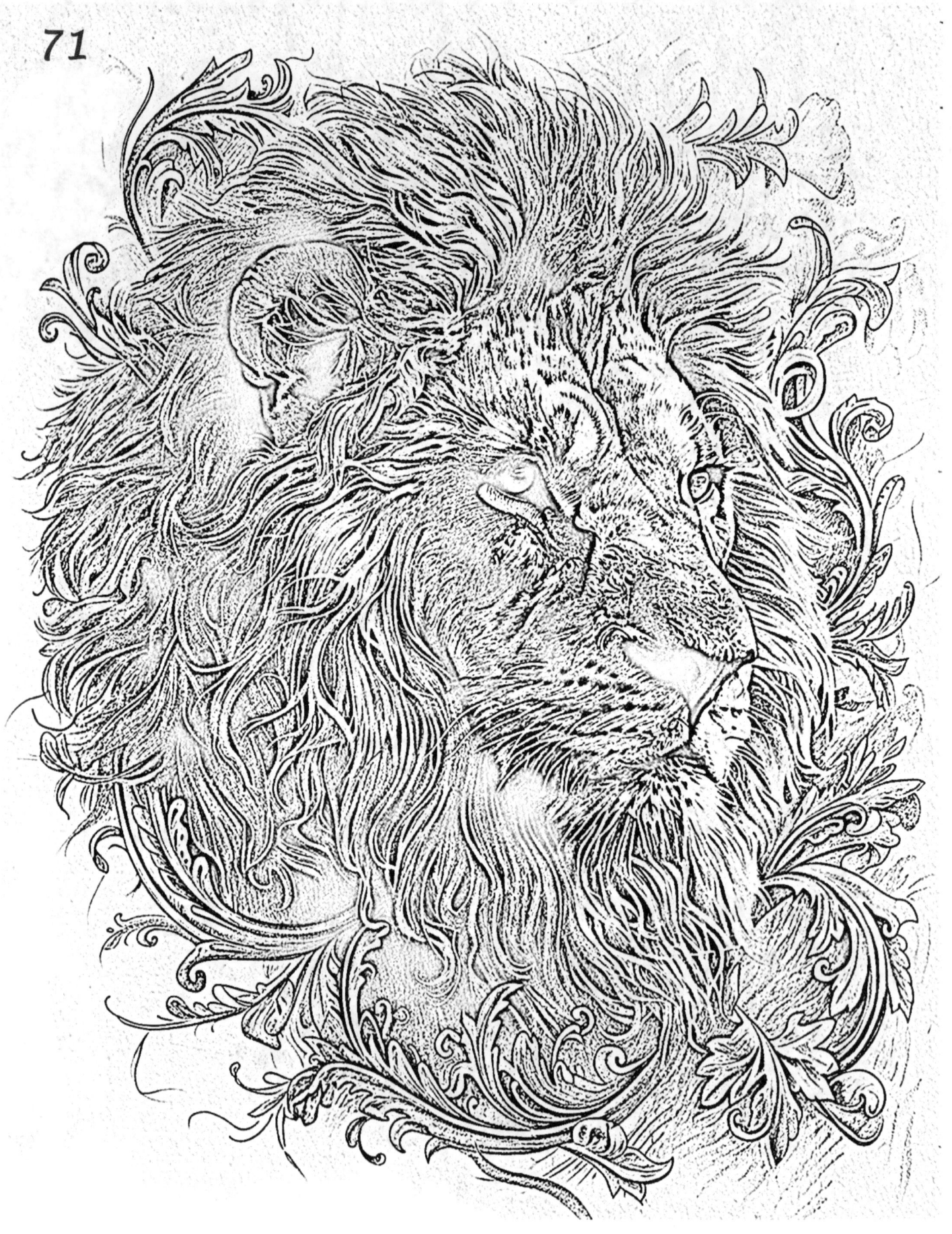

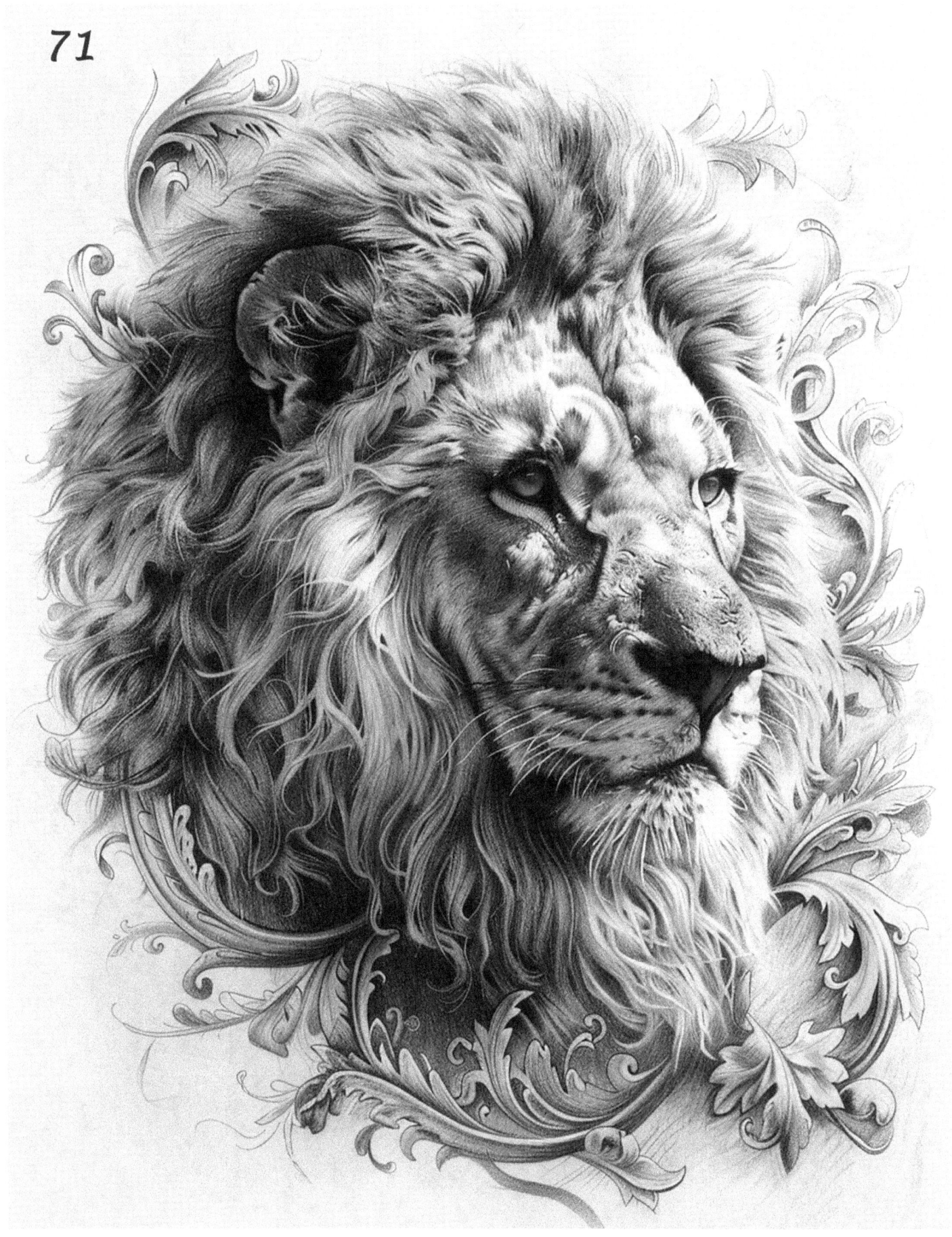

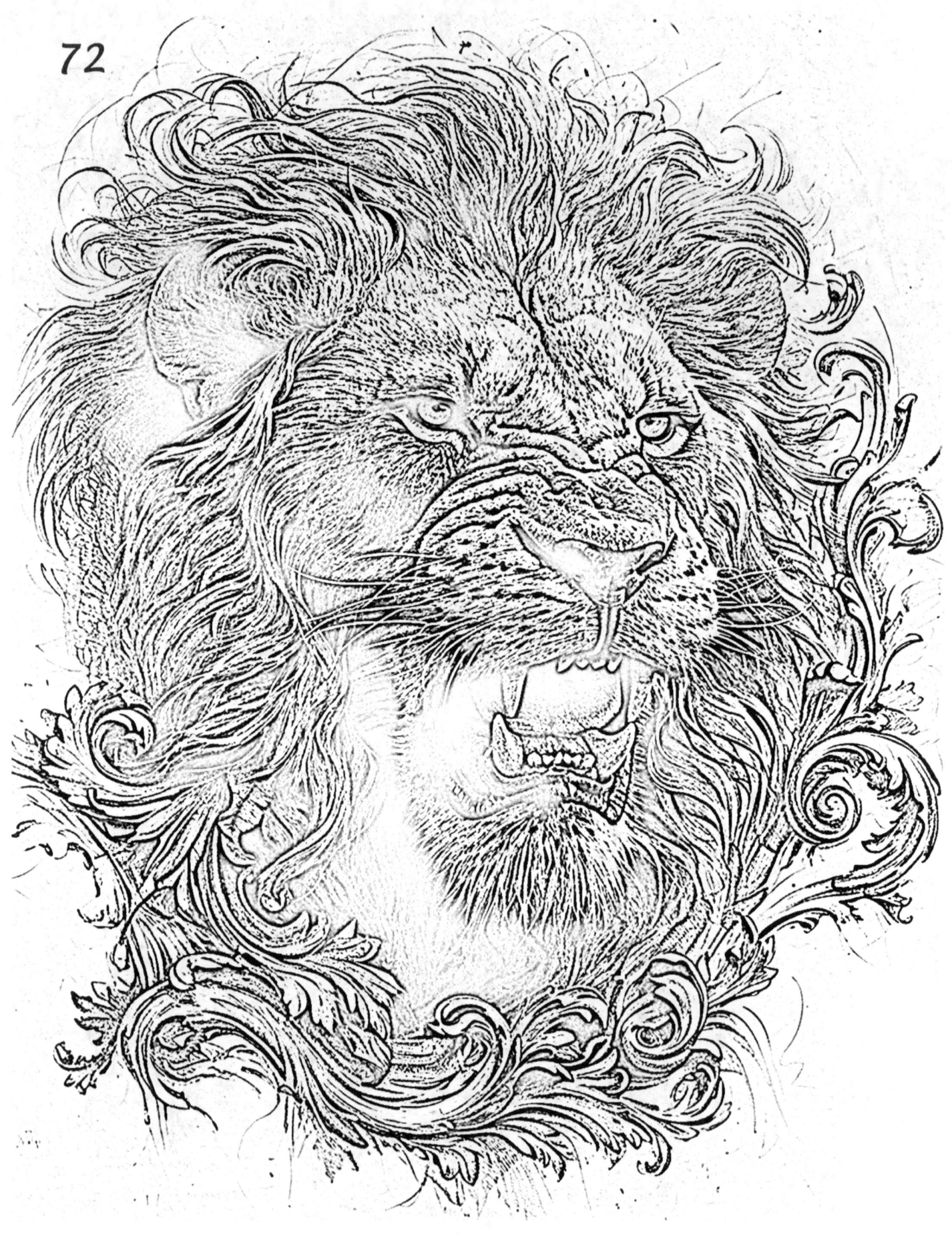

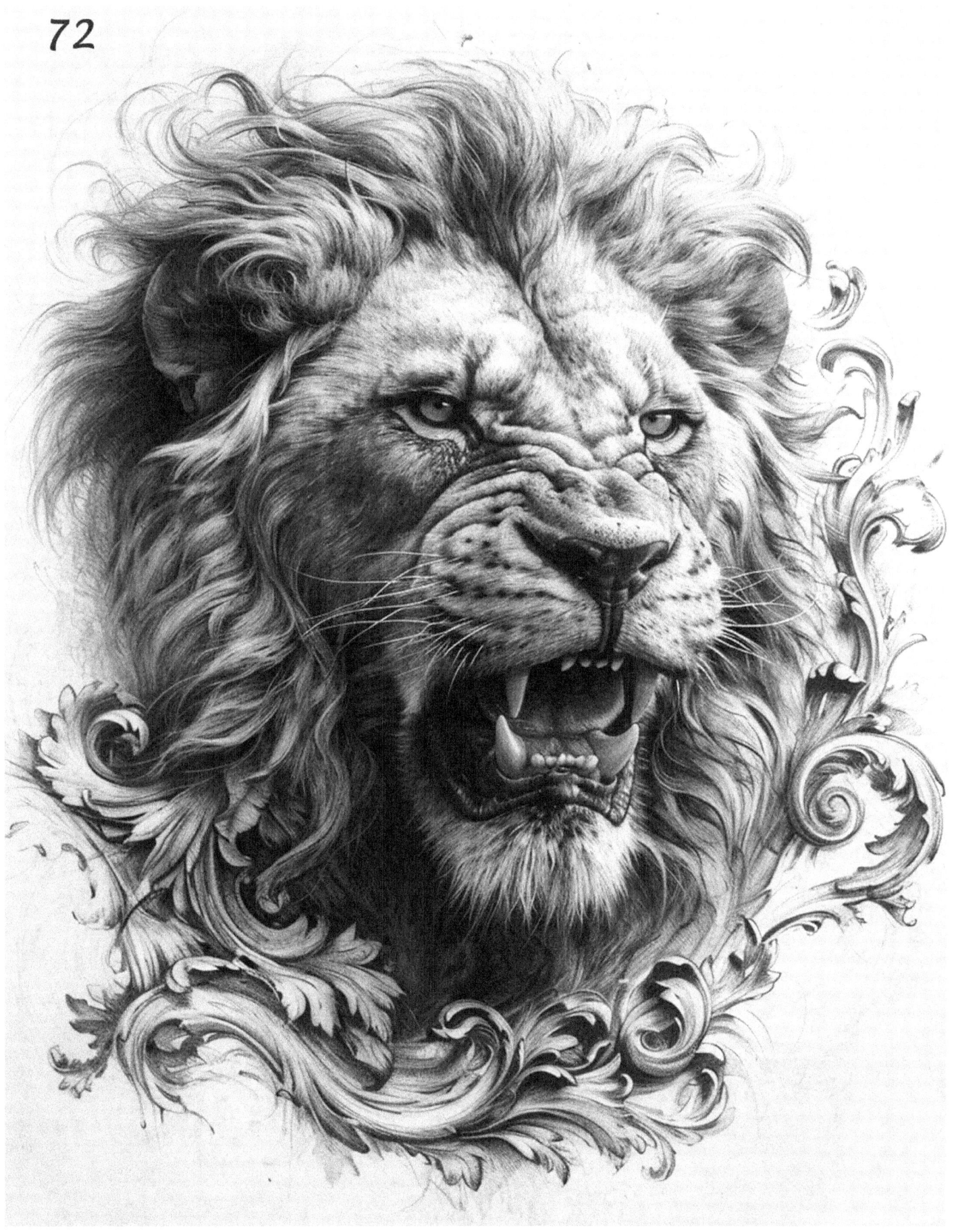

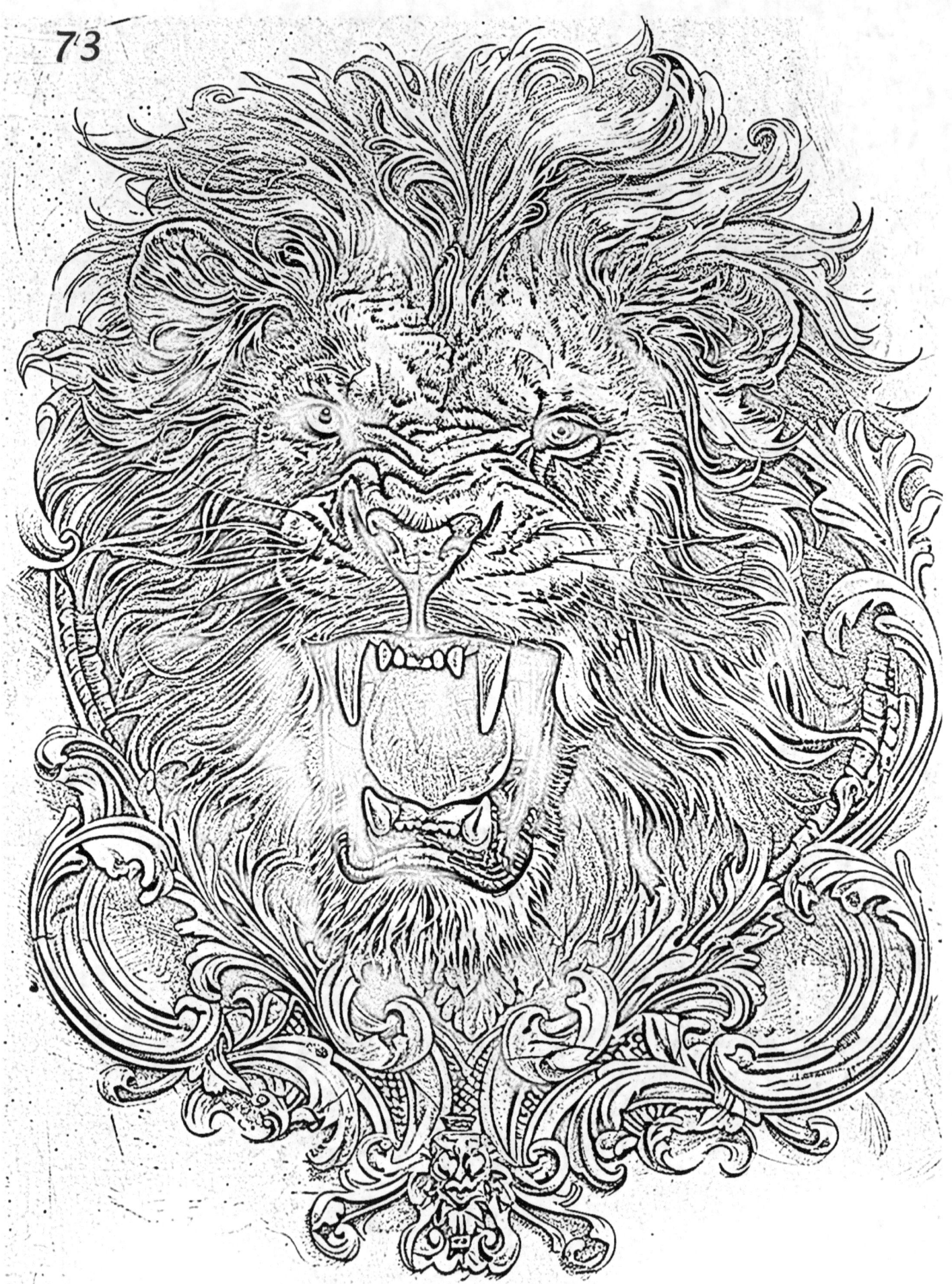

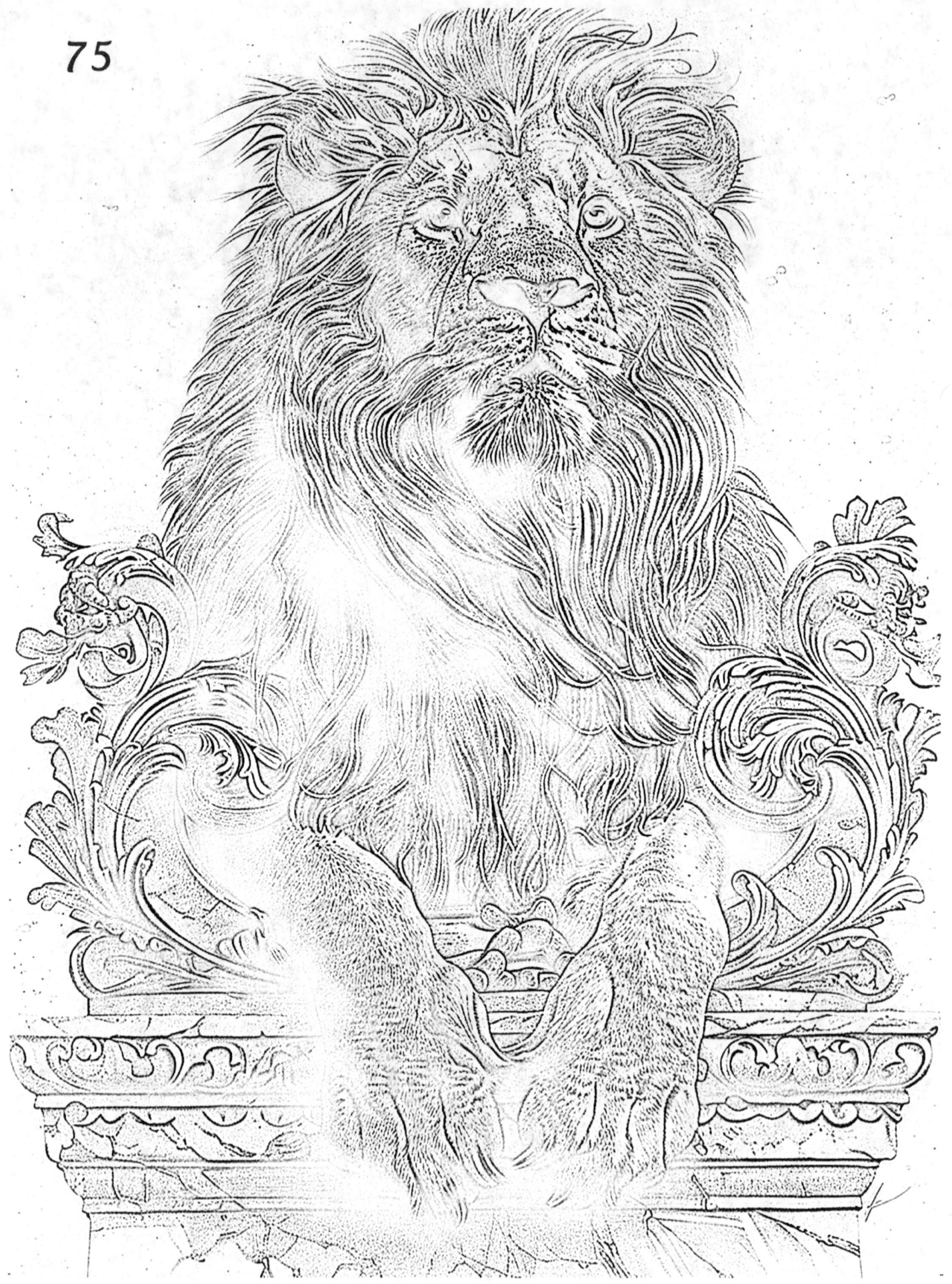

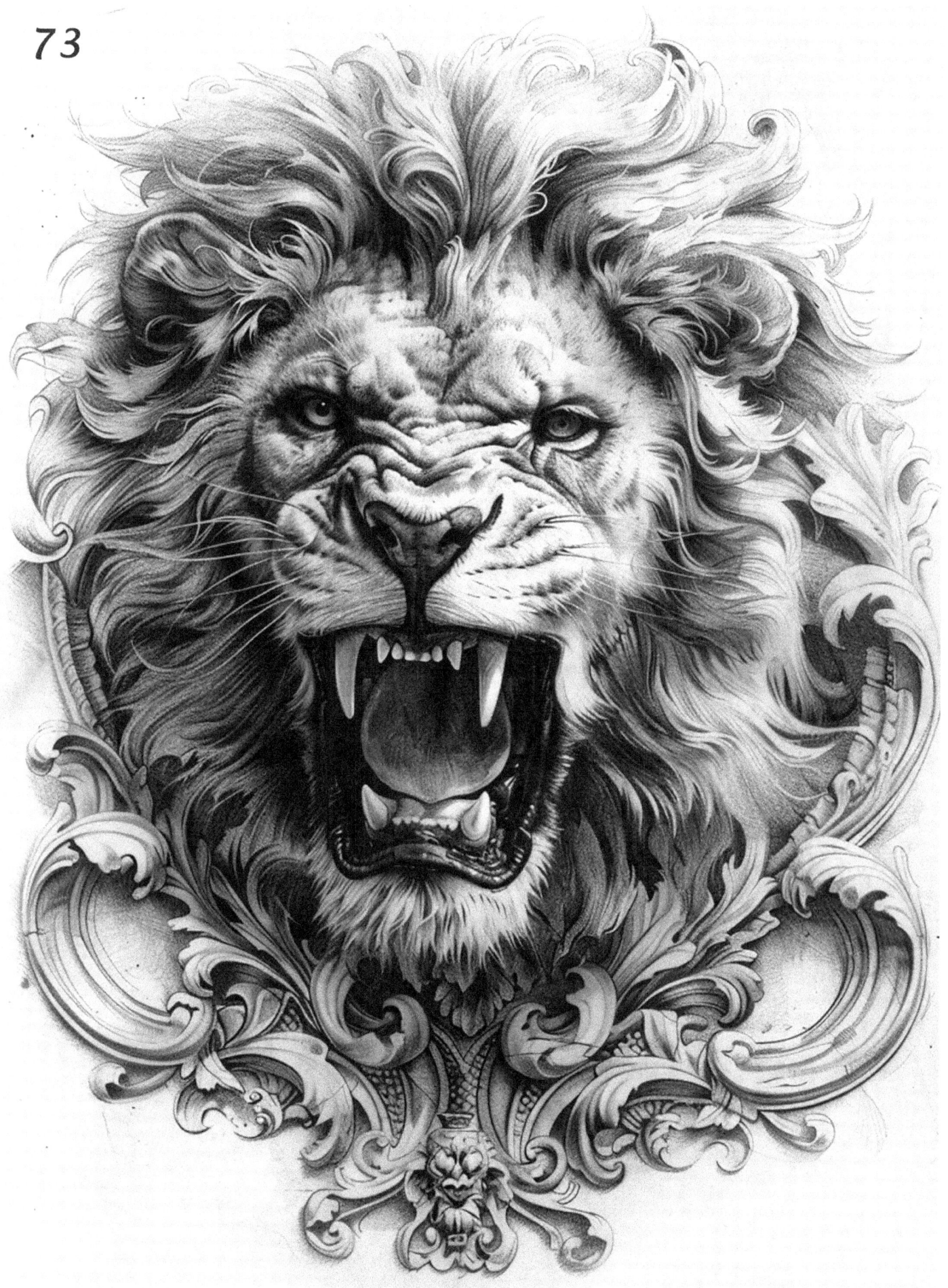

74

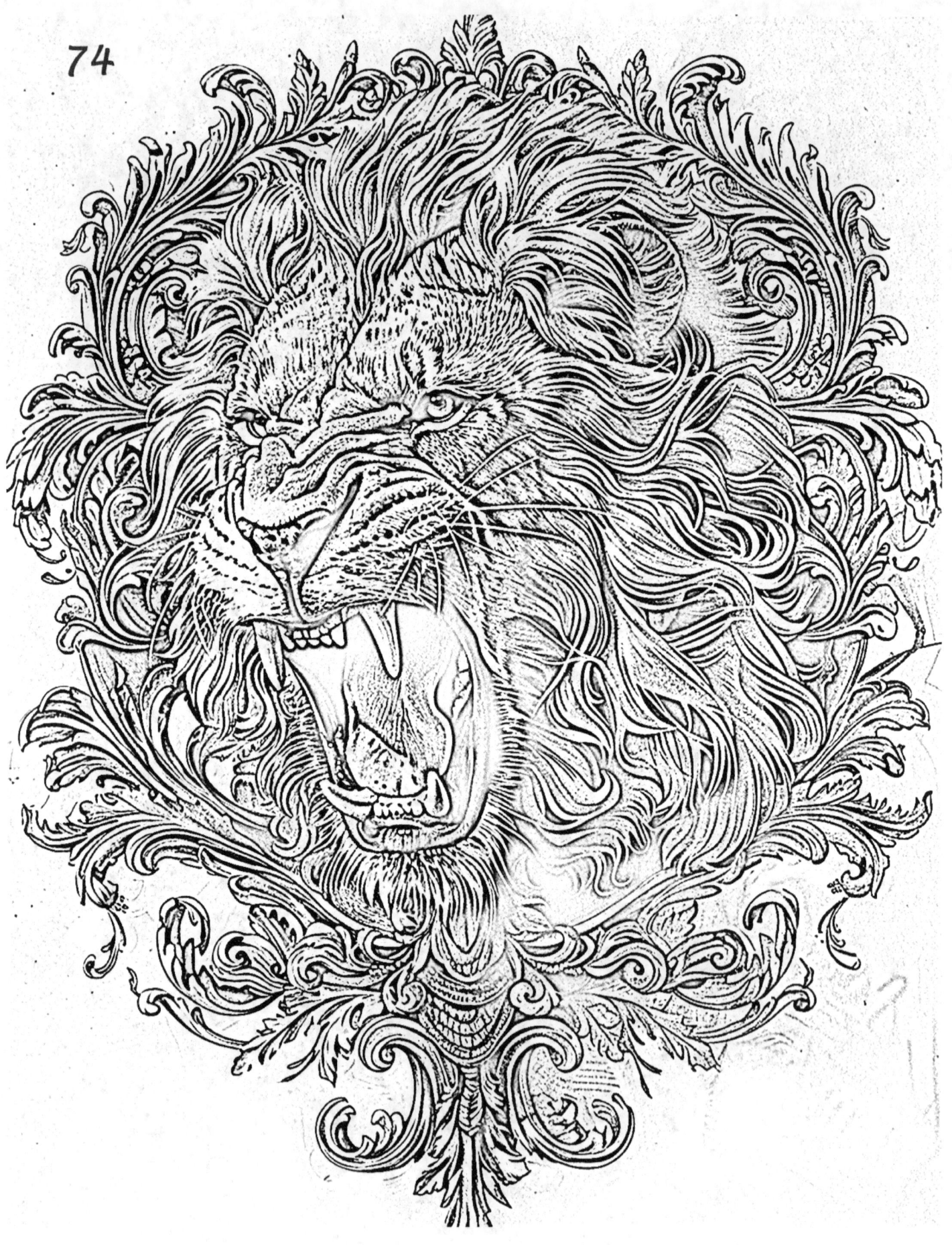

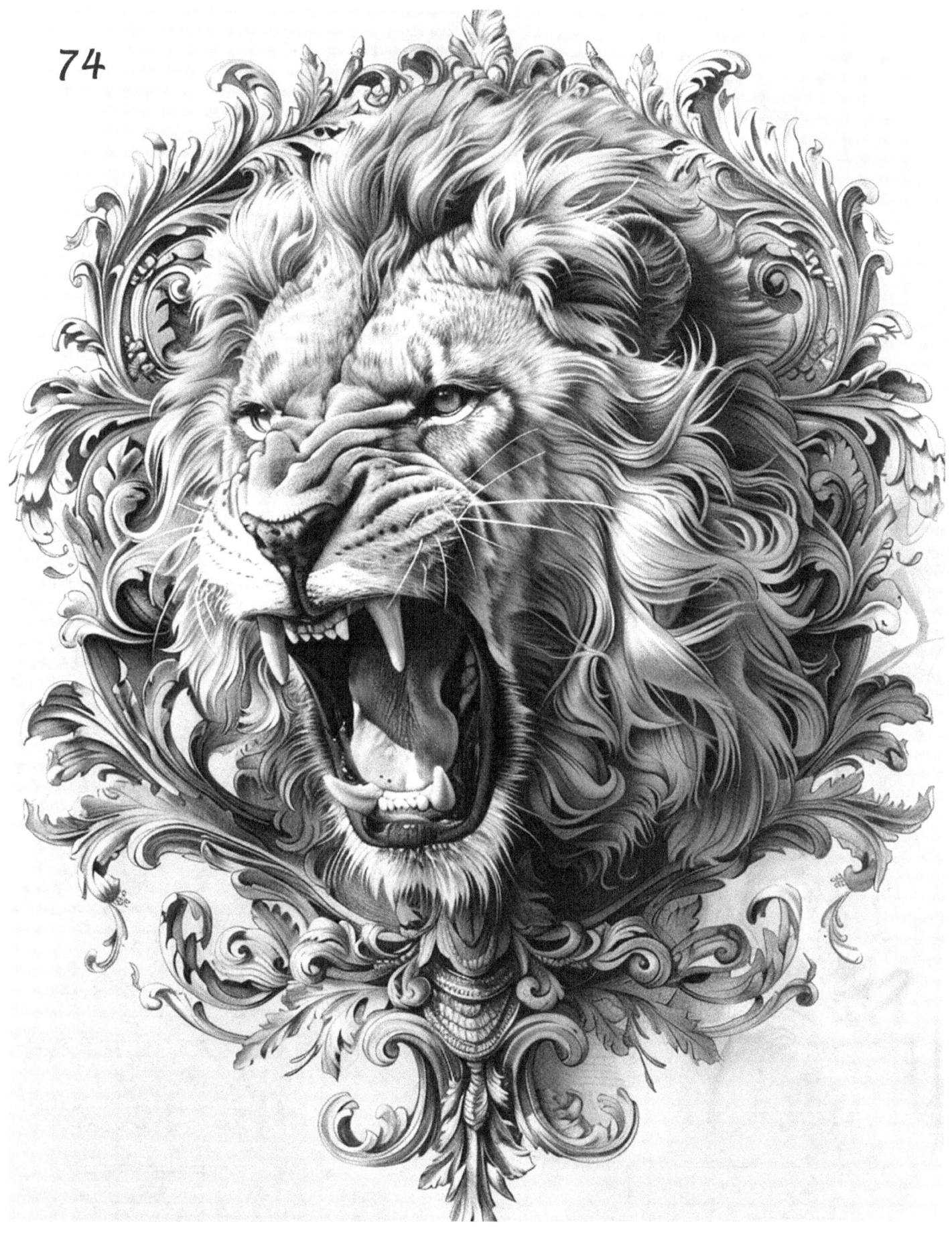

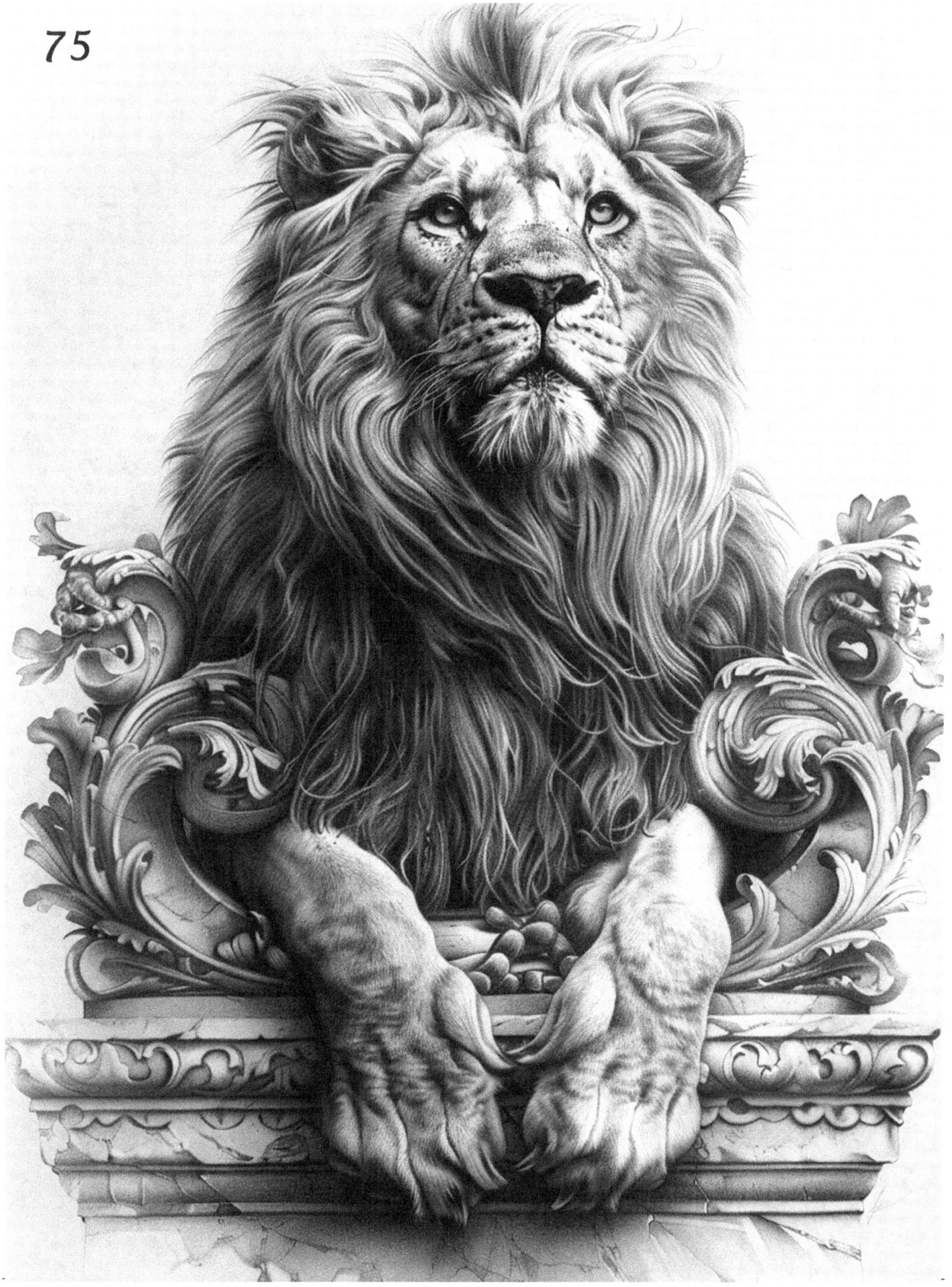

76

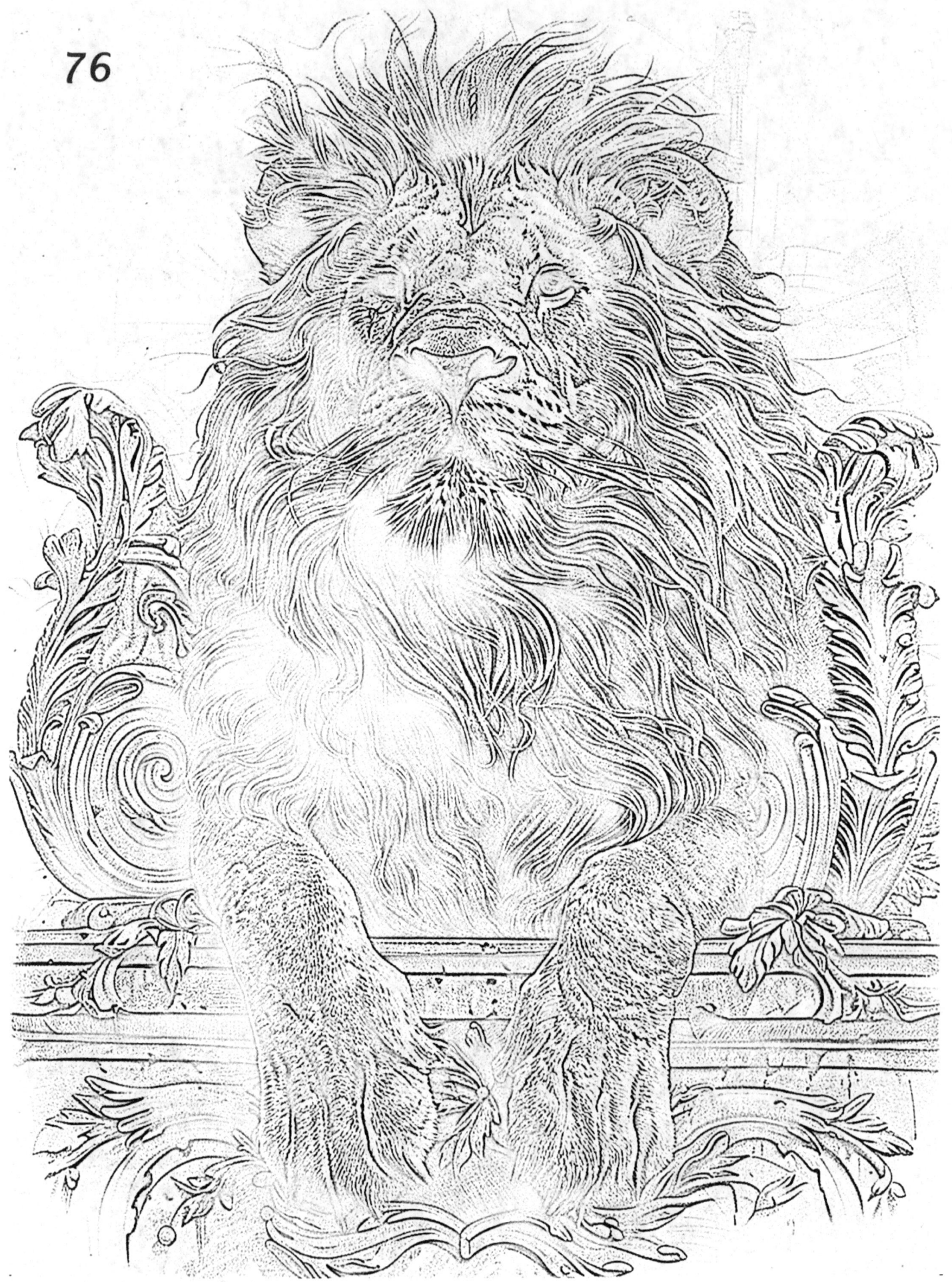

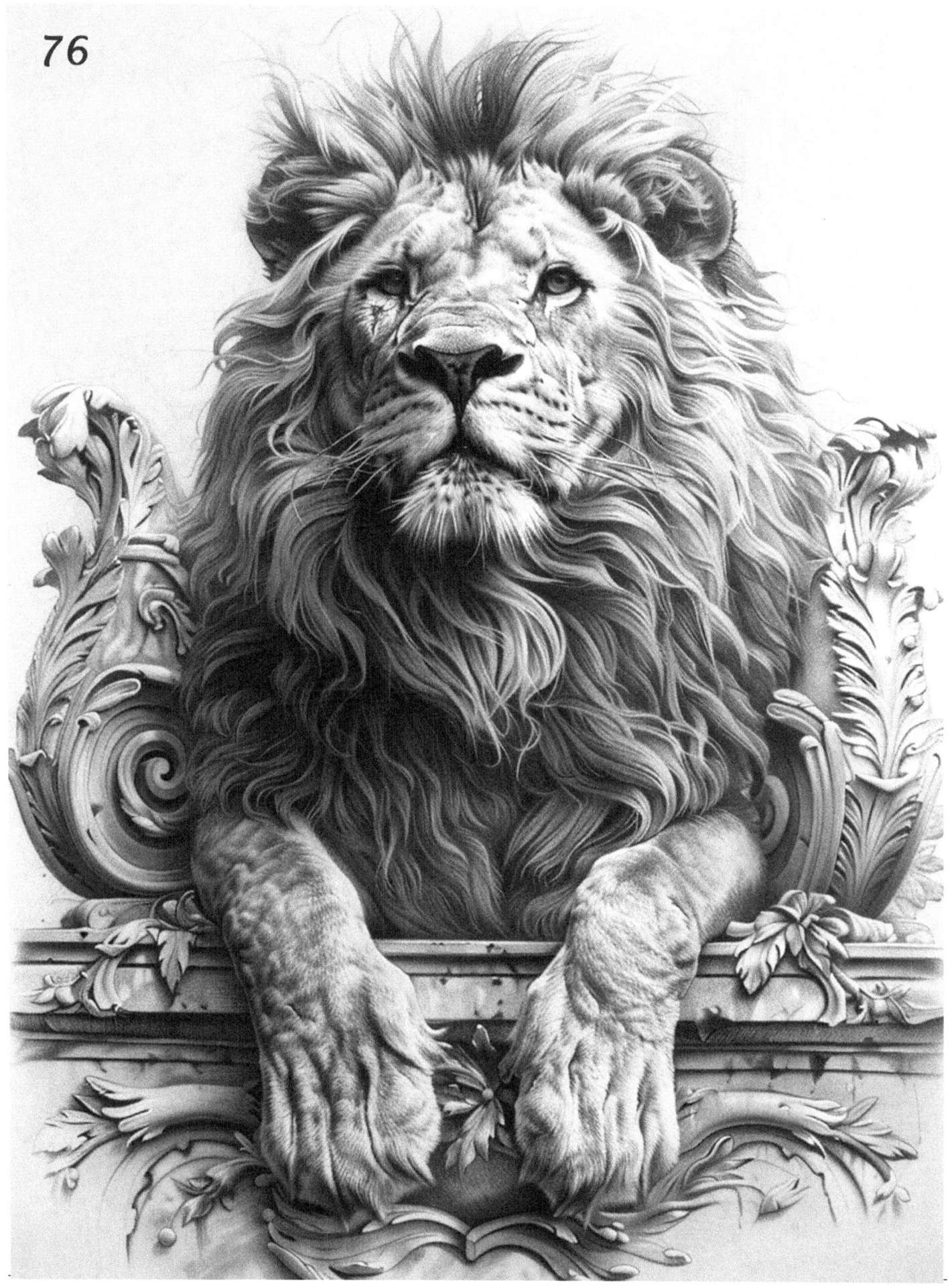

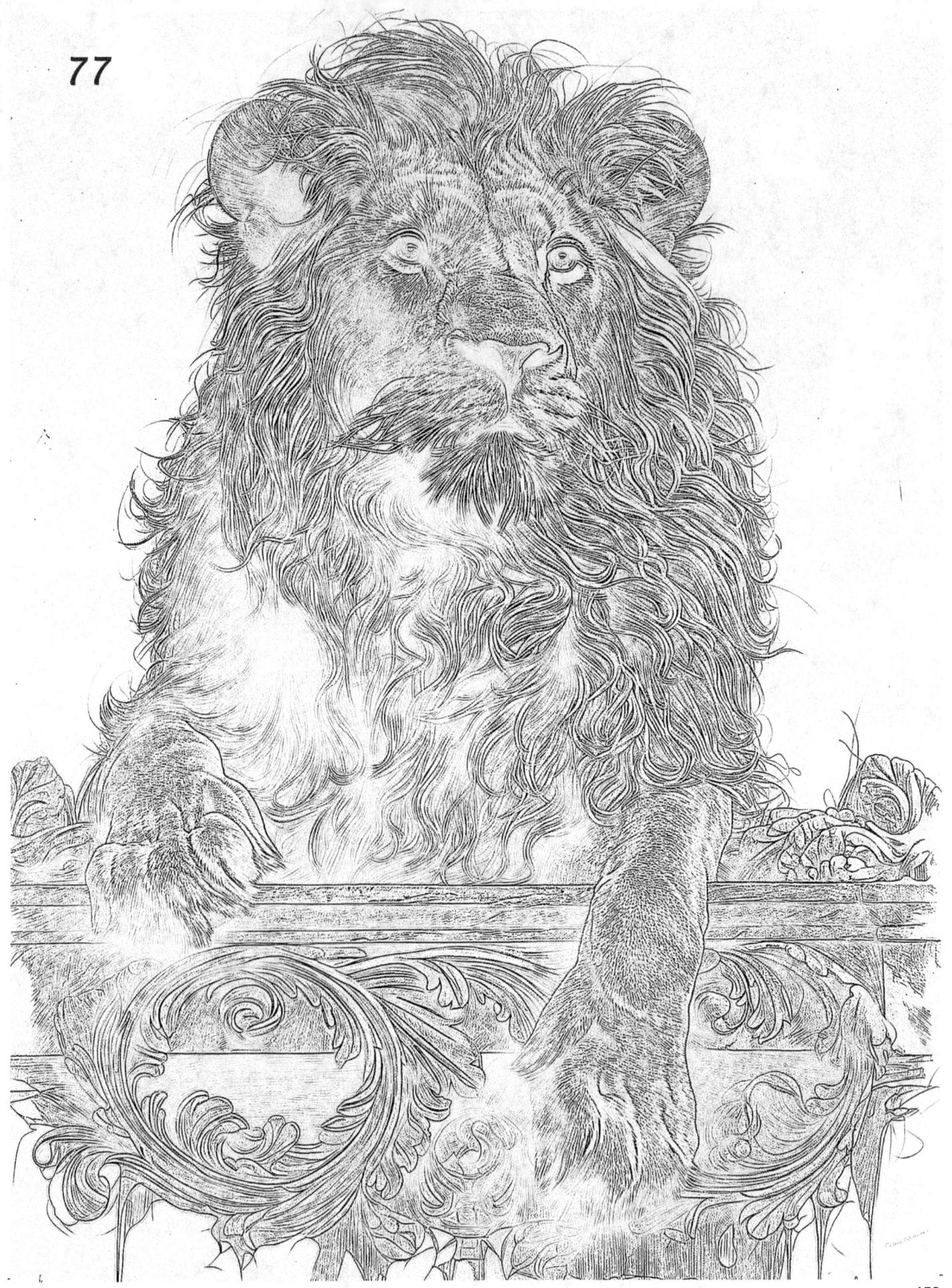

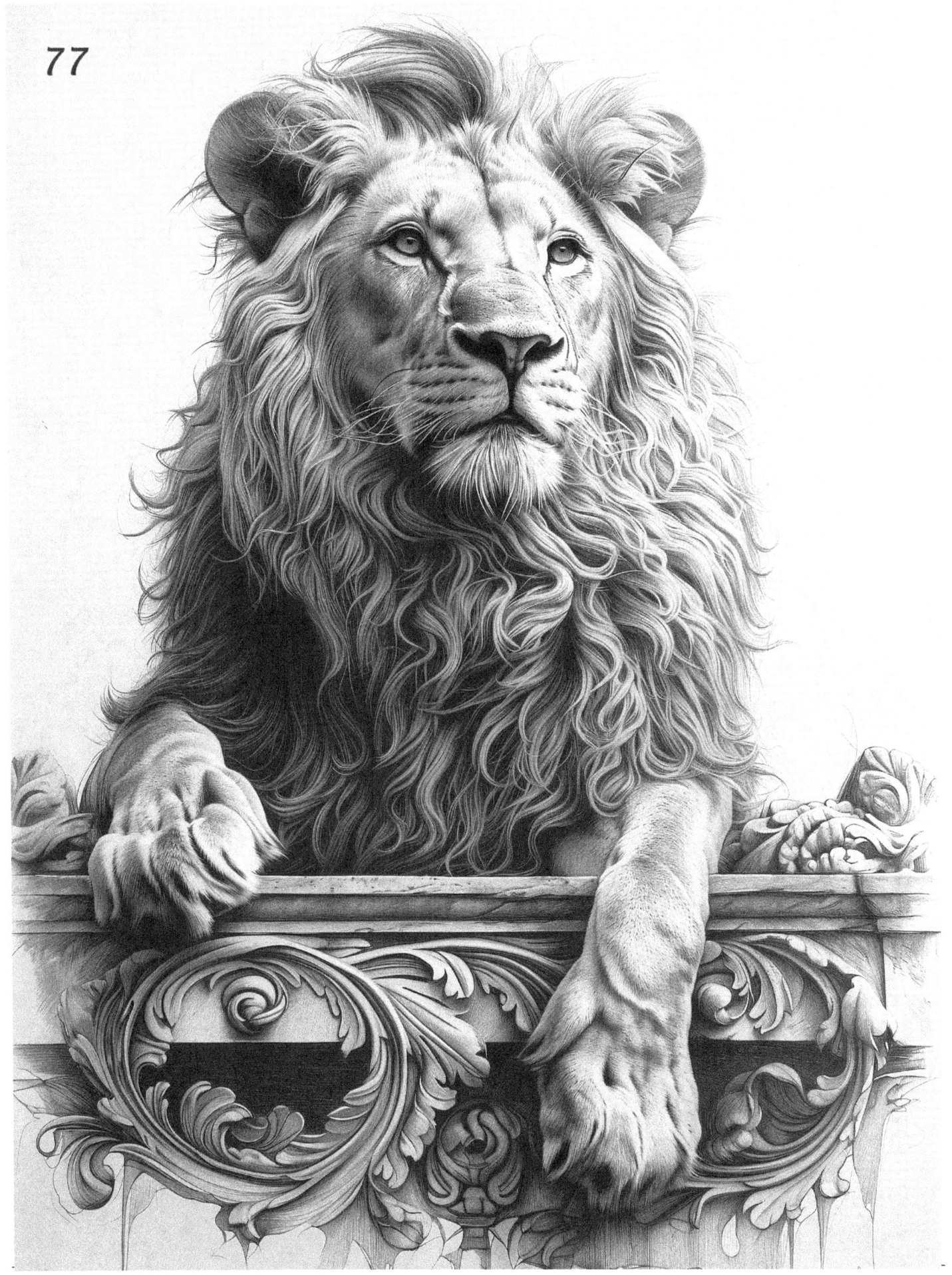

77b

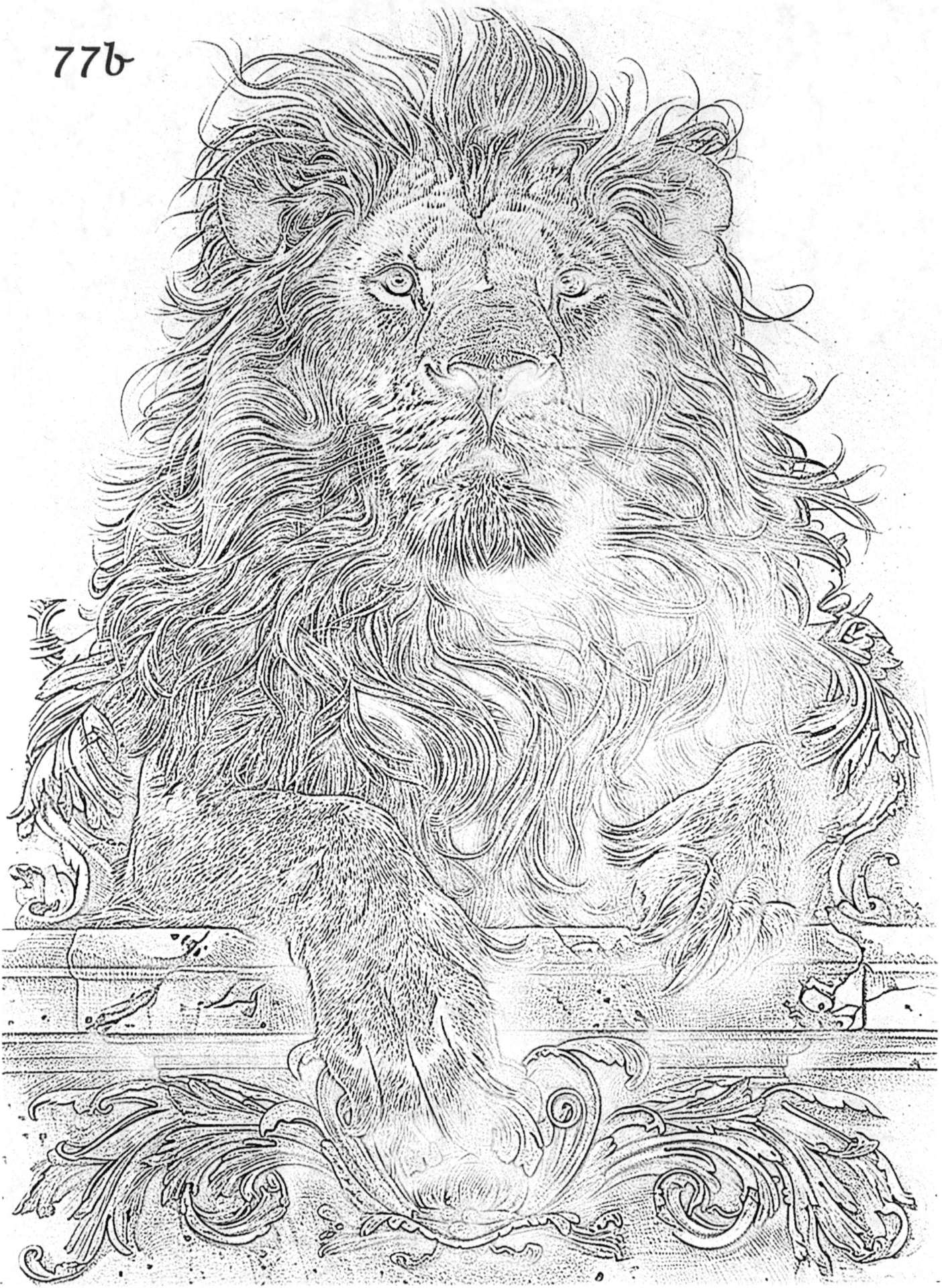

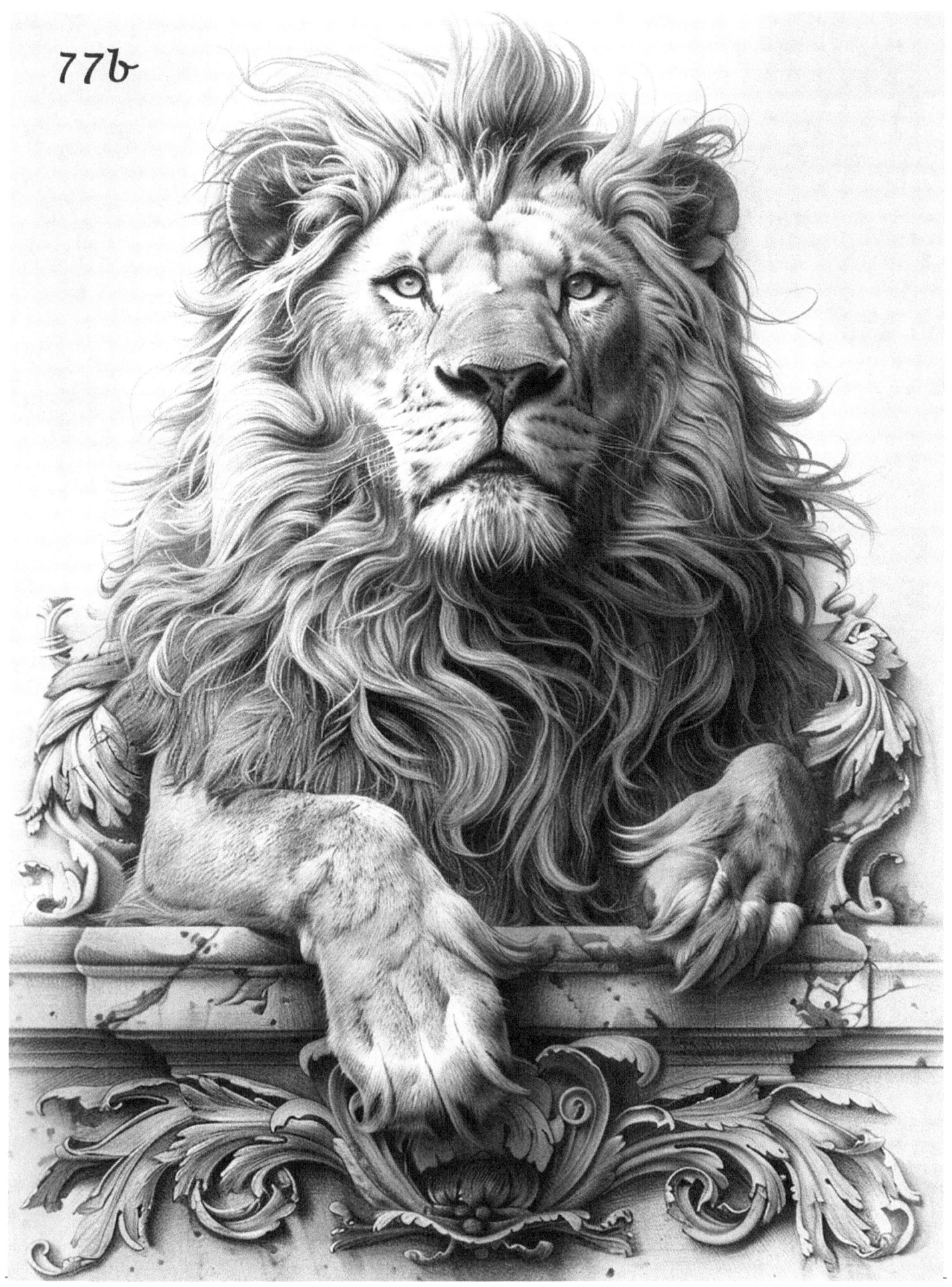

www.ingramcontent.com/pod-product-compliance
Lightning Source LLC
Chambersburg PA
CBHW062106220526
45471CB00010B/3615